Thinking and Speaking

Thinking and Speaking

A Guide

to Intelligent Oral

Communication

SECOND

EDITION

Otis M. Walter
Professor of Rhetorical Theory
University of Pittsburgh

and

Robert L. Scott
Professor of Speech
University of Minnesota

The Macmillan Company
NEW YORK

Collier-Macmillan Limited
LONDON

Third Printing, 1968

Earlier edition © copyright 1962 by The Macmillan Company.

Library of Congress catalog card number: 68–10185

The Macmillan Company, New York
Collier-Macmillan Canada, Ltd., Toronto, Ontario

Printed in the United States of America

Neither misery nor folly seems to me any part of the inevitable lot of man. And I am convinced that intelligence, patience and eloquence can, sooner or later, lead the human race out of its self-imposed tortures provided it does not exterminate itself meanwhile.

BERTRAND RUSSELL

Preface

We have written this book, first of all, because we believe that speech should be taught more as a liberal art than as a technical skill. Emerson remarked that speech was the greatest of the liberal arts. But what is a liberal art?

The term dates from ancient Rome when only freemen (*liberi*) were permitted to study that which was not immediately and solely applicable to job tasks. By association with freedom, the higher arts have become the signs of a free man. They are, moreover, that which make freedom meaningful, and that which make freedom possible. Speech belongs among them because it helps man do more than adjust to his environment; it enables him to change his environment. In giving man this power, speech frees him from domination by the world as it is, and equips him to reconstruct that world to bring it closer to his needs and dreams. Clearly, speaking belongs among the arts of free men. We have, accordingly, tried to emphasize those principles of speaking most important in a free society. Hence, we have emphasized the rhetorical problems involved in designing speeches about the forces that enfeeble and brutalize mankind; we have emphasized the analysis of the causes of these forces, the development of solutions to them, and the place of values in establishing the ultimate goals of man.

We have written this book, secondly, because we believe that in the last twenty-five years the intellectual competence of college students has improved markedly and that it will continue to improve. These students should be given a course in speech that will exercise their abilities vigorously. There is, moreover, a strong interest in increasing the depth, significance, and rigor of instruction. We have, therefore, selected those skills of rhetoric that will require the most careful thought, the maximum study, the most incisive analysis, and the greatest imagination. We hope we shall be able to engage the better student's interest, especially as his speaking is most likely to produce the greatest benefits for all of us.

For these reasons, it has been necessary for us to omit much that is often included in beginning-speech books. At the same time, we believe that we have furnished the student with enough fundamental concepts to enable him to enter successfully into the examination of problems, the analysis of causes, the presentation of solutions, and the clarification of values.

We owe much to others. We can never repay our own professors, colleagues, and students in seven universities who have stimulated us. We are indebted to disciplines outside our own; many philosophers, psychologists, and sociologists have been energized by the same problems that produced this book. Especially do we owe a heavy debt to the great rhetoricians of the past 2,500 years whose visions we may have only partly caught. If the book has merit, it is traceable to these sources. If it lacks merit, the fault is ours rather than of those who taught so well and who saw so much so clearly.

We would like especially to extend our appreciation to Professors Trevor Melia of Tufts University; Donald K. Smith of the University of Minnesota; George Shapiro of the University of Minnesota; Kenneth Erickson of Northern State College, Aberdeen, South Dakota; Bradlee Karen of Michigan State University; Ralph Nichols of the University of Minnesota (for his research on listening on which we have drawn in writing Chapter 8), and to Mr. John Dennis Moore, Editor, The Macmillan Company.

In this second edition, we have expanded several chapters and added a new one. For this edition, we wish to re-avow our thanks to the aforementioned scholars and, in addition, to thank the following for their suggestions for the revisions: Professors Robert P. Newman and William S. Tacey of the University of Pittsburgh; Franklyn Karns of the University of Florida; William K. Price of the University of Massachusetts; Mr. Allen Fitchen, Speech Editor, The Macmillan Company, and Mr. Ralph Boggia, Production Editor, The Macmillan Company.

The primary responsibility for writing Chapters 1, 2, 3, 4, 5, 7, 8, and 14 was Robert L. Scott's; the primary responsibility for writing Chapters 6, 9, 10, 11, 12, and 13 was Otis M. Walter's. The preface was composed jointly.

O. M. W.
R. L. S.

Contents

Part I ▮ Fundamental Concepts

1 | Our Rhetorical World

In speechmaking, as in life, not failure, but low aim, is crime.

W. M. PARRISH

You are undertaking the study of speech either because you thought it was a good idea to do so or because someone else thought so and either advised or required you to enroll in the course. But why study speech? This is a legitimate question for you to ask or for someone to ask you. Many answers can be given to that question. We hope that you will examine your own answers and expect you to find reason to recognize additional ones, not just in this course but throughout your life. We shall make some suggestions for you to weigh in considering the essential question: "Why study speech?"

MEN SPEAK IN RESPONSE TO PROBLEMS

The fact that men live together in social bodies generates problems which threaten the well-being of individuals and of the groups with which they identify. Speechmaking is a chief instrument men use in grasping, examining, and settling their problems. The decision to speak may be a critical one for a man and for the group of which he is a part. Let us illustrate this assertion by glancing briefly at the life of one of the most famous speakers in American history.

A little more than a hundred years ago, a man no longer young turned from a relatively comfortable professional life to politics, a career from which he had retired some years before in disillusion, having had so little success as to justify the epithet *failure*. But he had come to believe that his country was adopting policies that would be tragic. The proposal of popular sovereignty embodied in the Nebraska Bill and a movement to repeal the principles of the Missouri Compromise threatened to guarantee the growth of slavery. To prevent the growth of an institution which he believed to be only legally sufferable in limited circumstances, he plunged actively into the campaign for the re-election of the United States Representative from his district who had been fighting the legislation he feared. "Stand with anybody that stands right. Stand with him while he is right, and part from him when he goes wrong," he told an audience.

As Abraham Lincoln spoke to audiences, he felt reactions in himself and among his listeners that he had never felt before, although he had always been a crowd pleaser.[1] He began traveling farther from Springfield to speak, although he was not a candidate for an office. People quickly identified him with the opposition to the Nebraska Bill and those who shared his position turned to him for leadership. He spoke and was elected to the Illinois legislature in which he had served years before. He spoke and was nominated a candidate for the United States Senate. During his campaign for the Senate he engaged in that unprecedented series of debates with Stephen Douglas. Although the Republicans polled more votes than the Douglas Democrats, he was defeated for the office in the election held in the Illinois legislature. But he continued to speak and in 1860 was nominated for the Presidency.

From 1854 to 1861 Lincoln spoke in order to bring about a just settlement of the issues that divided the nation. He sought a peaceful means to his end; but the forces of division, for a multitude of reasons the relative influences of which are still undetermined, were too strong. As President in a nation torn by war, he put the ideals of democratic liberty into words that still live.

Other men arose to speak during these times. The names of many mark the pages of history—Stephen Douglas, John C. Calhoun, Wendell Phillips, William Lowndes Yancey, Charles Sumner. There were many others whose names we have never heard, persons who spoke in mass meetings, in frontier churches, in lecture halls, and in polite parlors. They also lived with the issues of the time and felt compelled to speak, to exert what persuasive influence they could, and to give expression to the feelings that moved within them.

In the debate at Alton, Illinois, Lincoln said, "That is the real issue.

[1] See the editor's introduction to *Created Equal? The Complete Lincoln-Douglas Debates of 1858*, ed. Paul M. Angle, Chicago, University of Chicago Press, 1958, p.x.

That is the issue that will continue in this country, when these poor tongues of Judge Douglas and myself shall be silent. It is the eternal struggle between two principles—right and wrong—throughout the world. They are the two principles that have stood face to face from the beginning of time and will ever continue to struggle."[2] Lincoln spoke of the will to oppress and the will to be free. Men have oppressed others, do oppress others, and will continue to oppress others, but the issues that have united and divided men are much more complex than this simple statement indicates. We cannot recount all of them, but in general men have dealt with them in two ways—by force and by persuasive discourse. Perhaps Cicero overstated the case when he claimed that persuasion is the very spring from which civilization flows,[3] *but the history of man's attempts to live together seems to indicate that forbearance and persuasion are the alternatives to terror and force.*

The lessons that we have drawn from the brief examination of Abraham Lincoln's speaking are scarcely unique to him or to his times. Consider for a moment one more historical example.

After a revolution had driven the tyrants out of the Greek city of Syracuse in the fifth century B.C., the citizens had to lay the basis for a renewed civil life. One of the most perplexing questions was the ownership of land. Much of the land had been seized and held by the ruling clique for years. How was the land to be restored to its rightful owners? Claims, often conflicting ones, arose. The city could easily have disintegrated into a chaos of grab-and-hold with killings, reprisals, and counter-reprisals. Instead the citizens established courts into which claims could be brought orally and decided by juries. Effective speaking had been useful undoubtedly in many places at many times, but this historical instance is unique because it was at this time, as far as we know, that men first tried to develop a systematic art of speaking which could be taught and learned.

The ancient Greeks had a name for this art; they called it *rhetoric,* a word which now has taken on much more limited meaning and for which consequently no satisfactory modern equivalent exists. Rhetoric was the art of prose composition, and in those times almost all prose was communicated orally. The ancient Greeks had uses for their art in the democratic assemblies, in which at least hypothetically any citizen could speak. They also spoke in the lawcourts, in which any citizen could bring a charge against another; the man who brought the charge had to prosecute and the man against whom it was brought, to defend himself. They spoke in great gatherings to commemorate occasions of public interest. *The principles and teachings of rhetoric* (today often known und r other names) *have persisted because the conditions that make ours a rhetorical*

[2] *Ibid.*, p. 393.
[3] See *De Inventione*, Bk. I, ch. 1, sec. 2.

*world are the innate results of man's need to communicate with his fel-
lows.* Recognizing the sort of world in which he lived, Aristole said that
it was absurd for any man to be ashamed of being unable to defend himself with his limbs and not be ashamed of being unable to defend himself
with his mind and tongue, because the use of rational speech is more
distinctive of a human being than the use of his limbs![4]

OUR RHETORICAL WORLD

We stand today where the men of Syracuse stood and where Lincoln
stood. This is not to say that we can lay no claim to accomplishments
unknown to them. We have, for example, made great strides in providing
for the material needs and desires of a large population, and this is no
mean achievement; throughout history no human problem has so ground
the humanity out of great masses of people as poverty. Still there are
issues that demand our attention as speakers.

What are the issues of our times? Actually they are pretty much what
they have always been even though the context may be significantly different—war, freedom, poverty, health, knowledge, and individual values, all
these words give rise to a twisted skein of particular issues both private
and public. To be more specific: "How shall we fight the pockets of poverty remaining in the midst of our plenty?" "What is our obligation, if
any, toward those nations who have not reached material abundance?"
"How can we live peacefully with Russia?" "How can we live peacefully
with our wives and husbands?" "How free shall we be—in our homes, in
our schools, in our jobs?" "Is bigness—big government, big business, big
unions, big universities—consistent with the development of each individual into a person of worth?" "Can we provide for our health needs as
individuals?" "Will sprawling metropolises bring potentially disabling
social problems?" The question game in indicating issues is endless; let's
try another. Think of the assertions that indicate issues: "The trouble
with religion in America is that we've made God into a 'good guy' who
can be counted on to sympathize with our self-indulgent whims." "Politics
are out of control; image makers are rushing us toward Orwell's *1984*."
"We must clean up our unions." "We must control prices demanded by
the big industrialists." "Intercollegiate athletics are show business, so
let's be honest and hire athletes openly." "Plan parenthood."

If we deserve the benefits of a materially rich society, we must become
involved in meeting the issues that face us. In so doing, we shall quite
likely find many opportunities to speak. This is not to claim that speaking
is the only way that men may meet the problems they face. Speech is only

---

[4] *Rhetoric*, Bk. I., ch. 1.

one of the activities by which man governs himself and learns to work out his problems in harmony with others, but it is one important human capability which most of us should learn to use as effectively as possible.

THE CIRCLE OF INFLUENCE

Our world is bewilderingly complex, and its issues may be too perilous for ordinary hands. "After all," we may be led to say, "even though he didn't have the advantages of a highly organized formal education, Lincoln was a genius, a man born to be great." The examples of great speakers, verbal geniuses from Cicero to Churchill, may discourage us; we may think, "Let the geniuses lead; let them speak." To take this attitude, however, is to have too narrow a view of speaking and, much more important, of ourselves and our society.

Every person using this book will almost inevitably associate himself with a number of groups—business, social, political, leisure, and religious. These groups conduct themselves through speaking. Members speak and listen to speakers. In these groups we shall inevitably come to grips in some way with the issues that face our times. In these circles we may be influential, and no matter how small the circle or how limited our influence, it is important. Our society—economic, political, religious—is composed of a tangle of interwoven circles within which men talk and exert influence. The influences exerted have a way of transmitting themselves back and forth throughout the skein. Take an example: What should be done with atomic energy? To what extent will government control its peaceful development? Who will profit and how? What will be done with the atomic wastes? What sort of agreements shall we enter into with other nations concerning the uses of atomic power? These and many more questions are not out of our reach. They will be decided and the decisions will seem to be made by the heads of state, but what about the climate in which our leaders act? What kinds of leaders shall we have? What will be the influence of their home environments, of their school environments, of their civic environments? What will be the values that will inevitably affect these decisions? These questions are too complex to answer, but the answer will depend upon the circles of influence that will inevitably operate and of which we shall be a part. The way that they operate, how openly and freely they operate, will also be determined by ourselves—how we think, what we say, what we do.

Our problems are manifested on many different levels. We tend to see the obviously great manifestation of our problems and sometimes overlook the manifestations in which we may be intimately involved. Take human conflict as an example. In living together human beings come into conflict. What shall be done? We tend to think of global conflicts, but we find human conflict in the home, in the neighborhood, in the school, in the community. We must deal with human conflict in thousands of cases and in many different ways, and we shall often want to speak.

THE EXPRESSIVE VALUE OF SPEECH

We have been emphasizing the communicative function of speaking. This is an altogether proper emphasis and is, indeed, primarily important. Too often, however, we are led to be unsympathetic with speakers and fail to recognize another important possible value of speaking. Our impatience is sometimes indicated with statements such as, "There's altogether too much useless talk in the world." "People should talk less and listen more." "He has nothing to say that I haven't heard. It's all been said a thousand times." No doubt some of this complaining is justified and may be healthful to the degree that it stimulates speakers to make worthwhile demands on themselves. Ralph Waldo Emerson put the criticism neatly in a single phrase; we do hear too much of the "small-pot-soon-hot style of eloquence."[5] Still the criticism is too easily made and may well lead us to turn quickly toward great men, failing to see our potential roles in our own circles of influence. Moreover we may fail to recognize an important value of speaking.

We should emphasize, especially as students and teachers, the value speaking has not only as communication but as expression. As men we live together in societies and share problems, but each of us is a unique human individual. The lessons we learn may be ancient ones; the answers we find may be common ones. But we must learn lessons and find answers ourselves; we must appropriate them to make them ours. We may listen; we may read; we may experience in a hundred different ways multitudes of forces that communicate meaning to us. But do we *know* unless we ourselves express the ideas that we find moving within us as a result of our varied experiences?

When we say that each person must express for himself the lessons he learns from books and experiences, we are saying more than simply that he must recite. He commits himself to an idea—to understanding, to analyzing, to solving—and stands responsible for that idea in recommending it as good information or opinion to others. Although the student may feel modest in the presence of what others have accomplished, and although he may feel grateful for the advantage of studying what others have left for him to study, he must make his knowledge for himself. If his concept of what knowledge can and should be does not include the responsibility to make it active, we can only say that in our opinion he has a stunted concept.

[5] *Of Eloquence.*

To put the matter another way, expression is an innately human need. This need will create tensions that seek resolution just as do the commonly recognized physiological needs. Speaking, of course, is only one means of expression. Some men may manipulate lines, colors, or musical notes meaningfully, but most of us must depend primarily upon the use of verbal symbols to fulfill our expressive needs.

When Cervantes wrote, "Make it thy business to know thyself," he echoed a lesson more than 2,000 years old, but in over 400 years more it is still, as we know, "the most difficult lesson in the world."[6] Speaking is one road we may take in our search for knowledge of ourselves. In confronting other men we may come face to face with ourselves. We may choose to speak or not; we may choose to speak on trivial matters or try to grasp important problems; we may choose to search for important meaning that we sense in what seems trivial to others and so lift ourselves a trifle and, perhaps, them; or we may make anything we touch trivial. But we shall choose, and by our choices we shall form ourselves.

SPEECH AS A HUMANE STUDY

In discussing the expressive value of speech, we indicated that speaking is one way of learning about oneself. In speaking one must face problems— problems that have a history and a relationship to other people, groups, and traditions we have formed for living together. If one takes this point of view, he cannot be satisfied with looking at speech simply as a skill. We are not arguing that skill is in no way involved in good speaking; we do argue that speech has little meaning if taken as something wholly apart from the matrix of human involvement, which has given rise to a fascinating skein of studies all of which are, from their own particular angles, the study of man. We conclude that the study of speech belongs in that area of the liberal arts traditionally designated the humanities.

Speech is commonly called a *tool*. Whether or not this label is healthful depends on one's attitude in applying it. Human tools are nothing to be taken lightly. In order to help determine whether or not certain fossils should be designated as human, archeologists seek in the strata where they find the remains for tools that might be associated with the fossils. Truly man is a tool using animal. But we must step beyond this simple observation.

Arguing along lines similar to those we have taken, Michael Polanyi has written:

Every time we assimilate a tool to our body our identity undergoes some change; our person expands into new modes of being. I have shown before

[6] *Don Quixote*, Part II, Bk. 4.

that the whole realm of human intelligence is grounded on the use of language. We can reformulate this now by saying that all mental life by which we surpass the animals is evoked in us as we assimilate the articulate framework of our culture.[7]

This book, and the course in which you are involved, are modest efforts in the enterprise Polanyi has identified.

From another point of view, speech is a humane study. We are surrounded by phenomena. Education is largely a matter of coming to understand these phenomena. A part of our world is composed of speakers and speeches. If we are interested in understanding our world, we ought to be interested in what is a uniquely human product. Certainly a speech is a work representative of man. If it is important to study the art, the music, and the literature that man has produced as representative of the characteristics of human potentialities, it is important to study speeches. If we are to understand the forces within and outside ourselves that urge us to expression, we must be interested in the efforts of others to communicate. To become a student of speech is to develop an intellectual disposition that will help make a man humane.

Speech has a history, many theories, and a body of literature. You could study speech as history, as theory, or as literature without speaking. This book, however, emphasizes your role as a speaker. In studying the chapters that follow, you should gain a deeper understanding of what a speech is, of how speeches are made, of the problems that speakers face. In so doing, you will come to understand better a pervasive part of your human environment.

This understanding is an end in itself. It is also a tool. Finally it may be viewed as a foundation for the further study of speech, study that may range from the theories of persuasion in ancient cultures through the outstanding speeches produced by the leaders who have built our nation to contemporary theories of communication. Frankly we believe that these studies will be more meaningful to a student who has himself struggled with the commitment to ideas that has led to attempts to gain the understanding or belief of others.

THE RESPONSIBILITIES OF A SPEAKER[8]

A speaker exercises rights, but these rights carry contingent responsibilities. The speaker has a right to communicate thought and feeling; he has the right to give expression to the needs of his own personality. On the

---

[7] *The Study of Man*, Chicago, Phoenix Books, 1963, p. 31.

[8] This section draws from the analysis of Karl R. Wallace, "An Ethical Basis of Communication," *Speech Teacher* (January, 1955).

other hand, these rights are assured only by the cooperation of a society in which they are valued. In our particular society we have been assured certain rights as a part of political system. *The speaker, basically, may speak freely, but he must speak in such a way as to protect and extend this right. Any action that weakens the right of free speech is irresponsible.*

As a speaker speaks he must realize that for the moment he is the source of knowledge for his audience about ideas and occurrences. He has a right to his opinions, but he has the responsibility for stating openly and as clearly as possible those opinions and the grounds upon which they are based. To mislead an audience concerning one's ideas or to distort the facts that he sees relevant to them is irresponsible.

The speaker, then, has the responsibility to understand the subject about which he speaks as completely as possible. This burden is not an easy one to bear. Often extremely conscientious persons are nearly paralyzed, refusing to take action on the grounds that they do not know enough. This sort of person is more to be respected than the man who is ready to give his opinion on anything with scarcely a second thought. But our argument is that being human and finite we cannot expect perfect insight nor can we wait indefinitely if we are to fulfill our obligations to ourselves and our fellows. The situations that demand our participation come and go. We can fail in two ways—by not preparing sufficiently to meet them as well as we can be expected to and by refusing to act at all.

Recognizing his right to his own opinions, the good speaker respects the right of his listeners to form their own opinions. He will then shun any opportunity to foist his views upon others. He will try to foster those circumstances in which ideas and the speakers who hold them may be freely confronted by other speakers and questioned by listeners. "In the end," Walter Lippmann has written, "what men will most ardently desire is to suppress those who disagree with them and, therefore, stand in the way of their desires."[9] Lippmann sees this desire as the outcome of the right of speaking freely unattended by the concomitant responsibility to entertain direct confrontation of contrary opinions.

We have discussed briefly two responsibilities: to act with the best knowledge one can obtain in the circumstances and to act in such a way as to encourage the freedom of response, the more direct the response, the better. There is a third we would mention: to act openly in one's self-interest.

Each speaker will inevitably have his own interests in subjects with which he is concerned. He has a right to be committed to ideas, to persons, to groups; but in speaking to others he must be responsible for these commitments. He must, in short, be willing to disclose his own interests.

[9] *The Public Philosophy,* New York, Mentor Books, 1956, p. 100.

Although it is not easy to gauge the motives out of which we act, willful distortion of these motives in speaking to others is irresponsible.

Some social scientists see the lack of this responsibility to be a serious threat to the soundness of the social fabric in mid-twentieth century America. For example, in his study of the Kate Smith war bond radio marathon during World War II, sociologist Robert K. Merton was struck by the way men and women emphasized Kate Smith's integrity. He commented:

> The emphasis on this theme reflects a social disorder . . . in which common values have been submerged in a welter of private interests seeking satisfaction by virtually any means which are effective. It is a product of a society in which "salesmanship"—in the sense of selling through deft pretense of concern with the other fellow—has run riot.[10]

Unfortunately the widespread feeling that "everyone's out to get you" was not a momentary phenomenon of the Second World War. Everyone knows only too well the tendency to joke cynically about the motivation of politicians, labor leaders, businessmen, students, college professors, and everyone else.

We can respond in one of two ways, we can use "everyone else" to rationalize our own disposition to distort for public consumption our own motivation, or we can act as openly as we are truly able.

As you gain experience in speaking, weigh the good sense of these three responsibilities. We ask you to consider one test—effects. A speaker is accountable for the effects at which he aims and for the means he uses to gain these ends. To answer the question, "What are good means and good ends?" is no simple matter that we can settle with finality for each reader. This is a question which you will constantly meet in many different contexts and applications—many of these will not directly involve speaking but the insights you gain will be relevant to your problems as a speaker.

As a speaker you must be concerned with the effects of your speech. John Dewey has argued compellingly, "Certainly nothing can justify or condemn means except results. But we must include consequences impartially. . . . It is willful folly to fasten upon some single end or consequence which is liked, and permit the view of that to blot from perception all other undesired and undesirable consequences."[11]

The man who says, "He gets good effects, but his methods are bad," speaks nonsense. Methods are bad because they have bad results. Often these bad results will be long range and difficult to predict. This fact does

[10] *Mass Persuasion: The Social Psychology of a War Bond Drive*, New York, Harpers, 1946, p. 10.

[11] *Human Nature and Conduct*, New York, Henry Holt and Company, 1922, pp. 228–229.

not relieve one of his responsibility for them. For example, I may get you to take good actions immediately by keeping you ignorant, but I shall be responsible, at least in part, for both your immediate desirable action and for the ignorance out of which other undesirable action may grow. Often the bad results will be the weakening of some societal values; for example, if one in speaking attains a laudable goal at which he aims in such a way as to lessen an audience's ability to make free decisions, both effects must be weighed, and the speaker is responsible for both.

The speaker must make a commitment to the group within which he acts. As a speaker he benefits from the institution of free speech and abuses his rights only at the peril of the value which he enjoys. He who jeopardizes the rights of others in speaking is no less immoral than he who steals from another or injures him physically.

SUMMARY

We have discussed briefly the forces that make ours a rhetorical world. We have mentioned some advantages to be gained by speaking and some responsibilities of the speaker. In undertaking the study of speech you are helping to prepare yourself to live effectively in a world of human, verbal interaction; you will gain insight into the advantages and responsibilities of speaking by your own experience. You may come to disagree in some ways with our interpretation of speech and the situation of the speaker. These are complex issues as are most of the issues we face as individuals and as groups. But we must struggle with these issues if we are to deserve the advantages of a materially rich society that has provided the instruments and the freedom necessary to participate in working out our own goals and the directions to be taken in reaching these goals.

In undertaking the study of speech you will be gaining increased ability and opportunity to express yourself. "An idea," says the Swedish film maker Ingmar Bergman, "is a brightly colored thread sticking out of the dark sack of the unconscious. If I begin to wind up this thread, and do it carefully, a complete film will emerge."[12] We may not be artists and the film may not be our medium of expression; we may never become the speakers that Lincoln or Churchill were, nor be moved by the circumstances that moved them. But we too must find ideas and express them for ourselves, making them *our* ideas.

In undertaking the study of speech, you should expect a deep pleasure. It will be the pleasure that comes from acquiring important knowledge, from learning to speak with increased skill, and from committing yourself to meaningful social values.

[12] Hollis Alpert, "Bergman as a Writer," *Saturday Review* (August 27, 1960), p. 23.

2 ⦚ Forming Ideas

It would be pleasant if textbook writers could assume readers brimming with ideas for speeches, possessing notebooks filled with their ideas, and only awaiting some suggestions for embodying those ideas effectively in speeches. As a matter of fact, allowing for a mild degree of hyperbole, the bright, well-educated adult (a description the college student should be striving to fulfill) should be eager to communicate a great number of ideas which he has formed and is forming in our rhetorical world. Free speech is worthless to men and women who have nothing to say.

Fortunately, most students do have something to say. The problem is to help them make the discovery that worthwhile subjects of discourse lie within them and their environment. Once students begin to find and manipulate ideas, the habit grows and the notebooks fill. The problem often becomes one of restraining rather than encouraging them.

Beginning students almost universally complain, "If I could only find a subject. . . ." Although we do not pretend that finding a subject is no trouble at all, we do believe that students make too much of it. Although the "right subject" is important, one should not expect sudden, immense revelations more than once or twice in a lifetime. Our advice is no secret formula; almost every creative artist has attested to it: *Start!* You may start with vague notions or less, but start. Start reading, start conversing,

14

start making notes. Ideas form slowly. Even those that seem to burst in sudden flashes of insight come to persons who at the moment are resting or engaged in other tasks but who have been working on problems to which the "inspiration" is related. Everything else may come to him who waits, but inspiration comes to him who works.

The beginner may agree with what we have said, but still want more specific instruction. We shall try to comply with his quite proper desire. But we must warn, as we shall repeatedly, that if the general suggestions we shall make are to be at all meaningful, they must become so as individuals apply them in specific, personal efforts to compose speeches.

It is common to hear statements like these: "The speaker needs a good idea." "Good ideas make good speeches." "If I only had a good idea. . . ." But these statements raise a question: *What makes an idea a good idea for a speech?* To approach an answer, let us consider two other questions, the first of which we have already dealt with quite generally: "Where does one find ideas for speeches?" and "How should one state ideas for speeches?"

Finding Ideas for Speeches

Let us imagine a conversation. Two boys leave speech class after having been assigned a speech. The instructor has not assigned specific subjects. The students are free to choose their own, ". . . as long as you choose something that you feel quite strongly about. Something you *want* to talk about. You should choose something significant." The two friends walk across campus.

First Boy: I believe I'll talk about boats.
Second Boy: Boats? Why boats?
First: Oh, I don't know. I've always been interested in boats.
Second: Sounds trivial to me. You know what the instructor said about choosing significant subjects.
First: Trivial! That shows what you know. A boat takes a man to handle it.
Second: A man? You buy a big motor and stick it on the back of a fiberglass hull. That takes a man? It might take money . . .
First (*Interrupting*): Who's talking about motor boats? I'm not interested in those hot rods. I'm talking about sail boats. There's something about sailing. A challenge. You feel the wind and watch the water; you know you're alive.
Second: You're going to tell us how to sail a boat, huh?
First: No, you don't get the point. I see I'm going to have plenty of work to do. Besides, I couldn't tell you how to sail a boat in a five-minute speech.
Second: Whatcha going to talk about then? Are you selling boats?
First: In a way I guess I am. It's a matter of attitude. I enjoy sailing, and

I don't think enough people know about the kind of enjoyment you can get. There's something about going places. Not just sitting back and being taken, but working to use the elements. Didn't you ever read sea stories? I was reading just the other day . . .

"First boy" has a good deal of work to do before he is ready to speak, or even before he is ready to say with precision what he'll speak about. But he has a start, and he has started properly, by turning to himself. It is apparent that he is drawing from what he does, what he talks about, and what he reads about.

Personal Experience

The beginning speaker too often neglects badly what he has seen, what he has done, what he has thought. There is not a freshman college student who has not played, worked, and studied with some degree of intensity. The beginner should ask himself questions like these: "What hobbies or leisure activities do I enjoy?" "What jobs have I held?" "What subjects have I studied?"

Often personal experience will only start the beginner toward a subject. He is not yet an expert who can bring to bear immense knowledge and understanding. But at the same time the beginner ought not underestimate what he has done. Some useful beginnings are indicated in these remarks: "I met a Buddhist yesterday. I knew a little about Buddhism and would like to know more. . . ." "I used to help make ice cream in a little plant in my home town. I wonder where ice cream got started anyway. What I mean is. . . ." "I visited the United Nations. . . ." You could multiply the list endlessly.

We shall discuss material, what we shall call supporting material, in Chapter 3. We might remark in anticipation of that chapter that the beginner should not fail to search his own experience for the material that goes with ideas. A near traffic accident may lead a student to want to talk about problems of safe driving. At the same time the story of his experience may well be useful in communicating his ideas to an audience.

Although most students underestimate the worth of their own experience, a few overestimate the sufficiency of what they have seen, done, and thought. "I know all about the attitude of Canadians toward the United States. After all I spent all last summer there." This example may seem too patently absurd, but a number of speakers, not all of them beginners, display similar attitudes toward their subjects. Most of the men and women we have met who deserve to be called "experts" are just those who seem the quickest to express their limitations and seek even more information.

Conversation

What do you talk about ordinarily? Much that is frivolous without doubt; we all do. But on the other hand, not everything that you and your friends discuss is of no potential concern to audiences you might address. The very student who in the morning says, "I have nothing to talk about. How can I make a speech?" will probably, before the day is over, discuss with his friends at least two or three subjects that potentially might be the bases of speeches.

Women talk about clothes. Clothes have history, utility, and meaning. On one level, talk about clothes might be the sheerest sort of trivia; on other levels, the same women might discover ideas that would be well worth communicating. Clothing as a social symbol, for example, is indicated by the title of the novel, *The Man in the Gray Flannel Suit.* Campaigns have been waged for sensible women's shoes. Clothing involves color and, necessarily, fascinating theories about the psychological effects of color.

The student of speech may well wish to sharpen his conversation by pointing it more directly toward ideas which he is considering using in speeches. There is no better way to work some of the vagueness out of the early ideas for speeches than to try them in conversation. The speaker may find himself becoming more and more interested in his subject and developing a desire to learn more about it. On the other hand, conversation may be discouraging. The speaker may discover that his great idea (almost all untried ideas are *great*) when scrutinized is rather flat. But in this case too, he might be challenged to learn more. At any rate, it is better to become disillusioned about the merit of an idea before one uses it in a speech.

Conversation, of course, is one means of gathering ideas and materials from one's friends. Often the speaker will want to formalize the process, will want to talk to an expert or two; in other words, he may find interviews to be valuable. Students are usually surprised at how readily businessmen, labor leaders, politicians, college professors, experts of all sorts will take time to talk with them. The student, of course, should make a definite appointment, telling the person from whom the interview is sought the purpose of the request. It is extremely important that the student prepare for the interview carefully. He should formulate his own thoughts as definitely as possible, preparing specific questions he would like to ask. The student speaker who "wants to know something about the purposes and techniques of interviewing persons applying for employment" and asks a personnel manager to "just tell me everything you know about interviewing applicants," will be met with either disgust or a deluge of information that will sweep him hopelessly adrift.

Reading

The first impulse of many beginning speakers is to run to the library to collect material. And, if the beginner is not unaware of the potential profit of assessing his own past experience and using conversation in his preparation, this is an excellent impulse. For most of us, no general source will be as profitable as our reading. We should do two kinds of reading to help us form initial, tentative ideas for speech and to help us gather the material to refine our ideas and support them: general, daily reading and specialized reading to find data on whatever particular topics we tentatively think we might pursue.

The speech student who suffers from a paucity of ideas probably reads neither regularly nor from substantial sources. There is no "program" which everyone should follow to be well informed, but there are some general recommendations that might be made. Read a newspaper daily, and read it carefully. The columns and editorials may be especially stimulating of ideas for speeches, but the news sections will not prove barren to a good mind. Often students complain that they live in communities in which the daily newspaper is inadequate. Although we ought not be too quick to despise our local newspapers, the thorough, inquisitive student (in or out of college) may want to make use of library facilities to read one of the well-known metropolitan newspapers. *The New York Times* and the *Christian Science Monitor* probably come to your mind, but there are other fine newspapers—*The Washington Post*, the *St. Louis Post-Dispatch*, and the *Atlanta Constitution*, to mention a few. The student may, and probably should, read one of the popular news magazines regularly, although it might be wiser to rotate one's reading among them. The alert student probably already reads at least one magazine of the *Harper's*, *Atlantic Monthly*, *Fortune* sort rather regularly. A person with a mind that is at all active will probably read several nonfiction books each year. If there are too many people, in college classes and out, with too few ideas, our reading habits may give at least a partial explanation. The student who reads only when he is forced to and who says, "I don't know what to talk about," deserves no sympathy.

There is another grave weakness in our reading habits. Most of us, when we do read about controversial problems, select material written from points of view that match our own predilections precisely. We make certain that our minds are not exposed to new ideas. If for no reason other than to find out what the devils on the other side are up to, we should read from sources with which we differ, and, if we intend to speak to audiences composed of people other than enthusiastic mirror-images of ourselves, nothing could be wiser.

Many experienced speakers keep notebooks or files of ideas and materials. The beginning speech student would be well advised to keep an idea notebook. Buy a notebook that is handy to carry with you. Then assess your past experience, your ordinary conversation, your past reading for potential ideas. Jot down any ideas that occur to you; do not hesitate because they may seem vague or wild or stale. You can make them grow. A good idea that occurs to you now and goes unrecorded may be unrecallable later. Add to your notebook day by day. If you are in the least conscientious in this enterprise, you will not need to complain later, "I have nothing to talk about!"

Special Reading

Once the speaker has a tentative idea for a speech, one perhaps that he's tested in conversation, he will want to dig out some relevant materials to help refine and support it. This desire will carry him to the library. We could at this point add highly detailed information on finding material in the library, but we shall not. It is our opinion that many students reading this book will not need such information, and those who do will profit little from such explanations. We shall give the latter only a brief introduction.

One should not assume too readily that he knows all about library resources. The only way to discover what sorts of materials are available and to learn how to use them is by visiting the library repeatedly with specific projects and the object in mind of discovering as much as possible about what's there. Most libraries can furnish printed guides, but for the person who has had no opportunity to use a library, personal help may well be advisable. Library personnel are usually among the world's most helpful people. Your speech instructor is able and willing to give you guidance; you will find some exercises at the end of this chapter which may be helpful. As you use library facilities time after time, you will become quite at home and be amazed at the amount of material available and at the different ways you can track down the necessary material.

Books. Most students are fully aware that a library lists its book holdings in a card catalog. Ordinarily each book has three cards appearing in different places in the alphabetical file: an author card, a title card, and subject matter card. If you know either the author or title of a book, you can find it easily. If you are interested in discovering all the books in the library on some given subject matter, you can look for the general heading, e.g., League of Nations. Because the cataloger may not have used the topical headings you think of, you may have to look under various associated headings. Usually the subject matter cards will list other headings used in the catalog for related subjects.

If you have a book related to the ideas you are interested in exploring, check the author's bibliography and footnotes for references to other books (periodicals, reports, pamphlets, and so on), which you might find useful. Most students report that this simple expedient usually yields a helpful list of sources quite quickly.

By glancing through the table of contents and index, you can often locate specific discussions in which you may be interested. You may well miss some important matter in so doing, but this is a risk all must run. For the sake of conscience one can recall Francis Bacon's famous remark: "Some books are to be tasted, others to be swallowed, and some few to be chewed and digested." Unfortunately, Bacon did not state once and for all which are which.

PERIODICALS. In his regular reading, the student of speech should locate a number of articles relevant to ideas he wishes to develop. But as you begin to work on your ideas you will find quickly that your store of information has obvious lacunas, and that you want to compare your ideas and materials with other views.

Most students have used *The Reader's Guide to Periodical Literature.* Ordinarily you will be checking subject matter headings in this source and must, as when you use the card catalog, do a good deal of cross referencing. Occasionally you will have the name of a specific writer and can check the alphabetical listing by his name.

Quite often you should not be satisfied with the popular periodicals indexed in *The Reader's Guide.* As good as many of these sources may be, you will often want to check more technical or professional work. *The American Psychologist* or *The Economics Quarterly* may contain articles that will give you the ideas and materials to carry your analysis beyond what your audience might typically be faced with.

You should become acquainted with special indexes. *The Social Sciences and Humanities Index* (before June, 1965, *The International Index*) is useful for speech students. You should certainly become acquainted with indexes to materials in areas in which you are especially interested. Education students should be familiar with *The Education Index;* engineering students, with *The Engineering Index.*

NEWSPAPERS. Students with good reading habits long ago may have begun to keep a clipping file. If you have, you may discover that you have a rough sort of index to help you find information in newspapers. If you have clipped newspaper articles relevant to some idea you'd like to develop in a speech, you probably can find similar reports in other newspapers of about the same date. Checking different newspaper versions of events is sometimes highly informative. Major libraries will subscribe to a wide variety of newspapers.

The New York Times Index lists its articles by subject matter and by author, if the article is by-lined. It is the only indexed newspaper in the

United States. Again, the date on which an event is reported or discussed will be an excellent clue to tracing down similar items in other newspapers.

PAMPHLETS. Pamphlets are usually more difficult to use in most libraries than are books or periodicals, but often they will yield specific information that you will find useful. *The Vertical File Service Catalog* lists pamphlets issued by a wide variety of organizations. Publications of the various departments, agencies, and bureaus of the federal government are listed in *The Monthly Catalog—United States Government Publications*. Most major libraries have special reference rooms and a reference librarian who can assist you in using the available resources.

OTHER SOURCES. The speaker may need all sorts of special information and may have recourse to many more sources than we shall discuss here. For example, one of the authors recalled the quotation from Francis Bacon used earlier and needed to check to see that he had it accurately. He turned to H. L. Mencken's *A New Dictionary of Quotations*[1]; a more familiar book of the same sort is *Bartlett's Familiar Quotations*.

Almanacs (*The World Almanac, Information Please Almanac,* and so on) will yield all sorts of statistical and other factual information. The *Statistical Abstract of the United States,* published yearly, is an even richer source of statistical information. Sources such as these are usually held in the reference room of large libraries; in looking for them, a student may find *The Statesman's Yearbook: Statistical and Historical Annual of the States of the World.* Quite often encyclopaedias will be well worth consulting for specific, factual information.

In looking for information about the authors of information, speakers may consult such sources as *Who's Who in America* (or one of the regional versions of this reference book), *Current Biography, The Directory of American Scholars,* or *International Who's Who.*

Making Notes

As you read, you will want to make notes. What should you note? You will want specific pieces of information (Chapter 3 should help indicate what sorts); you will refine your ideas and, perhaps, begin to build outlines (Chapter 4, as well as the rest of this chapter, should help indicate how you may proceed).

In making notes of specific pieces of information, the speaker will be wise to arm himself with a good supply of index cards, either 4″ × 6″ or 3″ × 5″. Learning to jot separate bits of information on separate cards

[1] New York, Alfred A. Knopf, 1962.

will prove to be advantageous. It is easy to sort cards, to classify and re-classify, to put aside those that turn out not to be directly useful, and to rearrange those that are.

You should put three things on each card: (1) a heading indicating what's on the card so that you can sort and rearrange easily, (2) the information itself, and (3) the source. There are various formats you might follow, but a common one looks like this:

1→   The extent of Klee's influence: present and potential

2→   "Klee's influence has not been superficial: it penetrates to the sources of inspiration and is still at work, like a ferment in the heart of our culture. If that culture survives the threat of atomic warfare, and if the new epoch of art initiated in the first half of the twentieth century is allowed to develop in creative freedom, then the work of Klee, visual and pedagogical, will inevitably be the main sap and impulsive force of its growth."

3→   Sir Herbert Read, *A Concise History of Modern Painting*, New York, Praeger, 1959, p. 187.

1→   Using "models" to predict weather

2→   "Each mathematical model represents a theory for the way in which the physical processes within the earth's fluid envelop, interact and bring about changes in its future state. The adequacy of each theory can be tested by comparing real time changes of the true environment to the changes indicated by the mathematical models in advance. If the predicted changes occur in fact, the models can be said to possess fidelity in that they have portrayed the true course of events."

3→   Robert M. White (Head of the Federal Government's Environmental Sciences Administration), "By Simulating Catastrophe," *Saturday Review* (May 7, 1966), p. 63.

Notice that an indication of the author's position is included with the source in the second example. Some note takers like to indicate the author's name just after the heading rather than at the bottom with the source. Others like to indicate the complete source—author's name, article and periodical, or book, date, page numbers—second, and then the quotation or paraphrase of the material.

Some note takers, to avoid the labor of copying the complete source several times on different cards, use a code number that matches a bibliography list. This method may save time *if* the note taker is an orderly person who never misplaces lists.

It is often wise to delay affixing headings to notecards until a later re-reading. At that time, the speaker may have a clearer idea of the shape that his ideas are likely to take in the speech and, therefore, be able to label his information in a more useful fashion.

STATING IDEAS

It is impossible to separate getting ideas from stating ideas. In practice the two are inseparable. In phrasing ideas the speaker should turn to his own past experience, to conversations, and to reading and in so doing hold in mind that he seeks to communicate to an audience possessing knowledge, abilities, needs, and attitudes. He should begin to jot down any idea that occurs to him. Most beginners make the mistake of wanting to wait until the idea seems fully formed and satisfactory before attempting to write it down as the beginning for working out a speech.

Most ideas for speeches begin as what we call *topics* but ought not to remain in this form long. "First student" in our hypothetical conversation had a topic—boats. The United Nations, personnel practices, Bernard Shaw, world law, water conservation, radiation, censorship, mutual funds, megalopolism, scholarships, Christianity, NATO, and so on represent topics. These represent more or less vague centers of interest for the persons who might jot down any of them.

The speaker might soon modify his topics: strengthening the United Nations, personnel practices in universities and colleges, Bernard Shaw's theory of humor, world peace through world law, progress in water conservation. These topics are narrower than their first versions. The speaker should seek progressively to narrow his topics, realizing that like the small, unattended boy in a cafeteria, he is apt to take more than he can handle.

All too often we hear speakers, in the classroom and out, who undertake to talk about "problems in the Near East," "maps, map-makers, and map-readers," "reviewing election procedures," and the like, but we are never quite sure just what they are talking about. Whereas topics make good places to begin and might serve well as titles for printed programs or announcements, the speaker must have a much more precise statement of his idea. If the speaker cannot state his subject with precision and clarity, he has no right to expect his audience to be able to do so.

A good speech should be unified; it should be governed by a single idea toward which all other ideas and materials in the speech should point. This central idea can be indicated by a number of different labels, but for the sake of convenience we shall use only one and that is a very common one—*thesis. The thesis should be stated as a single declarative sentence.* It may take many attempts to phrase the thesis in a way that will satisfy the speaker that it expresses his idea properly. Before discussing the statement of thesis further, another point should be considered. In arriving at a position to view his subject in relationship to his audience in such a way as to make a satisfactory statement of the thesis possible, the speaker should consider quite carefully the purpose with which he speaks.

Stating the Purpose

The speaker speaks to communicate, true; but that is the most general statement of his purpose. He must communicate something to someone. The best way to think of the purpose is in terms of the *response* that you want from your audience. What do you want them to think, to understand, to say, to feel, to know, to do, to value, to despise? The audience will respond in some way, if only to decide (although the decision is not always a highly conscious one) that the speaker is not worth listening to and that dozing or staring out the window will be more pleasurable. You must realize that an audience will respond and you must seek to guide those responses. *The way to start is by deciding what response to the speech you want the audience to have.*

Traditionally, purposes are classified generally by three infinitives: to entertain, to inform, and to persuade. A speech "to entertain" may be thought of as one in which the speaker desires to keep the audience pleasurably engaged in listening to him for five, ten, twenty minutes or so. Beyond the recollection of having enjoyed listening, the speaker does not care how the listeners respond. A speech "to inform" may be thought of as one in which the speaker has some body of knowledge which he wants the audience to understand and to remember. A speech "to persuade" may be thought of as one in which the speaker undertakes to change the attitudes or actions of an audience. Traditionally, the speech "to persuade" is sub-divided into speeches "to stimulate," "to convince," and "to actuate." The speech "to stimulate" is one in which the speaker assumes that the audience's attitudes are much like his own (they, too, believe in the doctrine, the candidate, the program, the principle) but that these attitudes need to be sharpened, to be made more immediate and important to the listeners. The speech "to convince" is one in which the speaker assumes that the listeners possess attitudes that differ to some degree from his own; he speaks to modify those attitudes by making them more like his. In the speech "to actuate" the speaker aims at getting his audience to take some observable action.

The speaker may state his purpose for a specific speech by extending the infinitive to make a phrase. He may, for example, speak to entertain his listeners with a series of anecdotes concerning a small boy's difficulty in communicating with the adult world of his parents, to inform his listeners of the methods of merchandising paperback books, or to convince his listeners that the federal government must operate under a balanced budget this year. This sort of statement may be called the "specific purpose."

Although viewing purpose in speaking as taking three general forms and using one of these general forms to state a specific purpose for a speech may be useful procedures, they are limited and too often misleading. For his own use the speaker should try to state his purpose in terms that seem to him uniquely proper for expressing his particular subject in terms of the desired response of his listeners. In doing so, the infinitive form will probably occur. Further, the traditional forms of "to entertain," "to inform," and "to convince," may be useful if they are viewed as points of departure rather than as necessary categories into which all speeches will fit neatly.

When one examines a specific speech to determine purpose, he rarely finds a clean example of a speech to entertain or to inform. Almost inevitably speeches, which seem at first to fit into these categories, take on persuasive colorations, sometimes quite strong ones. "Pure" speeches to entertain are rare. This is not to say that a speaker who may aim only to relieve the tensions of daily living by amusing an audience is not performing a legitimate speech purpose, although such distraction may be better served by means other than speeches. Most speeches that are highly amusing attempt to change attitudes, values, and behavior. The speech to entertain an audience with a series of anecdotes concerning a small boy's difficulty in communicating to the adult world may bring the audience to be more sympathetic with the attempts of children to communicate and to be more sensitive to the nature of the problems children face. "Pure" speeches to inform are also rare. Many speeches to inform may demand that the audience listen because the information is important if not vital to its interests. If indeed the information is important, it will probably have some effects upon the attitudes of the audience. For the speaker to say, "I don't care about these possible effects," is blind at best and dishonest at worst. It may be that the speaker will not want to make evaluations or demands explicit, but he ought to examine clearly the implications of the material and take into account what effects these may have in planning his purpose.

Every speech will be at once a speech to entertain (in that the audience will find pleasure in listening or probably won't listen at all), to inform (in that even a conscious effort to give no information will probably fail, the speaker ought recognize that he will be dealing with information of some sort), and to persuade (in that at least the speaker will want the audience to value what is done and at most will want to direct specific beliefs or actions). It is possible in a well-unified speech to serve several rather distinct purposes if the speaker works carefully; ordinarily, however, one purpose will tend to be dominant.

We feel that it is quite useful for the speaker to write a paragraph, or even more, setting out the purpose for which he speaks—the response or group of interrelated responses he desires from his audience. This paragraph will not be part of the speech as such but will be a preliminary step in composition. There is a danger in this procedure. Speakers are apt to be too indefinite in their aims, and indefiniteness may arise in writing at length about purpose just as it may in the most terse statement of a topic. However, if a speaker also states a thesis quite carefully, he can avoid this danger.

Let us consider an example of the statement of a speech purpose adapted from the work of a speech student.

My audience expects a speech to entertain, and I hope not to disappoint them; however, I have a rather specific attitude that I hope to communicate to my listeners and perhaps at least shake their predispositions to respond heartily to the subject with which I shall deal, the so-called "adult TV westerns." In my opinion adult westerns are adult only in superficialities—the heroes sometimes drink, smoke and carry on romantic relationships but in the end, "good" triumphs. The emphasis is mainly on the distractions of physical violence, but, in addition, violence is enthroned as a means to an end.

Basically "adult westerns" are not much different from old-fashioned "children's westerns." I shall, therefore, advocate the return to "children's westerns" which are at least morally superior in that the heroes do not drink, smoke nor consort with women. I hope in so doing to make it clear that westerns are childish. Making my point of view clear will be difficult, but I shall aim at convincing my audience, or at least upsetting them a little, and to do so in a way that will entertain them.[2]

This statement is not perfect nor was the speech perfect. But the speaker did have rather clear ideas of the sort of response he wanted from his audience. Full statements of purpose are apt to bring speakers to the clearest possible understanding of what it is that they are attempting.

Stating the Thesis

The thesis should be stated as a complete declarative sentence and as precisely and vividly as possible. Sometimes the statement of a thesis will come quickly; often the speaker will find it difficult to state and will revise his phraseology time and again. The more carefully the speaker has

[2] Adapted from an outline prepared by Donald Marti, University of Minnesota student, 1959.

worked out his purpose, the more confidently he will be able to state his thesis.

Try to think of the thesis as an assertion. We make assertions constantly: we ought to go to work earlier; nutritious lunches can be inexpensive, tasty, and easy to prepare; this dictionary is better than that one. Let your assertion represent the subject with which you want to deal and reflect your consideration of the particular audience to whom you will speak. Here are some samples.

Final examinations are designed to stimulate the student to learn, to help him evaluate his accomplishments, and to provide the instructor with a basis for assigning a grade.
Final examinations are absurd.
Final examinations should be abolished.

Any one of these three examples might serve as the thesis for a speech. The first will probably be basically a speech "to inform"; the other two, speeches "to persuade." The second, however, might be the basis of a quite entertaining speech. You will notice that each succeeding example is broader. The second might be included as a part of a speech for which the third example stood as the thesis.

WHAT ARE GOOD IDEAS FOR SPEECHES?

Good ideas for speeches are those that the speaker has drawn from his experience—either his own past experience, or from his reading, or, preferably, both—and which he has tested in conversation. Good ideas for speeches must be chosen and limited in terms of the listeners for whom they are intended. Good ideas for speeches must be well stated. The wise speaker will consider his purpose carefully and state it fully; he will state a thesis as a single declarative sentence.

Good ideas are those that the speaker wants to talk about. He should not, however, feel that a strong desire to speak must fasten on him unbidden and with a terrible swiftness. A strong desire to speak will probably grow as the speaker considers his own experiences, values, and convictions, as he thinks through and talks through his vague ideas, and as he relates these ideas to his audience's knowledge, needs, and attitudes.

Library Assignments

Note: In making bibliographical citations of sources, use these forms.

FOR BOOKS
Loring, L. M., *Two Kinds of Values*, London, Routledge and Kegan Paul, 1966.

Whitton, John B., and Arthur Larson, *Propaganda, Toward Disarmament in the War of Words,* Dobbs Ferry, New York, Oceana Publications, Inc., 1964.

For Periodicals
Gavin, James M., "Military Power: The Limits of Persuasion," *Saturday Review* (July 30, 1966), pp. 18–22, 64.

For Periodical Articles with No Listed Author
"Black Power: Road to Disaster?" *Newsweek* (August 22, 1966), pp. 32–36.

1. Using *Reader's Guide to Periodical Literature,* look up "conscientious objectors" (or some other topic assigned by your instructor).
   a. What cross references are given?
   b. What magazines are cited with which you are not familiar?
   c. List articles from at least three magazines, preferably from magazines unfamiliar to you. Browse through several issues of each of these magazines just to get acquainted with them.
2. Using *The Social Sciences and Humanities Index,* repeat the steps for number one. What is the difference between these two indexes?
3. What other indexes to periodical literature can you find in your library?
4. Using the card catalog
   a. Look up either *pacifism* or *guerrilla warfare.*
      (1) What cross references are given?
      (2) List at least three books on one of these topics.
   b. Does your library have a copy of the Loring book listed earlier? Does it have a copy of Clive Bell's *Old Friends?* Of A. H. Maslow's *Toward a Psychology of Being?* Of Allen Tate's *The Forlorn Demon?* Of Thomas Wolfe's *You Can't Go Home Again?*
5. Using Thomas Wolfe (or some other major author assigned by your instructor)
   a. What books *by* the author does your library have?
   b. What books *about* the author does your library have?
   c. What periodical articles published during the last four years about the man or his work can you find through the use of relevant indexes?
   d. What problems did you face in this project growing from the fact that other men have the same or similar names?
6. Compare articles on the same subject from at least three encyclopedias.
   a. Which article do you consider best?
   b. Why?

For Class Discussion

1. Come to class with a topic which you feel has the potential to become a good subject for a speech.
2. Working as a class, or in smaller groups, try to phrase different purposes upon which speeches might be made selecting from among the topics individuals suggest.
3. Discuss the merits of the statements of purpose. Select those which seem to be most interesting to the group.
4. Try to phrase a thesis for each statement of purpose selected.
5. To supplement this exercise, choose one thesis. Go to the library to find relevant material. Make an annotated bibliography of not less than five items. (By *annotated* we mean add to the bibliographical citation of the source a paragraph or more in which you summarize the material presented in whatever source you cite. Strive to be concise.)

3 ❙ Supporting Ideas

They do not understand me; I am not the mouth for these ears.

NIETZSCHE

True beauty and usefulness always go hand in hand.

QUINTILIAN

As a speaker formulates ideas in relationship to his audience and his own purposes, he asserts these ideas for his own analysis and ultimately he will either assert or imply them in the speech itself. One of his primary tasks in his speech will be to make his ideas clear, interesting, and acceptable to his listeners. All of us can sympathize with Nietzsche's Zarathustra. Like him we may wish to withdraw to the mountains. But Nietzsche makes Zarathustra come down from the heights repeatedly to preach in the town and to the passersby.

The tendencies to rail at listeners for being obtuse or to stand haughtily aloof are all too familiar. Rather than turning away from audiences it may be wiser to turn toward our *truths* and our development of them. Consider, for example, these assertions: "When the Russians use the word *coexistence*, they do not mean by it what we Americans are apt to assume." "The principles upon which the slide rule is constructed are simple ones that can be readily understood and applied by anyone." "If we are to fulfill our responsibilities toward ourselves and others, we must be governed by the concept of self-determination." "Norman Mailer's *Cannibals and Christians* is a bad book." How many of these assertions are clear, interesting, and acceptable? The speaker cannot, of course, answer this question without first modifying it by asking another: *To whom?* But assume yourself to be the audience to whom the assertions are addressed. What ones meet all three criteria? Imagine yourself making these assertions to any audience. What kind of responses might you get? "What do you mean 'bad book'?" "Slide rules! I never could understand math." "Another moralist is about to tell me how I should behave."

The point should be clear. Whereas some assertions may be instantly clear, interesting, and acceptable to audiences and then may be used to help support other assertions, most assertions cannot stand alone; and most ideas, asserted or implied without support, deserve the application of the often-heard *mere assertion* with all the negative evaluations it implies.

If an intelligent person who had never studied theories of speech-making were to listen carefully to a large number of speeches or were to read the best speeches of the ages, he would soon discover that good speakers tend to make use of recognizable means of making assertions clear, interesting, and acceptable. These means have traditionally been isolated and discussed in speech textbooks usually under the heading of *supporting materials*.

The term *supporting materials* is a good one. Think for a moment about the function of *supporting;* think in a physical sense of things that need supporting and of what supports. You and the chairs you sit in have legs; houses have foundations; battles have supporting actions; he who is destitute has "no means of support." Think for a moment about the word *material*. "That which gives substance" is material. "We can't build a bookcase. We just don't have the material." Football coaches are often heard to make similar statements. Too often speakers "just don't have the material" necessary to build ideas—clearly, interestingly, and acceptably.

He who would become a speaker must concern himself with three questions. *What sorts of supporting materials are there? Where can I discover supporting materials for my speeches? How can I distinguish good material from poor or just passable material?* We have dealt with the second question in Chapter 2. We shall now give some terms and suggestions that may help speakers answer the two other questions. But one must remember that these are not the sorts of questions that can be answered "once and for all." Each speaker must continually endeavor to increase his understanding of the answers, and to find fresh answers as well, as he deals with specific subjects and specific audiences. Our answers will be somewhat arbitrary. With the third question especially, one might well work endlessly, and we shall make only a beginning in answering it.

What sorts of supporting materials are there? An answer to this question must be arbitrary and artificial. In the first place, many different divisions and labels are possible. We shall choose a list of categories which we believe is simple and useful. In the second place, a given passage may be composed of the intertwined elements of several different kinds of supporting materials. A good speaker, for example, may make simultaneous use of testimony, statistics, and visual aids. The student ought not to be misled by any textbook's categorization of materials into believing that the types necessarily stand neatly apart. But in general, supporting materials may be classified as

EXAMPLES
STATISTICS
TESTIMONY
ANALOGIES
VISUAL AIDS

EXAMPLES

In Alberto Moravia's novel *The Lie,* the protagonist, an intellectual, undertakes to explain an idea to his wife, a shrewd, complex woman, but no intellectual. He says to her:

"Ah, yes, there may be some truth in that. I was looking . . . I was looking for something which I then called 'genuineness' and which it seemed to me I had found in you."
"Genuineness?"
"Yes."
"What does 'genuine' mean?"
"Genuine, in the sense in which I use it, means 'sincere.' "
"Sincere?"
"Yes—that is, real, authentic, not false, not a parody."
"A parody?"
"A parody—that is, an ironical imitation."
"Well, tell me something that's genuine, give me an example."

If this conversation makes any reader smile slightly, his amusement may result partly from its familiarity. All of us have demanded of someone, "Give me an example of that." And we have all had similar demands made on us. Listen carefully today to see how many times you hear the words *for example* used. In trying to make ideas clear and compelling in conversation, we all use examples and often label them as such.

In trying to understand an idea or to get another to accept an idea, a critical question is, "Has the thing happened?" If so, when? Where? How? A speaker bewailing the moral decay he sees among his contemporaries and wishing to stress the danger may point to the oft-used example of imperial Rome. A speaker desiring to make viable the idea of patient, persistent commitment to a goal in spite of staggering obstacles may tell us in some detail about the work of Marie and Pierre Curie. An entire speech may be composed of a single example. Although rare, such speeches can be impelling, as Wendell Phillips' famous "Toussaint L'Ouverture" demonstrates.[1]

A speaker who knows what examples are, who is continually looking for examples, is apt to find them. The more examples a speaker finds, evaluates, and uses, the more he will learn about examples. Some elementary classifications of examples may prove useful. Examples are either detailed or undetailed, factual or hypothetical.

Undetailed Examples

Who these days hasn't heard someone remark, "The pollsters can be wrong. Look what Harry Truman did in 1948." Almost everyone has heard some speaker or another say, in effect, "Great handicaps can be overcome, as Helen Keller's life proves." Neither of these examples is detailed, although they could be. The speaker assumes that the examples are well known to his audience and that he merely needs mention them.

Although undetailed examples may stand singly, it is common and highly effective to compound them. The great advantage of an undetailed example is that it is short, that it takes little time; the speaker may, therefore, pile example on example as Frederick Douglass, an ex-slave, did in Rochester, New York, in 1852, when he *refused* "to prove that the slave is a man":

> For the present, it is enough to affirm the equal manhood of the Negro race. Is it not astonishing that, while we are plowing, planting, and reaping, using all kinds of mechanical tools, erecting houses, constructing bridges, building ships, working in metals of brass, iron, copper, silver, and gold; that, while we are reading, writing, and ciphering, acting as clerks, merchants, and secretaries, having among us lawyers, doctors, ministers, poets, authors, editors, orators, and teachers; that, while we are engaged in all manner of enterprises common to other men, digging gold in California, capturing the whale in the Pacific, feeding sheep and cattle on the hillside, living, moving, acting, thinking, planning, living in families as husbands, wives, children, and, above all, confessing and worshiping the Christian's God, and looking hopefully for life and immortality beyond the grave, we are called upon to prove that we are men!!

Although some of Douglass' audience might have known a Negro clerk or have seen a Negro working in metals, many probably had never seen or perhaps heard of Negro poets or gold miners. Yet all the activities

---

[1] This rather long address is an excellent one for the serious student of speech to study. See Wendell Phillips, *Speeches, Lectures, and Letters*, Boston, Lothrup, Lee and Shepard, 1893, pp. 468–494. The speech may also be found in W. M. Parrish and Marie Hochmuth (eds.), *American Speeches*, New York, Longmans, Green and Company, 1954, pp. 311–322.

referred to might plausibly be undertaken by Negroes, and at any rate, the examples need no detailing. Probably the audience understood and was held and compelled by Douglass' multiplication of examples.

Detailed Examples

In praising the qualities of the Negro leader in the Haitian revolution Wendell Phillips uses this detailed example in his "Toussaint L'Ouverture":

The second story told of him is this. About the time he reached the camp, the army had been subjected to two insults. First, their commissioners, summoned to meet the French Committee were ignominiously and insultingly dismissed; and when, afterwards, Francois, their general, was summoned to a second conference, and went to it on horseback, accompanied by two officers, a young lieutenant, who had known him as a slave, angered at seeing him in the uniform of an officer raised his riding-whip and struck him over the shoulders. If he had been the savage which the Negro is painted to us, he had only to breathe the insult to his twenty-five thousand soldiers, and they would have trodden out the Frenchmen in blood. But the indignant chief rode back in silence to his tent, and it was twenty-four hours before his troops heard of this insult to their general. Then the word went forth, "Death to every white man!" They had fifteen hundred prisoners. Ranged in front of the camp, they were about to be shot. Toussaint, who had a vein of religious fanaticism, like most great leaders—like Mohammed, like Napoleon, like Cromwell, like John Brown [Cheers]—he could preach as well as fight—mounting a hillock, and getting the ear of the crowd, exclaimed: "Brothers, this blood will not wipe out the insult to our chief; only the blood in yonder French camp can wipe it out. To shed that is courage; to shed this is cowardice and cruelty besides;"—and he saved fifteen hundred lives.

Inasmuch as Phillips cannot assume that his audience knows about the incident or that they accept his assertions, he must tell about the occurrence in detail. "I cannot stop to give in detail every one of his efforts," said Phillips, knowing that detailed examples take time and that, therefore, they must be used judiciously. But he also knew that a carefully selected, well-detailed example is worth the time it takes. (Notice that within this detailed example the phrase "like Mohammed, like Napoleon, like Cromwell, like John Brown . . ." is a quick series of undetailed examples.)

Hypothetical Examples

The categories of examples we have listed overlap. Every example referred to in the previous discussion of detailed and undetailed examples is also factual. Whereas the meaning of *factual* should be clear enough in this context, a few words concerning *hypothetical* examples may prove useful.

In fighting for the Compromise of 1850, Henry Clay stated the issues that threatened to lead to disunion, and then argued, "Well, now, let us suppose that the Union has been dissolved. What remedy does it furnish for the grievances complained of in its united condition?" Twenty years earlier in his famous reply to Hayne, Daniel Webster used the hypothetical mode of dealing with the threat of disunion by imagining in some detail the circumstances—the actions of the states and of the representatives of the federal government—that would probably occur in order to emphasize the impossibility of peaceful secession.

The hypothetical example, the "supposed" case, is an ancient device, but too often the beginning speaker overlooks the possibilities. The speaker with vigor and imagination can often invent hypothetical examples to make his ideas clear, interesting, and acceptable. In speaking to fellow managers on employer-employee relations, Charles J. Stilwell invited his listeners to imagine with him:

Let's put ourselves in the other fellow's place. If you got no satisfaction out of your job as employer, if you had no pride in the sense of accomplishment, if you didn't feel yourself a vital part of a dynamic organization, all the pay you would get would be money. Take away all those things that make up your compensation, and every one of you would demand that your pay be doubled, because money would be all that was left.

Out in your shop a man comes to work at 7 A.M. He doesn't know too much about his job and almost nothing about his company or how his work fits into it. He works eight hours and goes home—with what? His pay and nothing more. Nobody (except the union steward) took much if any notice of him. Nobody complimented him if he did do well because nobody realized that fact. Nobody ever flattered him by asking his opinion about something. In millions of cases nobody ever told him the importance of his work.

At night he goes home to his family and neighbors—unimportant, with nothing to boast about or even talk about. And the union calls a meeting to discuss a grievance—that workman can get up on his feet and sound off while people listen, he can be an officer with a title, he can boast to his family and friends how he "gave those big shots of the company what-for!" A strike vote is exciting! Being a picket is important! He gets looked at and talked about; he wears a badge!

Again, let's be honest. If you and I were in that worker's situation, wouldn't we do pretty much what he's doing?[2]

Quite often the speaker is warned against the use of hypothetical examples. Even though most authorities grant that such examples may be

---

[2] "Effective Leadersip for Better Employee Relations," *Vital Speeches*, (Dec. 15, 1947), p. 156.

useful for making ideas clear and interesting, "they don't prove anything." Whether or not hypothetical examples "prove anything" depends on the examples and what one means by "prove." Did Stilwell "prove anything" with his example? Probably the example did help listeners to see his point. In this case as in many, understanding could help lead to belief.[3]

Selecting and Using Examples

The alert speaker will continually search for examples—undetailed and detailed, factual and hypothetical. He will search for examples to support specific ideas he wishes to make clear, interesting, and acceptable to prospective listeners. Finding examples, in turn, may bring the speaker himself to new insights. In composing a speech, the speaker will constantly ask himself, "What is a good example? Is this example phrased as it should be? Which of these examples should I use?" Although there are no criteria that can be applied as set, unchanging rules, the beginning speaker will raise these questions:

1. Is the example clearly relevant to the idea?
2. Is the example appropriate to the audience?
3. Is the example typical?
4. Is the example properly detailed?

We must emphasize that these suggested questions are not iron rules. Take, for example, the third question. When will an audience accept an example as being typical? Often this question will depend on the number of examples used and the context in which the example or examples are used. A speaker might, by citing examples of dishonest policemen in a given city, charge that "Our police force needs reform." How many examples would warrant such a generalization? Surely we would not have to wait until 50 per cent of the force were shown to be dishonest; the assertion is a limited one and in this case even a few examples would constitute cause for concern. The rule must, therefore, be applied sensibly, not rigidly—a statement that applies to any of the other "rules" presented in this and in any other book about speaking. On the other hand, if the idea the speaker were making is that "Our police officers are corrupt," one or two examples would in no way establish the generalization.

How many examples should a speaker use? In general it is safe to say that he should use as many as possible. It is often useful to demonstrate that the examples are typical either by producing enough of them to satisfy one's listeners or by demonstrating statistically that the examples

---

[3] For an interesting and deailed discussion of "real" and "invented" examples, see Richard Whately, *Elements of Rhetoric*, (London: B. Fellows), 1836, Chap. II, sec. 7.

used fit the average for the sort of example. Thus a speaker might give a single detailed example about the condition of the Southern sharecropper, describing his home, his family and their circumstances, his hopes and frustrations, his dreams and his realities. If the speaker follows this description with statistics to show that this sharecropper makes about the same amount of money per year that the average sharecropper does, he will have demonstrated that the example he has used is typical and may have made the sharecropper he described a symbol, in the minds of his audience, for all sharecroppers.

Attention to the detail of an example will often help solve some of the problems that arise in answering the previous questions. "Can I cut the detail out entirely so that I can overwhelm my audience with a number of examples as Frederick Douglass did?" the speaker may ask. "Can I add detail that will make the example more vivid? Can I add detail that will help my listeners relate the incident and the idea to their own needs, experiences, interests, and knowledge?"

Reread the examples used by Wendell Phillips and Charles Stilwell. These examples are vivid and specific. Notice how both speakers introduce touches of dialogue. Some speakers make extensive use of dialogue in examples. Phillips introduced the name of John Brown and brought cheers from New Englanders for whom Brown was a recent martyr. Both speakers bring their stories to a climax.

Consider a part of the speech which Henry R. Luce, then Editor in Chief of *Time, Life,* and *Fortune,* gave at the 1953 commencement of Temple University. Mr. Luce opened by telling his audience about being in Rome and asking "a middle-aged gentleman: 'What is the name of this bridge?' 'This,' said he, 'is Ponte Garibaldi.' And then, his eyes lighting up, he continued: 'And there, the next one is Ponte Mazzini and beyond, at the bend of the river, Ponte Cavour." Luce talked about the meaning of his phrase, "The Great Liberal Tradition," and then said:

Let me tell you a little about Garibaldi, Mazzini, and Cavour. Garibaldi ran away from home when he was 15, fired by what he had heard about liberty. He became the master of revolutionary war, the first great guerrilla leader. For a decade he was an exile in South America. He established liberty in Uruguay, one South American country which has kept it ever since. And he found in Brazil the great love of his life, Anita, who shared hardship and danger in the cause she also loved. Finally Garibaldi came home and with his 1,000 Red Shirts landed in Sicily, swept down the rotten defense of a long, rotten regime, and a few years later rode into Rome with Victor Emmanuel II, the constitutional king to whom he had given his allegiance. Today, high above the banks of the Tiber is a huge statue of Garibaldi on a horse, overlooking the whole of Rome—and not far from him is a statue of Anita, carrying her infant child in the saddle as she, too, rides for liberty!

Garibaldi, the man of action, the soldier. And there was Mazzini, an entirely different character. The idealist, the impassioned intellectual, the ceaseless propagandist for what we would call today the brotherhood of man under the Fatherhood of God. Like Garibaldi, he was often exiled and suffered torture. He failed in all his particular schemes, he never entered Rome or anywhere in triumph. But historians call him the soul of the Italian Risorgimento.

And there was Cavour—the practical man, who made dreams come true. An aristocrat and a businessman, as many of these nineteenth century liberals were, he started with a tiny little kingdom in Northern Italy, he built the first railroad, he encouraged commerce, he went into politics and, maneuvering among the great powers—France, Germany, Austria, Britain—he parlayed his tiny kingdom into a key position and he made Italy united and free. Historians, noting all the many great men of the nineteenth century, call Cavour the ablest statesman of that age.

What has all this to do with America?[4]

Luce's question indicates clearly that he saw the necessity of making the relevance of his examples clear. He went on to assert that America stood as an inspiration to these Italian liberals. Later in his speech, after he had developed his ideas in more detail, he referred to these examples:

The work of the Liberal Tradition can not be done by a single party or a single style of mind. It requires the combined work of thinkers and dreamers like Mazzini, fighters like Garibaldi, negotiators like Cavour.[5]

In this mixture the examples are undetailed. The speaker may simply refer to them because he has acquainted his audience with them earlier. The listeners can see the relevance of the examples easily.

Were these examples appropriate to his audience? Probably so. The speaker had before him primarily a group of college graduates, men and women who had studied history or at least felt that their minds could or should be able to cope with the meaning of the people, places, and events referred to.

Are these examples typical? This is a more difficult question to answer. But probably the situation, the assertions made, did not call the question to the minds of the audience.

These three examples are relatively short. The speaker wanted all three and could not assume that he could use them as undetailed examples. He had to give enough detail to make them lively and meaningful for his audience and yet keep them rather strictly limited within a complex speech. He gives us the most detail for Garibaldi, making him a living man not only with a mission but with a wife and a child. The detail

---

[4] The Great Liberal Tradition," a speech delivered by Henry R. Luce, Editor in Chief, *Time*, *Life* and *Fortune*, at the Sixty-seventh Annual Commencement of Temple University, Philadelphia, Pa., copyright, Time Inc., pp. 1, 3–4.
    [5] *Ibid.*, p. 8.

of the first example enables the speaker to deal much more quickly with Mazzini and Cavour without losing the feeling that here are real men uniquely involved in great reforms.

On the Use of Humor in Examples

"May I use humor in my speech?" a student will often ask. Of course the question may involve plans to use material other than examples, but it most often arises when a speaker believes that he has a "funny story" to tell. The question is a most difficult one to answer; any reply must be prefaced with "yes, if. . . ."

There are a few occasions upon which humor would not be appropriate, but very few. The speaker should not equate a long face with serious purpose. The man who has never learned to smile at adversity, who has never sensed the absurdity that permeates so much of human conduct, may be the most frivolous thinker of all. When one thinks of the coupling of humor with serious intent one almost inevitably remembers the great dramatists from Aristophanes to Moliere to Shaw who certainly caught the attention of their contemporaries and whose work remains an important part of the accumulation of human thought. Speakers have been no less aware of the utility of humor than have the dramatists. The reports of the Lincoln-Douglas debates in 1858 are heavily interspersed with the reporters' notes of "laughter."

"The theory of comedy in general is perhaps the most elusive and tenuous among all theories in polite learning," Marvin T. Herrick has observed, "and certainly the theory of what makes people laugh is the most baffling element in comedy."[6] Although we cannot analyze at length the theory of the laughable, we ought to look for humor in incongruity; any statement, situation, or action that upon closer examination is not what it seems at first to be is potentially humorous.[7] Bernard Shaw claimed that humor lies in the discrepancy between what man is and what he pretends to be, in man's attempt to romanticize fallible human institutions.[8] At any rate, the speaker who is alert to problems will see manifestations of them, which present opportunities to make use of examples that are humorous.

[6] "The Theory of the Laughable in the Sixteenth Century," *Quarterly Journal of Speech*, XXV (February 1949), p. 1.
[7] For classical discussions of humor see Aristotle, *De Poetica*, chapter 5, and Cicero, *De Oratore*, Book II. Aristotle defined the ridiculous as "a mistake or deformity, not productive of pain or harm to others . . ." (1449a 34–35). Although it is difficult sometimes to determine what produces pain or harm, the speaker should take care that his humor is not at the expense of others. Many successful speakers have learned that it is often wise to make oneself the butt of one's jokes.
[8] See the preface to *Plays Pleasant in Prefaces by Bernard Shaw*, London, Constable and Company, 1934, pp. 701–702.

We recognize, however, that although humor can be useful in gaining the attention of an audience and making others remember an idea presented, many speakers err badly in making use of humor. The wise speaker will keep his mind's eye squarely upon his subject, for material which he believes humorous, no less than any other material, must be relevant to the matter at hand. The most common mistake the beginner makes (and many others who should know better from experience) is to tell an allegedly funny story for its own sake. Resist that temptation. If the ideas are worthwhile, they deserve the speaker's effort to make them clear and interesting; by no means should he distract the audience's attention with irrelevant though humorous examples. The best humor is that which grows out of the ideas and the situation in which the speaker is engaged.

By no means should a speaker adopt a "stop me if you've heard this" attitude. He must determine in advance whether or not the material is relevant. If it is, perhaps, it will bear retelling even though some of the audience may have heard it, but the speaker should be cautious, knowing that retelling wears a story thin quickly. There is no easy way to tell whether or not material will really be humorous. Actual trial is best; practice before listeners whom one respects may help the speaker decide upon the appropriateness of his material.

Unfortunately many speakers, not only college students, need to be cautioned concerning the propriety of some sorts of humor. Too many speakers learn to their chagrin that the embarrassment level of an audience is much more quickly reached than that of the individuals who may compose it. What may well be appropriate in an informal gathering even of "mixed company" may not be responded to at all well in a public speaking situation. As a student once put it, "When in doubt, leave it out."

The answer to the student's question, "May I use humor in my speech?" is yes, *if* . . . if it is relevant to the ideas of the speech, if it really is humorous, and if it is appropriate for the audience to whom one speaks.

Statistics

Statistics are closely related to examples. If a speaker wishes to impress his audience with the poverty of a given geographical section of the country, he might use detailed factual examples of several families residing there. But, probably, because of the inevitable demand, "Typical?" he may add, "Only 10 per cent of the families live on incomes of more than $3,000 a year, while more than 50 per cent live on incomes of less than

$1,500 yearly." Statistics serve to give an orderly summary of many examples.

Technically, the term *figures* may be used to indicate numbers referring to simple quantity: "There are twenty students present." *Statistics* may be used to refer to a statement of ratio or proportion: "Only half of the students were present." For ordinary purposes, however, the terms may be interchanged, which is fortunate for the many speakers who find *statistics* a difficult combination of sounds to utter.

Call them *figures* or *statistics* but use them. President Franklin D. Roosevelt speaking before a labor audience in 1944 said, "Labor baiters forget that, at our peak, American labor and management have turned out airplanes at the rate of 109,000 per year; tanks, 57,000 per year; combat vessels, 573 per year; landing vessels, 31,000 per year; cargo ships, 19,000,000 tons per year, and small arms ammunition, 23 billion rounds per year."[9]

As Roosevelt knew, the simple weight of figures may make an idea dramatic. Lt. Gen. James M. Gavin. (Ret.) uses figures in a similar fashion to give his thought impact:

In 1966 our Gross National Product will be in excess of $700 billion. Our industry is doing very well. During the decade beginning in 1955 combined annual sales of the 500 largest industrial corporations increased by $100 billion (from $161 billion to $266 billion). Corporate profits last year before taxes were $73 billion, an increase of $9 billion over the previous year. Per-capita income reached $2,700 last year, a 6 per cent increase over 1964 income. Personal income was a record high of $528 billion, up $35 billion over the previous year.

These are impressive statistics. We should have no apprehension about the outcome of any competition with the Communist countries in the realm of economics. Our apprehension, if any, should be concerned with whether or not we use our resources wisely and well: to provide a good society at home, to aid the emerging young nations abroad, while at the same time we provide our armed forces with weapons to meet the broad spectrum of challenges that will confront us. We must give serious attention to the problems of exporting our economy abroad.[10]

Gavin uses his material to make a point, "We should have no apprehension . . .," a point that is immediate and clear. The statistics prepare the way for another argument: in the face of our increased prosperity, we are doing proportionately less and less to encourage the developing nations.

[9] Keeping Political Faith," *Representative American Speeches: 1944–45*, A. Craig Baird, ed., New York, H. W. Wilson Company, 1945, p. 138.
[10] "Military Power: The Limits of Persuasion," *Saturday Review* (July 30, 1966), p. 20.

Gavin finds it useful to put this idea statistically, "We have steadily reduced the amount of foreign aid until today, in 1966, it is but .48 per cent of our Gross National Product, compared to 1.75 per cent at its inception in the late 1940's."

Some Complexities of Statistics

A good speaker should understand something about the nature of statistics. Various professional fields require special courses in statistics. With the increasing use of statistical statements, any citizen who desires to act intelligently will need some knowledge of statistics. Disraeli is supposed to have quipped, "There are three categories of liars: plain liars, damned liars, and statisticians." Unfortunately, in this chapter we can say little more than, "Take care," and offer a few general remarks for the speaker's guidance.

CENTRAL TENDENCIES.   Many statistics that speakers use are statements of central tendency. The most common statement of central tendency is the mean, or arithmetical average. Averages may be misleading. Take this hypothetical example: "These men have an average salary of $7,000. This figure is very close to the national average." If "these men" are five, two of whom earn $3,000; one, $5,000; one, $7,000; and one, $17,000, the average is quite misleading.

Two other common sorts of statements of central tendency are: the mode and the median. The mode is that item of those in the range which appears most frequently. The medium is the middle item. In the hypothetical example of incomes, the mode is 3,000; the median, $5,000. In this case, both are considerably lower than the mean.

Often, to be meaningful, statements of central tendency should be accompanied with some information about the distribution of the data. What is the top; what is the bottom? What per cent of the total falls between different intervals on the scale? A normal distribution is one in which most cases fall near the average (the mean) with about an equal number above and below. If the distribution is near normal, the mean, median, and mode will be about the same. To present some statistical statements clearly may necessitate using visual aids.

A critical question that the speaker (or listener) should ask is, "Just who are involved?" Suppose that a speaker says, "The average salary paid by University X is Y dollars." Does he mean *faculty* salary? Or does his average represent custodians and typists as well? If he means faculty salary, are part-time faculty included? The careful speaker, of course, will say that "the average full-time faculty salary at University X is Y dollars."

SAMPLES.   The question "Just who are involved?" is important when one is dealing with statistics based on samples. "Four out of five students at our University favor the administration's policy controlling the rights of student groups to sponsor public meetings," may not be a meaningful statement if the speaker queried the first five students he met among the 25,000 in attendance. Most professional polling services employ dependable sampling techniques, but even so, sampling will give at best an *approximation*. The margin of error for the famous 1948 polls that indicated Thomas Dewey's election over Truman was small but significant. The problem was that communicators of the results of the polls were not careful in pointing out the *margin of error* and its meaning. In this case the margin of error was about 2 per cent, which means that the prediction was not that the vote would fall at a certain point but within a narrow range. Inasmuch as the difference between the two candidates indicated by the poll was slight, no confident prediction as to which would poll the more votes could be made.

Recently a "straw vote" taken at a state fair indicated that one candidate for governor of the state was favored by a large margin over the other candidates. This phenomenon was less perplexing after a newspaper reporter pointed out that the booth of the organization taking the "straw vote" was next door to a booth sponsored by one of the major political parties and a considerable distance from the one sponsored by the other major party.

SOURCES.   The problems the speaker will encounter in evaluating the sources of statistics will be quite like those of evaluating testimony generally, a topic to which we shall turn immediately. Often speakers and listeners will have to depend upon what appears to them to be reputable sources for statistical statements, although this fact does not relieve anyone of the responsibility for knowing something about the use of such statements. Both the speaker and listener should be especially wary of unidentified sources. Vague references to "figures indicate that . . ." or "statisticians tell us . . ." and their variants are usually the signs at best of uncritical mouthings of whatever the speaker may have stumbled across.

The following example of the questionable use of statistics is so patent as nearly to lead one to believe that the author intends it to be amusing:

So far as longevity is concerned, it has been proved by statistics that the greater the smoker the longer he lives. A number of centenarians have been fiends for smoking. Statistics, again, prove that the expectation of life has been longer since the introduction of tobacco and its use by the ordinary man. Taking the example of France: in 1830 the average duration of life was no more than twenty-eight years; in 1953 it is forty-five years, the consumption of tobacco in proportion to the population having trebled in the period. This increase in the average duration of life is most marked among those peoples who beat the record for the consumption of tobacco, such as the Dutch and the Swiss.[11]

Selecting and Using Statistics

The alert speaker will raise the same sort of questions about statistics that he raised about examples. Is this material *relevant, appropriate, typical,* and *properly detailed?* But the speaker will want to raise some special questions about statistics.

1. Are the statistics dependable?
2. Are the statistics clear?
3. Are the statistics interesting?

In discussing the nature of statistics, we have touched on the problem of dependability. It should be apparent that this problem is a complex one that the speaker will have to struggle with. He should be prepared to defend the objectivity of agencies upon whom he depends for his statistics. If a current claim is made, the statistics should be current.

It may seem surprising that statistics, which like other supporting materials may be used to make ideas clear and interesting, should themselves be examined for clarity and interest. But statistics tend to be dull and are often anything but clear. Some figures are so large or small as to carry little meaning to an audience. This is why we may hear a speaker in addition to the number of feet say, "The wingspan of that plane is as great as the length of this building in which we are sitting." The explosive power of modern nuclear bombs is sometimes given in multiples of "Hiroshima bombs." Often a speaker will (and should) round off a number if exactness is not a critical question, thus "nearly 50,000 people rallied in the square" has more immediate clarity and impact than "49,450." To bring his figures home clearly and interestingly to his radio audience, Billy Graham said, "Alcoholics are being produced in the U.S. at the rate of more than twelve hundred a day—over fifty an hour—around the clock."[12]

Finally, when he uses statistics, the speaker should ask himself:

1. Can I simplify the statistics in any way?
2. Am I using so many statistics without relief that I'll lose my audience's interest?

[11] Georges Herment, *The Pipe*, trans. Arthur L. Hayward, New York, Simon and Schuster, 1954, p. 150.
[12] "Alcoholism," The Billy Graham Evangelistic Association, Minneapolis, Minn., 1959, p. 1.

3. Can I use these statistics in conjunction with other supporting materials, particularly with visual aids or analogies, to increase clarity or interest?

Testimony

In our complex society we are becoming increasingly dependent upon testimony. Our small world is filled with incidents that we are unable to observe or which, if we could observe, we are unable to interpret intelligently for ourselves. Therefore we must listen to the scientist describe the effects of radiation; we must weigh the opinions of military experts as to the feasibility of so-called "limited war"; we seek out the reports of journalists on political demonstrations in other countries. But the dependence upon testimony is no modern phenomenon; our history ranges from ancient testimony of the efficacy of the worship of the Sun or a Tree-god to modern testimony that certain toiletries transform ordinary men into objects highly desired by women.

Quotations are useful because they give the weight of authority to an opinion (which accounts for the myriad times George Washington's advice to steer clear of permanent alliances with any part of the foreign world has been quoted by American politicians), or because they phrase an idea in a particularly striking manner (which accounts for the frequent use of Shakespeare's words), or both (which accounts for the frequent use of that most-quoted book, the Bible). The speaker, then, may wish to use testimony to lend his statements particularly apt phrasing or authority.

Consider the copious use of testimony in this passage from a speech given by a college student:

One may be prompted to ask at this point what it is about the man of high education which discourages certainty, creates doubt, and thus "causes him to lose the name of action?" Hamlet said that "conscience makes cowards of us all," that "the native hue of resolution is sicklied o'er with the pale cast of thought." What Hamlet called conscience we recognize as the product of intelligence. Coleridge tells us that "conscience is but the pulse of intellect." Hamlet refused to take the word of an apparition, even though it assumed his father's shape and confirmed his own suspicions. He preferred to put his trust in reason. "The play's the thing," he said, "wherein I'll catch the conscience of the king." In this manner he sought to remove his doubts. Schiller spoke of "the constraint intellect imposes upon the imagination"; he also might have mentioned the constraint intellect imposes upon a man's actions.[13]

[13] From a speech prepared by Frank Louis Greenagel, University of Minnesota student, 1961.

This passage also indicates the tendency for types of supporting materials to become intermingled in use, for more than testimony is involved. In a sense, Hamlet is used as an example.

In building an argument defending the role of the United States in Vietnam, Senator Gale W. McGee of Wyoming, speaking before his colleagues in the Senate, drew mainly from testimony of two sorts: first, from American leaders whom his colleagues, and especially the critics of the policy, would be likely to respect, and, second, from Asian Communists, whose statements were used to suggest that force must be met with force. Quotations of the second sort tended to be quite short:

> But unfortunately mainland China is still in the hands of men who believe —as Mao Tse-Tung has said again and again—that "all political power grows out of the barrel of a gun." And his disciples have turned to a new form of aggression which they offer to the world behind a false face called "wars of national liberation."

Quotations of the first sort tended to be much longer:

> It is well worthwhile to recall here today the key passage of that historical proposal which came to be known as the Truman doctrine. The President pointed out that the survival of Greece was threatened by terrorists led by Communists—that Greece must have our assistance—that there was no other place to turn except the United States—that the future of Turkey as an independent state likewise was threatened. And then the President enunciated the policy he was recommending to the Congress and the people in these words:
>
> "I am fully aware of the broad implications involved. We shall not realize our objectives, however, unless we are willing to help free peoples to maintain their free institutions and their national integrity against aggressive movements that seek to impose upon them totalitarian regimes."[14]

McGee went on to argue the similarity of this situation and others to that in question. A number of questions could be raised concerning this material. We shall suggest a few lines for inquiring into the use of testimony.

Selecting and Using Testimony

Too often testimony is poorly and clumsily used. The speaker should raise questions like these:

1. Is the testimony precise?
2. Is the person cited known and respected?

[14] See the Congressional Record, Proceedings and Debates of the Eighty-ninth Congress, First Session, Volume III, No. 138, Washington, July 29, 1965.

3. Is the person cited a good source?
   a. Is he in a position to know?
   b. Has his opinion on similar problems proved to be sound?
   c. Has he a bias?
4. Have I indicated the source quickly and easily?

Speakers frequently use quotations that are quite lengthy. Sometimes the quotations are rather interesting, but often they contain data or opinions that bear on the speaker's point only obliquely if at all. In general, the speaker should prefer several short quotations to one long one. It is perfectly ethical to shorten quotations if one can do so without seriously changing the meaning intended. One may quote a United States Senator on a particular measure and then add the names of several other senators who agree without quoting them directly. Perhaps you noticed that Senator McGee first paraphrased much that President Truman said in his message on Greece before quoting him directly. Paraphrases, of course, should me made clear as such.

In debating affirmatively upon a proposal for socialized medicine before an American audience, a British university student said, "Let's hear what an English statesman has to say on this point." He then quoted a statement quite favorable to his position. "Who said this?" he asked, "Clement Atlee? Aneurin Bevan? No, Winston Churchill." "Now let an American speak." He quoted a statement quite similar to the first. "Who said this? President Truman? Oscar Ewing? No, Bernard Baruch." The speaker was warmly aware of whom his audience knew and respected.

One might suggest that if the audience knows and respects the source of a quotation that the source is a good one; in some cases the two questions may be synonymous, but not always. We may know and respect a man and recognize his disability on a given subject. Often the speaker will be wise to indicate that the person he cites is in a position to know about a particular problem and to indicate, perhaps, his reliability in the past. It is better, of course, if the testifier's credentials are obvious. If the audience will be inclined to dismiss a quotation because of a bias they attribute to the person cited, the speaker would be wise to find another quotation. It is quite effective to cite a person who testifies against his supposed bias, to bring the "reluctant witness." "Even my opponent admits . . ." is a much abused but familiar example.

In citing a source, be as simple as possible. The men the British student cited were familiar to *his* audience; he did not need to identify Aneurin Bevan or Oscar Ewing for his listeners. Sometimes the name of a good source will be unknown to an audience. In such cases it is ordinarily sufficient to indicate the person's position, e.g., "Arthur Larson, formerly Director of the United States Information Agency and later a special assistant to President Eisenhower, is now the head of the World Rule of

Law Center, Duke University. Larson warns that . . ." At times it may be advantageous to build in detail the basis of authority for a person cited, but the speaker should be conservative in deciding that he has such an occasion.

Ordinarily it is not necessary to indicate the book or magazine containing the quotation. The disposition of some speakers to say "I quote," or "quote" and then "unquote" is distracting and often makes the quotation less rather than more precise. Most speakers with perhaps a conscious effort to pause and probably an unconscious change in pitch can make perfectly clear what is and what is not quoted. There are, of course, exceptional cases in which "I quote his exact words . . ." of similar phrases may add emphasis to the material cited. In all cases, however, "I have a quote here . . . " is too obvious to warrant uttering. Likewise, "A well-known authority . . ." or "reliable sources . . ." should be avoided.

ANALOGIES

Department stores hire comparison shoppers. Reviewers will often compare several recorded versions of the same music. In evaluating essay examinations, college professors will often compare the answers students give to a model answer. Note the frequent use of such expressions as "better than," "not as good as," "similar to," "much like," and "resembles" in ordinary conversation. The impulse to make ideas clear, interesting, and impelling by using comparison is common. It is the principle of comparing that makes analogies useful in supporting ideas.

Analogies are ordinarily classified as literal or figurative. The literal analogy deals with two (or more) phenomena that are essentially alike —one political party as compared to others. The figurative analogy deals with phenomena that are essentially different (thus Plato compared the governor of a city to the steersman of a boat), but which nonetheless contain a critical common element (our destinies are in the hands of our political leaders just as our lives may be in the hands of the steersman).

Literal Analogies

One seldom hears analogies in ordinary speeches. This may be because analogies are more difficult to use than other types of supporting materials, or it may be that most speakers simply are not in the habit of seeking out analogies. On the other hand our observation leads us to assert that good speakers frequently use analogy. Consider this long analogy from a radio address by Billy Graham:

A student at an eastern university recently went to Mexico where, in the process of time and discovering true dedication in some Communist workers, he became a Communist. Shortly afterward, he wrote to his fiancee breaking off their engagement. This letter was given to me by a Presbyterian minister in Montreat, North Carolina, where I live. This is what it says:

"We Communists have a high casualty rate. We're the ones who get shot and hanged and lynched and tarred and feathered and jailed and slandered. . . . We live in virtual poverty. We turn back to the Party every penny we make above what is absolutely necessary to keep us alive.

"We Communists don't have the time or the money for any movies, or concerts, or T-bone steaks, or decent homes and new cars. We've been described as fanatics. We are fanatics. Our lives are dominated by one great overshadowing factor—the struggle for world Communism . . . We subordinate our petty personal selves into a great movement of humanity, and if our personal lives seem hard, or our egos appear to suffer through subordination to the Party, then we are adequately compensated by the thought that each of us in his small way is contributing something new and true and better for mankind.

"There is one thing in which I am in dead earnest and that is the Communist cause. It is my life, my business, my religion, my hobby, my sweetheart, my wife and mistress, my bread and meat. I work at it in the daytime and dream of it at night. Its hold on me grows, not lessens, as time goes on. Therefore I cannot carry on a friendship, a love affair or even a conversation without relating to this force which both drives and guides my life. I evaluate people, books, ideas and action according to how they affect the Communist cause and by their attitude toward it. I've already been in jail because of my ideas and, if necessary, I'm ready to go before a firing squad."

Do you have that much dedication to the Lord Jesus Christ? In Christ, God offers us everything, but He demands no less.[15]

Does Graham's analogy help make his point clear, interesting, and impelling? Notice how the detail of the young Communist's letter serves to indicate specific actions that emphasize sacrifice for a faith.

Speakers make analogies to indicate similarities, but the speaker should not overlook the possibility of making comparisons to indicate dissimilarities. This process, sometimes called contrast, was used by Laurence M. Gould, President of Carleton College, as a part of his argument for greatly increased support of education:

Of the Americans who have been able to observe Soviet education currently, all report the high quality of instruction. This we should expect. In Russia the top professor's total salary is in the range of $35,000 to $50,000 per year at the official rate of exchange. Added to this are low taxes, low rent, free health service, free education for his children, and in the case of particularly

15 "Call to Commitment," Billy Graham Evangelistic Association, Minneapolis, Minnesota, 1960, pp. 1–3.

outstanding work—paid vacations for himself and his family. But above all else the Soviet professor is looked up to! Contrast that with our own country . . . The average full professor's income is about one and one-half times that of the factory worker. In Russia the top scientist is worth as much as the top industrialist; whereas in the United States the top industrialist gets thirty to fifty times the salary of the top scientist.[16]

This is, of course, an example of the combination of supporting materials, because Gould uses statistics in making the contrast.

Figurative Analogies

Analogies, like examples, may be minutely detailed or undetailed. Robert G. Ingersoll uses a simple pair of figurative analogies in his famous speech "The Liberty of Man, Woman, and Child": Do not treat your children like orthodox posts to be set in a row. Treat them like trees that need light and sun and air." On the other hand the figurative analogy may be extended to show the basis of comparison in more detail:

A man's knowledge is like a lake fed by a stream. The volume of that lake will depend upon the breadth and depth of the stream feeding it. If we are to consider, then, the store of knowledge made available to a man by higher academic education, we must be interested not simply in the number of years he attends college, nor the number of courses he might take. The nature of the courses themselves, their depths, must be questioned. I am afraid that the modern college student is the victim of a broad but shallow education.[17]

Handled well, the figurative analogy can add clarity and interest to an idea, and it can, if the basis for analogy is strong and sharp enough, be impelling. A figurative analogy used by Abraham Lincoln in his "Cooper Union Address" demonstrates this assertion. Although he is standing before an audience in New York City, Lincoln has said that he is addressing some arguments to the South:

But you will not abide the election of a Republican President! In that supposed event, you say, you will destroy the Union; and then, you say, the great crime of having destroyed it will be upon us! That is cool. A highwayman holds a pistol to my ear, and mutters through his teeth, "Stand and deliver, or I shall kill you, and then you will be a murderer!"

To be sure, what the robber demanded of me—my money—was my own; and I had a clear right to keep it; but it was no more my own than my vote is my own; and the threat of death to me, to extort my vote, can scarcely be distinguished in principle.

[16] "Education and Survival," *Carleton College Bulletin*, LV, 1 (August, 1958), pp. 11–12.
[17] Adapted from a speech by Steven Larson, University of Minnesota student, 1961.

Selecting and Using Analogies

The speaker considering analogies should apply to them the same sort of questions that he should apply to examples:

1. Is the analogy clearly relevant to the idea?
2. Is the analogy appropriate to the audience?
3. Is the analogy properly detailed?

At times it is difficult to distinguish between example and analogy. Consider a passage from a speech delivered at a convocation of the Graduate School of Cornell University by Jacques Barzun, Provost of Columbia University. Barzun is arguing against what he calls the "philanthropic" tendencies that keep educators from the vigorous development of academic excellence:

Now if we step from this little utopia to the training quarters of a successful athletic team, we find a very different state of affairs. The boys being trained are indeed the same that we encounter in any of a thousand classrooms in the country; but on the field their view of life is suddenly and radically altered. To begin with, a special seriousness pervades the atmosphere; the boys are not contented but visibly anxious. One feels the concentration of many strong wills on one object. There is little aimless action. Everyone takes advantage of the intervals of free time to jump, swing, flex the muscles, to practice throwing, catching, running. The coach and his assistants are as much interested as the classroom instructor in individual development, and they are keen watchers of diverse aptitudes. But they clearly have in mind for each individual a fixed idea of what constitutes performance. Far from letting each set his own pace, they hold him to a standard of their own choosing. If he does not meet it, he fails. Let me make the point clear: if he fails, he fails. There may be reasons for the failure, but no excuse, and certainly no consolation prizes and no verbalized psycho-apologies to the parents. On the contrary, I am told that the verbalizing of football coaches in moments of stress is far from apologetic.[18]

The authors would classify this as an analogy, but we would hasten to add that such classifications are arbitrary. In so far as a system of labels may be useful in helping a speaker understand, seek, and use supporting material, it will be important. But it is not important to be able to put each piece of material neatly into a textbook category. In the case at hand, analogy or example, does Barzun's material meet the test questions?

In addition to those questions concerning the material's relevancy,

[18] "The Place and Price of Excellence," in *The Speaker's Resource Book*, ed. Carroll Arnold, Douglas Ehninger, and John Gerber, Chicago, Scott, Forsman and Company, 1961, pp. 28–29.

appropriateness, and detail, in using analogy the speaker should ask these questions:

1. Is the basis of the analogy clear?
2. Are there important dissimilarities in what is compared?

In any question of clarity, one of the best tests is to try the material on as many listeners as possible. Get them to react. The basis of the comparison should be clear with a minimum of explanation. Too often we hear speakers giving painfully inappropriate hints to the audience. In using the ancient story of the Arab who allowed his camel to put his nose in the tent and soon found the camel in and himself out, for example, the speaker ought not feel compelled to speak of "the tent of free enterprise" nor of "the camel of state control." The figurative analogy may be clear, but it becomes ludicrous instead of compelling.

There will be some dissimilarities in anything compared. Generally the speaker should not call attention to them; he should not try to explain them away. He should look for dissimilarities that will render his comparison ineffective and, if he believes he finds them, discard the analogy. Anyone wishing to press Barzun's argument would probably stress the differences in the aims of athletics and of education generally. Barzun recognizes this response, in fact he bids it. He doesn't try to explain away the differences, but builds another argument on a primary distinction. Again, consider the passage cited from Senator McGee's speech. We used the passage to illustrate testimony, but it is also a comparison of the situation in Vietnam in Lyndon Johnson's administration to that in Greece in Harry Truman's. More than one public leader has argued that these are not comparable.

Using analogies is difficult, but many fine speakers have used them to advantage.

Visual Aids

The use of a model, a chart, a graph, a diagram, or a picture may enable the speaker to clarify an idea that could not easily be made clear through words alone. The wise speaker, ordinarily pressed for time, soon discovers that he can often present material much more quickly by using visual aids.

A speaker might want to indicate the rapid rise in the employment of personnel working on manned spaceflight programs since 1961 and, perhaps, to stress the fact that after the phenomenal rise the tendency is now for the level of employment to fall. He could indicate the various numbers employed at various times. But how long would it take? Would the audience get a clear impression? Would his listeners retain the information? Certainly a simple line graph (see Figure 1) would help.

The typical student speaker may not have the access to the services of the commercial artists upon whom the editors of *Business Week* can call, but with some large sheets of paper (some students use ordinary wrapping paper), a marking pencil, and a little imagination student speakers can invent or imitate all sorts of visual aids. For example, one student talking about the advantages of the Metropolitan Opera's new house at New York City's Lincoln Center executed a drawing of the seating arrangements in the old and the new auditoriums. (see Figure 2). His was scarcely lovely art, but it did help him make his points more quickly and more clearly.

A speaker need not be especially skillful to prepare a simple graph or a diagram indicating the paths of various earth satellites or a map indicating the location of a slum clearance project. He simply needs a minimal creative aptitude and a little time. He might, for example, obtain a large map of the United States (ordinarily available quite cheaply at most

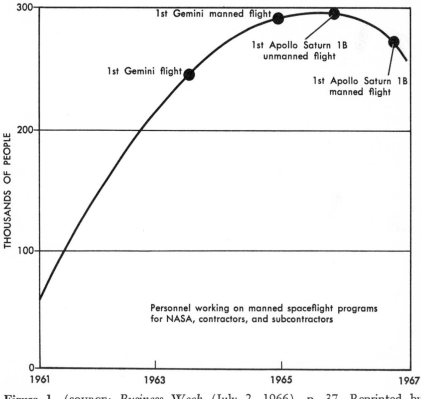

Figure 1. (SOURCE: *Business Week* (July 2, 1966), p. 37. Reprinted by permission.)

bookstores) and outline in vivid red the zones of polluted air around major population centers described in a periodical which he has read.

Most adults are familiar with line graphs, bar graphs, slices-of-pie (see Figure 3), and other methods of indicating statistical information visually. Line graphs are usually best for showing trends, although bar graphs will serve this purpose also. Slices-of-pie are excellent for showing the proportions of parts to the whole. Bar graphs are also useful in showing the proportion of one thing to another and often several lines on a line graph can be used to compare one trend to another.

THE "MET"

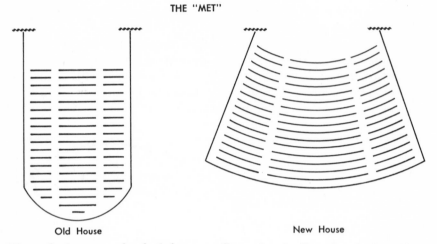

Old House   New House

Figure 2. (SOURCE: sketched from an illustration in *Saturday Review* (September 17, 1966), p. 48. Reproduced by permission.)

Visual aids may add impact to ideas that may seem at first to be adequately expressed verbally. The destructiveness of nuclear explosives may be described many ways, but enlarged aerial photographs of Hiroshima before and shortly after August 6, 1945, may startle even an audience that has responded quite positively before to other material. Unfortunately enlarged photographs are expensive. The student might find ways of diagramming from the epicenter of the blast outward in concentric rings the effects of a nuclear explosion, perhaps comparing the old-fashioned Hiroshima bomb to an up-to-date weapon.

Do not overlook the use of objects. If a speaker were to undertake to explain the steps in binding a book, he might well want the materials available to display during the speech. But the speaker ought not limit his imagination to inventing visual aids to help him make simple explanations. One speaker brought out a stick of dynamite (a dummy, he informed his audience a few moments later) with fuse attached and a match. "Would anyone of you care to light the fuse and put this stick of dynamite in his pocket?" he asked. "No? Why not? You probably have something in your pocket that is potentially just as dangerous. The keys to your car." And thus he made a rather arresting beginning to a speech on safe driving.

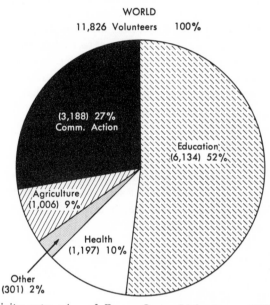

WORLD
11,826 Volunteers 100%

(3,188) 27% Comm. Action

Education (6,134) 52%

Agriculture (1,006) 9%

Health (1,197) 10%

Other (301) 2%

Figure 3. Activity categories of Peace Corps Volunteers, 1965. More than half of them teach, and half of these for the first time. (SOURCE: "Western Man at His Best," *Saturday Review* (April 23, 1966), p. 15. Reprinted by permission.)

Selecting and Using Visual Aids

The speaker who told his audience that a car is as dangerous as dynamite, used both a visual aid and a figurative analogy. Inasmuch as visual aids are usually used to present some other type of supporting material, the speaker ought not overlook questions relevant to whatever other type is involved.

Visual aids are so often poorly used that one is tempted to compose long lists of do's and don'ts. But most of the trouble could be avoided with only a little caution. Too many speakers never practice using their visual aids and therefore overlook some rather obvious problems. In addition to ordinary care, the speaker should raise questions like these:

1. Can the audience see the visual aids?
   a. Are they large enough?
   b. Are they simple enough?

2. Can I handle them?
3. Will they distract my audience?
4. Are they as striking as possible?

Visual aids that cannot be easily seen are worse than useless. The speaker must make them large enough to be seen in whatever situation he is to speak. If he cannot get the photograph enlarged enough, he should not use it. He should resist the temptation to pass a small object among the members of his audience, remembering that this is about as effective as sending a person among them to whisper an example to each in turn.

Often a visual aid can be seen but not comprehended because it is too complex. Be certain that the details are simplified so that only the essential ones are included. Often it is wise to use several graphs or diagrams instead of trying to put all the information in one.

Frequently a speaker will find himself before an audience with a diagram in mind and a piece of chalk in his hand only to discover that as he executes the drawing, it just doesn't look as he imagined it would. In addition, his drawing takes much longer than he expected and whatever attention his audience had given him has wandered in other directions. Unless he is a nearly professional artist, the speaker should restrict himself to putting simple items on a blackboard, and those should be well rehearsed. Whatever he does should not take his attention from his audience more than momentarily. He must practice changing charts, pointing out details on his graphs, and manipulating whatever objects he feels will be useful to show to his audience.

Too often a speaker will engage in a detailed explanation of a visual aid that is apparent to the audience immediately. If the visual aid needs detailed explanation, it probably isn't a good visual aid.

A large, colorful map pinned up at the front of the room at the beginning of a speech and not used immediately will probably command a great deal of the audience's attention while the speaker is concentrating on the ideas. The speaker must remember that visual aids are potentially highly distracting and, if at all possible, should display them only while he actually wants to use them. It takes very little foresight to cover a map (or a diagram or a graph) with a blank sheet of paper. Although a listener might wonder what's beneath, he will be much less distracted, probably, than he would be by the material itself.

Speakers are too easily satisfied with their visual aids, just as they often are with any piece of material. The speaker should ask himself: what can I do to make this material more striking? Perhaps he'll decide to use several bright colors to indicate different items on his graph. Perhaps he'll devise a simple method to keep the object out of sight until he's ready to use it.

Summary

Using supporting materials effectively is a matter of fixing some habits of thinking. Assertions should turn the speaker's mind immediately toward examples, statistics, testimony, analogies, and visual aids. The experienced speaker constantly looks for material to make ideas clear, interesting, and impelling. This is why one so often discovers that good speakers keep files and notebooks to save materials that seem to be useful in supporting ideas in which they are interested. Moreover, speakers continually become interested in an increasing range of ideas because their habits of thought find meaning in the events they meet. A good speaker stocks a full mind and draws from it, and he is rarely satisfied with what he has. He sorts and checks his ideas and the materials from which they are drawn and seeks fresh resources for both.

An Exercise

Work with this passage or another assigned by your instructor. It is taken from the article by Sidney Lens, "Guatemala: Invitation to Revolution," *The Progressive*, September 1966, pp. 31–32.

One Guatemalan economist estimates that seventy-five per cent of the peasants work only thirteen per cent of the land. There are twenty-two landowners who own fourteen per cent of the arable acreage, and 1,900 who hold three-fifths. At a model farm I visited near Antigua, a tourist mecca, the two hundred seasonal laborers earn about seventy cents a day for picking 100 pounds of coffee per man. Next door, at the Margarita farm, the rate was ten cents a day less—sixty cents—and this was in the economic center of the country, only twenty-eight miles from Guatemala City. In the backlands conditions are far worse.

The peasant works on great farms where two-thirds or three-quarters of the land is unused while he himself is usually landless. If he decides to become a squatter on some of this land he is frequently uprooted and sometimes thrown in jail. There is a law on the books taxing unused land as a means of forcing the landlord either to cultivate his holdings or sell them, but it has never been even partially enforced.

To make matters worse the few items such as salt or textiles that the peasant buys from the local store on credit—he seldom sees money—have gone up in price, while the commodities he sells to the city have stayed much the same. The rich have grown richer, the poor poorer. The Guatemalan economist I interviewed estimates that a few years ago eighty per cent of the national income went to twenty-five per cent of the population; today, he says, that eighty per cent of income goes to only twenty per cent of the population —a measure of how regressive has been the redistribution of income. Tax reform, sponsored by the Alliance for Progress to remedy such situations, has been a dud—only $8 million a year is collected in income taxes—and a considerable part of the taxes is evaded by the wealthy, particularly the landlords.

1. Using the questions applicable to the types of supporting materials, criticize this passage. Give special, but not exclusive attention to the source, e.g.,
   a. Who is Sidney Lens?
   b. Does the fact that he does not name the economist he interviews weaken the material? Can you think of any reasons that he does not, or should not, name the economist?
2. The use of statistics is evident, but the passage has the qualities of several other sorts of supporting materials. What are they? What details especially give Mr. Lens' material impact?
3. Using his statistics, sketch some visual aids that you believe might be effective if you were presenting some part of the material orally.

A Listening Assignment

1. Listen to a speech. (Do not use a classroom speech or a professor's lecture.)
2. Make a list of the pieces of supporting material the speaker uses.
3. Describe each briefly.
4. Evaluate each.

An Oral Exercise

1. The class should be divided into four groups.
2. Each person will make a two- to three-minute extemporaneous talk supporting an assertion.
3. Those in group one will use an example or examples to support their assertions; those in group two will use statistics; those in group three will use testimony; those in group four will use analogies.
4. Simply state your assertion and support it. Limit and phrase the assertion carefully. Search diligently and choose your supporting material critically. Do not consider this exercise to be a complete speech. Your beginning and ending will probably seem abrupt.
5. The presentation of the talks should serve as the basis of a thorough class discussion on the selection and use of supporting materials. Let this question be your theme: How can the use of material be improved? Talk about specific efforts made in class.

A One-Point Speech

1. Each person should prepare a three- to four-minute one-point speech.
2. The thesis must be carefully selected and limited. Make an assertion

which you can support directly with supporting material, not one which must be divided into subordinate assertions, which in turn may be supported.

3. Use this pattern: illustrate, state, amplify, and restate.

Illustrate. Begin with a detailed example, either factual or hypothetical, from which your assertion can be drawn. Do not bother with preliminaries: "I was wondering what to talk about when an idea struck me." "This morning I'd like to talk to you about one of my favorite subjects." Just open with the example.

State. Make your assertion. Try to state the thesis as clearly, concisely, and strikingly as possible. Do it in a single declarative sentence, al-

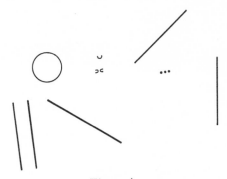

Figure 4.

though you may include several sentences of transition relating the illustration to it.

Amplify. Use other supporting material to make your assertion clear, interesting, and impelling. You may use any supporting material in any order that seems feasible.

Restate. Although you may wish to restate your thesis several times during your speech in relating supporting material to it, make a final restatement that will serve as a simple summation.

4. Discuss the speeches. As students, you should be striving to learn to use supporting material effectively.

4 ❘ Organizing Ideas

Each of us is surrounded by phenomena. For some of us listening to a Beethoven symphony is an enjoyable experience, for others it is not. Some of us find modern art meaningful, and some nuclear physics; some of us understand cost accounting and some Shakespeare's sonnets. In experiences with these phenomena we are more or less aware of the sorts of impressions we have, of why we enjoy, why we understand, or why we don't.

Whatever phenomenon we might be interested in—because it pleases us or because it puzzles us—the more meaningful it becomes, the more we recognize that a pattern of parts inheres in it. We recognize that the whole is made up of parts and that the parts stand in a given relationship to one another. To change the relationship of the parts is to alter or to destroy the whole.

We experience other physical beings in various ways. Man is a structure, or, rather, many interrelated structures. The physiologist can explain the relationships of the physical parts of a man in amazing detail. An artist can represent a man in a drawing, and Picasso may upset us by putting the parts in unusual relationships to one another.

At the end of the last chapter you came upon a senseless jumble of lines labeled Figure 4. You may have glanced at them and wondered what merry fool had slipped this plate into the presses, but chances are that the lines were not meaningful. Look again. It's a man, a stick man; it is not great art, but it is a man if one simply puts the parts into the proper relationship. You are well acquainted with what men look like and, if presented with a childish drawing, you recognize it. If the drawing has three arms and one leg, however, you are upset by the impropriety or irritated by the poor joke.

The point is clear. The person who wants to play, to compose, or who just wants to listen to music must become aware, to some degree, of the patterns of pitch and time. He soon recognizes that some patterns are traditional ones, that for example, the ordinary rhythmical patterns of Western music are made up of two's or three's. Eastern music, with its complex changes in time patterns may be an upsetting experience for Western ears. One may discover that the second movement of Tschaikovsky's sixth symphony is somehow slightly strange and come to realize that it is written in five beats to the measure. And so the person interested in music recognizes that the traditional patterns to which he is most accustomed may be modified with various effects.

The person who wishes to compose speeches will become aware that like most other phenomena, speeches follow more or less orderly patterns or interrelated groups of patterns. The speaker should come to realize that there are traditional patterns that can be used or modified with varying effects.

From the discussion thus far, several generalizations are possible. (1) Speeches should be made up of patterns of ideas and materials. (2) When one is presented with a speech that seems to be unpatterned or improperly patterned, he will probably be puzzled or irritated. (3) There are traditional speech patterns which one can learn. (4) The traditional patterns should be quite useful in helping a speaker construct his own speech, and because they are traditional and therefore familiar to listeners, should help his audience respond to his speech.

One way a person could learn to pattern ideas and materials in a speech would be by listening to and reading a great number of speeches to try to discover useful principles; he could then work with his own ideas and materials to test these principles. In the final analysis, only by this process can he learn in a deeply meaningful way to construct speeches. A book such as this one can only claim to give a few suggestions to make his observation, distillation, and practice somewhat easier and more immediately helpful.

We must say again, as we did in Chapter 3, that the principles we discuss will be abstract and, therefore, necessarily artificial and somewhat arbitrary. This observation does not mean that the principles will not prove useful nor that they should not be learned and applied. It does mean, however, that not all examples of well-organized speeches will fall neatly and clearly within the patterns described.

THE DEVELOPMENT

Inasmuch as most adults have heard many speeches and read some sort of theory that bears on the composition of discourse, to say that a speech should have a beginning, a middle, and an end—an introduction, a development, and a conclusion—will surprise almost no one. Although it is difficult to say where a speaker will start in his process of organization, he will probably not start, and should not start, at the beginning, that is, by composing the introduction. Because the introduction and conclusion serve definite functions in relation to the development, the development should be at least relatively well composed before the speaker plans how he will begin and end.

Patterns of Arrangement

Everything in the speech focuses on the central idea. We discussed in Chapter 2 problems of stating purposes and theses. The speaker should be willing to modify his statement of purpose and his statement of thesis as he composes his speech, because he should become increasingly aware of the content of his speech in relationship to his audience. The sooner, however, he can make definite, though tentative, statements of purpose and thesis, the better.

"Fraternities should be abolished." Here is an assertion (one used rather commonly for illustrative purposes) that might serve as the thesis of a speech. If I were to make such an assertion in your presence, you might reply, "What makes you think so?" or "Rot!" I would then be inclined to support my assertion. In doing so, probably I would make other assertions that stand in a subordinate relationship to the thesis:

Fraternities should be abolished.
  I. They distract the student from important activities.
 II. They build false sets of values.

Another person might use a different set of assertions to support the same thesis. Hearing such assertions, you might be inclined to defend fraternities:

We must correct some common misunderstandings about fraternities.
  I. The cinema stereotypes do not represent the average fraternity.
 II. The real aims of fraternities serve legitimate individual needs.

The hypothetical speeches attacking and supporting fraternities have barely been begun. These are only the first indications of what the speeches might become. The point is that the initial development of a speech is composed of a series of assertions. The thesis is divided into subordinate assertions which we shall call *main heads*. The main heads, in turn, may be subdivided. Hypothetically the process of division could be carried on toward infinity. In speeches, however, the pattern of division should be simple; the speaker should learn to come quickly to supporting material that will make an assertion clear, interesting, and impelling. When an assertion is well supported, it in turn supports the assertion that stands above it in the organizational pattern. Too often speeches become a skein of finely divided assertions, few of which are properly supported.

The speaker who is culling his past experiences and reading in order to enrich his understanding of ideas and to find material which he can bring to bear on them will probably begin to jot down related series of assertions, will start forming the development of a speech. When he does so he may gain increased insight into the possible patterns into which his ideas might be developed if he understood some traditional patterns of arrangement.

TIME PATTERNS. The parts of some ideas must necessarily stand in a chronological relationship to one another. First things must come first. If you find it necessary to explain a process, you will start at the beginning—what must be done first, second, third. If you wish to make a proposal, you may be inclined to indicate what steps will be necessary to initiate the proposal, what steps will be necessary in its operation, and what steps will be necessary to evaluate what is accomplished.

Suppose that you are a member of a group and feel that although it is founded around some excellent purposes and has some fine members, that the group has lost sight of its goals. You have an opportunity to address the group.

Purpose: to clarify and intensify the feelings of the members toward the group's goals.
  I. Our founders were men of vision who established a group with some rather remarkable principles.
 II. At the present time we are carrying forward many of the group's original projects.
III. In the future we can find exciting new work to do by turning again to the principles of our founders.

Perhaps the second point seems mild. If you decide that it will be more effective to chastise the group directly instead of merely suggesting stagnation, the second point might be:

II. We are failing miserably to live up to the principles of our founders.

A major portion of Vice-President Hubert H. Humphrey's speech before the national convention of the NAACP in Los Angeles, July 6, 1966, takes its shape from the time pattern. Although he does not explicitly underline *past, present,* and *future* as we have done in our hypothetical example, he speaks first of federal programs already in being, next of immediate action to be taken, and finally of work to be done in the future. A few excerpts from his speech will show the care with which he divides this portion of his speech.[1]

But there are certain problems demanding priority attention as we strive to translate legal promises of equality and freedom into reality.

First, the federal government accepts the job of meeting its growing responsibilities.
. . . .
Secondly, there exists an urgent need for new initiatives and responsibility in civil rights matters by our states and local governments.
. . . .
Thirdly, we must enlist new allies in our struggle against discrimination and deprivation—from business, labor, religious, and community groups

The time pattern will be useful in a variety of situations. The speaker may use the past, present, future in reference to any number of topics. He may, on the other hand, be dealing with the past only:

Thesis: The Old Testament contains several distinctly different conceptions of God.
  I. The God of the creation and the flood was an angry, powerful, jealous God.
 II. The God of Moses was a personal God—a lawgiver to a tribe.
III. The God of Micah was a gentler God of love.
IV. The God of Job was an inexplicable arguer.

As you looked at this series of main points, you probably remarked, "These assertions will need subdivision and support. And it may be wise to talk about Job before Micah!" The latter observation recognizes the potency of time order. The listener who is familiar with the Old Testament would be irritated, if not disgusted or outraged, by a speaker who reversed the order of the books of Job and Micah.

TOPICAL PATTERNS. If you were to make a speech describing Shakespeare's plays, you might choose a time pattern, talking in turn about the early plays, the middle plays, and the later plays. You would be more likely,

[1] *The Congressional Record,* July 12, 1966, p. A3608.

however, to talk about the histories, the comedies, and the tragedies. Some subjects have parts—aspects, qualities, types, branches—that tend to be more or less clearly a natural part of them. Some common element seems to recur in different manifestations making what may be called a topical pattern. Think of the speeches you have heard that were extensions of topics such as these: the *benefits* of physical activity (or adequate insurance or reading a newspaper regularly or studying speech); the *qualities* of a good fraternity member (or a cigar or a business letter or a college professor); the *types* of football formations (or poker players or sorority girls or patterns of arrangement).

Consider this series of statements culled from a work of Aldous Huxley's:[2]

Without an understanding of man's deep-seated urge to self-transcendence, of his very natural reluctance to take the hard, ascending way, and his search for some bogus liberation either below or to one side of his personality, we cannot hope to make sense of our own particular period of history or indeed of history in general, of life as it was lived in the past and as it is lived today. For this reason I propose to discuss some of the more common Grace-substitutes, into which and by means of which men and women have tried to escape from the tormenting consciousness of being merely themselves.

. . . .

Alcohol is but one of the many drugs employed by human beings as avenues of escape from the insulted self.

. . . .

Like intoxication, elementary sexuality, indulged in for its own sake and divorced from love, was once a god, worshipped not only as the principle of fecundity, but as a manifestation of the radical Otherness immanent in every human being.

. . . .

The professional moralists who inveigh against drunkenness are strangely silent about the equally disgusting vice of herd-intoxication—of downward self-transcendence into subhumanity by the process of getting together in a mob.

Although we do not find formal outline statements, the first paragraph indicates Huxley's thesis, and the next three statements the main divisions of his discussion. The pattern is topical.

One special manner of applying topical order is to consider it as giving rise to a series of contentions. Take any assertion you would have an audience accept; state it and then ask, "Why?" Your answers to this question will form a series of contentions in support of the thesis. Many television commercials are based on this process at its simplest; a demand is made and enticement is offered: Use this soap! (Why? . . .) Smoke this cigarette! (Why? . . .) Buy this refrigerator! (Why? . . .)

---

[2] *The Devils of Loudon*, London, Chatto and Windus, 1952, pp. 361, 363, 365.

In a previous example we imagined that you were about to address a group which you felt had lost sight of its goals. Apply a topical pattern:

Purpose: to clarify and intensify the feelings of the members toward the group's goals.
Explicit thesis: The goals our founders set for our organization should be carefully reconsidered by each of us. (Why?)
  I. (Because) by so doing we shall honor those men who by their vigor and imagination formed this group.
 II. (Because) by so doing we shall be better able to serve those purposes to which we have committed ourselves.
III. (Because) by so doing we shall gain personal satisfaction in fresh achievements.

Which pattern will better accomplish the speaker's purpose, the time pattern or the topical? The question is impossible to answer except for a specific speaker and a specific group. The speaker who sees more than one possibility, however, will be in a position to choose which appears to possess the greater potential effectiveness.

A special problem often arises in using a topical pattern: Which main head should be used first, which second, which third? Consider this simple application of the topical pattern:

Thesis: Intercollegiate football should be abolished.
  I. Intercollegiate football is detrimental to the participants.
 II. Intercollegiate football is deterimental to the nonparticipating student body.
III. Intercollegiate football degrades the colleges that sponsor it.

Which of these main heads should be used first, which second, which third? In answering the question the speaker should decide first which is his strongest, that is, his clearest, most interesting, and most impelling point, and which is the least strong. In the present case, the answer would probably be somewhat dependent upon the audience. Is the speaker addressing participants or nonparticipants? Students or a group of professors? Let us suppose that a speaker has decided that in order of strength his points may be ranked 1-2-3. He then has several choices. He may choose *climactic* order, that is, he may arrange his points 3-2-1, starting with the least strong and using the strongest last. He may choose *anticlimactic* order, 1-2-3, beginning with the strongest point. Although the evidence available is somewhat contradictory, in general the speaker should prefer anticlimactic order if his aim is to make the audience remember the points. A recommendation at least as old as Cicero is to begin with the strongest point and use the next strongest last (the old principle of putting the weak argument in the middle)—1-3-2, or with four points, 1-4-3-2. Based on the same inclination to arrange a speech to give a strong beginning and ending, Richard Whately recommended a little over a hundred years ago that one use anticlimactic order and then summarize in climactic order: 1-2-3; 3-2-1. Whatever advice the speaker may follow, he should not allow himself to arrange a topical pattern without a conscious effort to decide in what order the points should come. He should make his decisions with his eyes on his audience's possible responses.

In dividing and arranging the parts of a speech, the speaker, especially the inexperienced speaker, should strive for simplicity. A useful guide is to use from two to five main heads. Five is no magic upper limit, but a well-constructed and -supported speech of more than five main points will be a rare occurrence. It may be impossible to support five points effectively in a short speech. The speaker should ask himself questions like these, especially, if he believes he has five or more main points:

1. Are all my main heads really distinctly coordinate parts of the thesis, or should several of them be combined, or, perhaps one subordinated to another?
2. If I have more than five main points, and I'm sure that they all are distinctly coordinate parts of the thesis, might I be wiser to narrow my thesis, and therefore my span of points, allowing myself more time to develop each point?

Just as the thesis should be divided into main heads and these main heads should be arranged into some sort of pattern, so should the main heads in turn be divided and the subheads arranged. Let's allow one of our samples to grow a little.

We must correct some common misunderstandings about fraternities.
  I. The cinema stereotypes do not represent the average fraternity.
     A. There are three common stereotypes that are frequently presented as being representative of fraternity life.
     B. The sources of these grotesque pictures are rooted in a lack of direct experience with modern fraternities.
  II. The real aims of fraternities serve legitimate individual needs.
     A. Fraternities help serve legitimate scholastic needs.
     B. Fraternities help serve legitimate social needs.

This sample is a combination of topical patterns. The speaker must decide which subhead to use first when he uses a topical pattern; and, in arranging subheads, the speaker must be certain that he has real divisions and should hold their number to a minimum. Again two-to-five is a good guide.

PROBLEM-SOLUTION PATTERNS.   Consider these assertions, all of which are much like many that we have heard again and again: "To meet rising juvenile delinquency we need to re-establish father as the head of the family." "We can stem the tide of auto deaths if each of us will practice defensive driving." "The threat of world Communism can be met only by a vigilant, well-armed alliance of democracies." "We face total annihilation unless we can work out a system of mutual disarmament." Each of these statements suggests a problem and a solution. Speeches dealing with them will probably in some way or other utilize statements concerning the nature, extent, and effects of the problem and statements concerning the nature and efficacy of the solution in constructing an organizational pattern.

The simplest and most ordinary use of the problem-solution pattern is a two-step sequence:

I. The electoral college is a dangerous anachronism.
II. We should adopt a system for electing the president by a direct vote of the people.

or

I. Modern, materialist man inevitably suffers from a realization that he is wasting his life.
II. The individual can find complete human happiness only by dedicating himself to some cause higher than personal gratification.

Looking at these two examples, you may ask, "Where's the thesis?" *In a problem-solution pattern, the thesis is synonymous with the statement of solution; it should embody the aim of the speech.*

Recall the hypothetical speech we used to illustrate both the time and topical patterns. We might profit from reviewing the trial divisions and comparing our use of these patterns:

Purpose: to clarify and intensify the feelings of the members toward the goals of the group.
Thesis: The goals of our founders should be carefully reconsidered by each of us.
Time Pattern:
I. Our founders were men of vision who established a group with some remarkable principles.
II. At the present time we are carrying forward some of the group's original projects.
III. In the future we can find exciting new work to do by turning again to the principles of our founders.

Topical Pattern:

Each point is in answer to the question posed by asking "Why?" of the thesis:

I. (Because) by so doing we shall honor those men who by their vigor and imagination formed this group.

II. (Because) by so doing we shall be better able to serve those purposes to which we have committed ourselves.

III. (Because) by so doing we shall gain personal satisfaction in fresh achievements.

It is not difficult to invent a simple problem-solution pattern to embody the purpose of the speaker:

I. Our group is threatened by disintegration.

II. We can save our group by reconsidereding the goals of our founders.

As one glances at these trial divisions he may see the possibility of making the headings just suggested for the topical pattern the principal subdivisions of the solution. A combination of problem-solution as the over-all pattern with the topical as a subordinate pattern is quite common.

Obviously each of the three general patterns could be applied to the purpose with still other results. The wise speaker will work continually to find the structure that seems best for his particular subject and audience. The wider his range of choice, the better position he will be in to make an effective selection.

The simple two-step use of the problem-solution pattern is capable of being modified in a variety of ways. The speaker, for example, may suggest a solution that will raise some objections in the minds of his audience. The speaker must decide what he wants to do about these objections. If he feels that they are minor, he may decide simply to stress the virtues of his solution and not mention any possible objections. He may on the other hand believe that he cannot safely or legitimately ignore some possible arguments against his proposal; they may be, for example, so obvious as almost to demand consideration. In this case, he may decide to meet the objections as he discusses his solution keeping basically the two-step sequence. He may also decide to follow a pattern something like this:

I. Our present methods of controlling pollution on the upper Mississippi are woefully inadequate.

II. We should adopt the methods that have been successful in the Big Horn River valley.

III. The obvious objections of cost and cooperation can be met.

If the speaker wishes to utilize the last section of his development for refuting objections, he will probably wish to return to a positive approach to his solution in his conclusion.

The speaker may wish to modify the two-step problem-solution pattern to meet possible objections in a somewhat different sense, that is, there may be another solution or several solutions that would suggest themselves to members of his audience. In such a situation he might feel that he would have to eliminate obvious proposals before making his own recommendation:

 I. We must be able to meet aggression and civil turmoil anywhere in the world if civilization is to survive.
 II. Unilateral military action is not feasible.
 III. Action by regional alliances is little better.
 IV. We must evolve a permanent police force under the control of the United Nations.

Quite obviously, the more complex the modifications of the simple problem-solution pattern become, the more time the speaker must take to support the parts of the speech adequately.

There is one other important modification of the problem-solution pattern which we ought to consider. Thus far the pattern as modified has maintained what could be called a *sequential* form; the problem is developed and then the solution is developed. The pattern can take on what can be called a *parallel* form. One phase of the problem is developed and the solution applied; another phase of the problem is developed and the solution applied; and so on. The result is an alternation of aspects of the problem and aspects of the solution. This "parallel" form is particularly useful when the problem has several rather distinct aspects that can be treated as relatively independent subproblems and when the solution is a rather simple proposal that does not require detailed development to be clear. Consider this example:

 I. The electoral college can result in the election of a president who is not preferred by a majority of the voters.
 I'. Electing the president by a direct vote of the people is our best assurance that the will of the majority shall prevail.
 II. The electoral college system discourages the exercise of the franchise.
 II'. Giving the people a direct voice in electing the president would encourage them to exercise their democratic privilege of voting.

Many of the same problems arise in using the problem-solution pattern, especially when it is modified, as arise in using the time pattern or the topical pattern. The speaker should strive for simplicity, should be certain that his main heads really are coordinate parts of the whole, and should consider limiting his thesis if it seems that he cannot support all the assertions adequately in the time he has. If the problem is a fresh one for his audience or if the speaker's analysis is unique, he may wish to concentrate all his efforts on the problem, discarding at least for the moment any consideration of the solution. On the other hand, he may find that he is dealing with a problem that is clearly recognized as such by his audience. All he will have to do is mention it, or outline it briefly and concentrate on the solution he would have the audience accept.

The speaker, of course, must divide the main heads of a speech arranged in a problem-solution pattern into subheads. In so doing he must meet the unique demands of the situation, but there is a traditional group of questions that may help him discover useful subheads in a problem-solution speech:

Problem: 1. Is the problem serious enough to warrant a change?
2. What are the causes of the problem?
3. If no changes are made, will the problem persist? Or will it, perhaps, be resolved without making changes?
Solution: 1. Will the solution remove the causes of the problem?
2. Can the solution be put into operation?
3. Will the solution have desirable effects? Do the desirable outweigh any undesirable effects?

This list is not intended to suggest that these questions constitute a form which the speaker ought to follow in constructing the specific points of his speech. It would be a rare case in which a speaker would want to make explicit use of answers to each question in order. The listener as well as the speaker may find it useful to raise these questions in considering problems and solutions.

In this section we have made a few generalizations about patterning the developments of speeches. Orderly speeches are not simply a matter of making models of textbook instructions. Speeches have order in terms of the needs of specific subjects and specific audiences. Learning to make use of traditional patterns will necessitate thought, planning, and practice. The alert student will find a great deal of the material in the second part of this book which he may use to help him pattern his speeches, using or modifying traditional forms.

INTRODUCTION AND CONCLUSIONS

Few things can do so much for a speech as a good introduction and a good conclusion. All of us have heard speeches that began well, that were rather muddled and boring in the middle, and then, miraculously, were concluded with clarity and grace. The total effect was good. Such speeches, of course, are no argument for muddled, boring developments.

Much more often, however, we hear speeches that begin and end with remarkable awkwardness and obscurity.

Too often a speaker will begin with endless ham-handed references to all his friends present and to the world situation in general. He will quip pleasantly (if we are fortunate) and unfold what he considers to be delightful anecdotes. Somehow or another, we aren't quite sure how, when, or why, he gets into the speech.

If introductions are all too often weak in the speeches we ordinarily hear, the conclusions are worse. "In conclusion let me say to you . . ." may be the signal for fifteen minutes of dreary effort to bring some sort of order into a development that has been in disarray from the beginning. "Finally I would remind you . . . " from this speaker probably indicates at least another ten minutes. We prefer this man's opposite, the speaker who when we look up after politely having yawned, has suddenly disappeared. He doesn't conclude his speech; he just quits.

The main cause of ineffective introductions and conclusions does not lie in any insurmountable problems posed by these parts of the speech but in the simple lack of attention that speakers give them. Too often a speaker seems to say to himself, "Oh, I'll get started. I have a good speech and can end it." He who leaves anything to the "spur of the moment" is apt to discover that the moment usually arrives, but the spur often fails to function. If a speaker will prepare introductions and conclusions carefully and knows what it is that he's preparing, he can do a good job. Intelligent preparation does not assure success—we all make errors of judgment—but ignorance and indolence will go far in assuring failure. There are two words the speaker who would begin and end his speeches effectively should remember—*purpose* and *simplicity*.

Introductions

The speaker should realize that there are some legitimate openings which are nonintroductions, in terms of our meaning of the word *introduction*. Some occasions, for example, demand what might be called *preliminary remarks*. When the mayor is introduced to the audience, he will probably acknowledge the speech of introduction and recognize dignitaries, party faithful, the purposes of the organization, and so on. Many speakers face circumstances that call for such remarks. Often skilled speakers will be quite anecdotal in their remarks (that is, they will use detailed examples drawn from personal experience). The beginning speaker, however, seldom speaks in occasions that demand preliminaries beyond perhaps, "Mr. Chairman, ladies and gentlemen."

At other times the circumstances will make an introduction unnecessary. The audience knows who the speaker is; they know what subject he will speak about; they are highly motivated to listen and able to understand. The speaker may begin his development immediately; even, "You know that I'm here this evening to talk about. . . ." is superfluous. The beginning speaker seldom finds himself in such circumstances.

Ordinarily the speaker plans an introduction to fulfill some specific purposes. Three generalizations should guide the speaker:

1. The introduction should arouse the audience's interest.
2. The introduction should dispose the audience to respond favorably toward the speaker.
3. The introduction should give the audience at least a tentative acquaintance with the speaker's thesis.

Although the speaker may often safely ignore the second purpose listed, the first and third are essential—*arrest* and *clarify*.

Making a list of the purposes of an introduction should not mislead the speaker into thinking that his introduction will necessarily be composed of three distinct, chronological steps. The speaker might well fulfill these purposes in terms of a specific speech and a specific audience in a sentence or two. On the other hand, it is possible to have a rather elaborate introduction making two or three rather distinct steps. But the speaker should strive for simplicity. It may be that in facing a particularly hostile or apathetic audience the speaker will have to use a rather long introduction, but in general it should be short. The only "rule" possible is to make the introduction as short as possible while fulfilling the purposes demanded by the particular speech situation.

AROUSING INTEREST. The introduction should make the audience want to listen to the speech. Although there are some relatively traditional methods for accomplishing this end, the speaker should be constantly alert for methods that seem potentially useful for him. In general, any piece of supporting material may be used to open a speech if, in the speaker's opinion, it will arrest the attention of the audience or help clarify his subject. Let us make a variety of beginnings for a hypothetical speech that will deal with water conservation.

A SERIES OF RELATIVELY UNDETAILED EXAMPLES

Buried in the back pages of our daily newspaper we have seen a number of interesting little articles lately. For example, we read about the progress engineers are making in drilling a tunnel under a mountain in the Rockies to bring water to the city from the western side of the Continental Divide. Sounds like a lot of trouble for a little water, doesn't it? But without it Denver's industrial growth will come to a halt.

Ground water tables have dropped an average of 40 feet between Texas and

California. California is taking 1,000 billion gallons more a year out of underground supplies than rain replenishes.

There is very little water left underground at St. Louis.

Many coastal states are troubled by the seepage of the ocean's salt water into fresh water underground reserves.

A Detailed Example

Last August we experienced a water shortage. Watering lawns was banned, and we watched our grass go from green to brown. We were asked to conserve bath water, to fix leaky faucets—a drippy faucet could cost us 113 gallons of water a month, we were told. The radios and newspapers droned caution at us for weeks until we were bored and irritated by the whole business. But let's not forget that three manufacturers decided to locate plants elsewhere for fear that our water supplies would be inadequate. And let's not forget that unless we start acting with intelligent, long-range plans our water shortage will be more than an occasional three-week nuisance.

An Analogy

Last week a strike by gasoline truck drivers cut off our supply of motor fuel. Our tanks were soon dry and we were soon walking. Some business leaders predicted great financial losses, but the strike was settled and we were riding happily again. Even so we were brought to realize how dependent we've become on gasoline.

But suppose that our supply of another liquid had been cut off? Suppose that instead of dry gas tanks, we had turned on our water faucets and found them dry? What sort of problems would we face? You say, let them drink beer? But our local brewery used half a billion gallons of water last year.

Testimony

In our quest for "push-button" living, we have set up the "potentials for push button destruction." This is not the opinion of a physicist or a politician warning about atomic warfare, but the opinion of a man worried about the rate at which our modern gadgets are wasting water.

M. D. Hollis, assistant surgeon general of the United States Public Health Service, reminds us that "Man in his pursuits must seek some order of balance. In the physical environment, water, air, and food represent the basic triangle. Of the three, water thus far in history has been the most dominant influence on man's eternal struggle with his environment."[3]

Statistics

With our back yard swimming pools, automatic washers, and air conditioning, we Americans are increasing our consumption of water tremendously. Even the motors on our cars and boats spell water consumption; it takes 50 gallons of water to refine one gallon of gas.

Now we use 300 billion gallons of water a day. Within 20 years, if the

[3] "Push-Button Living Seen Dangerous," *Minneapolis Star*, August 2, 1960, p. 4A.

present trend continues, we'll need 600 billion gallons a day. This is 85 billion gallons per day more than nature provides through rain, snow, sleet, and fog.

Visual aids can be put to use in an introduction. Just as the student mentioned in Chapter 3 used fake dynamite to arrest his audience, a speaker dealing with water conservation might dramatize his statistics with colorful graphs or might display greatly enlarged pictures of the effects of a lack of water on land, plants, and people.

Often a speaker will be able to refer to a recent experience a member of the audience has had, another speech, some aspect of the occasion in which he and the audience are participating, or perhaps to something said by a speaker preceding him in such a way as to help arouse interest. The speaker must be alert and must weave such remarks into the fabric of his own speech.

DISPOSING THE AUDIENCE FAVORABLY TOWARD THE SPEAKER. In general, the best advice on this point for the beginning speaker is simply to plan carefully an introduction that fulfills the other purposes of an introduction. If one can do so, the audience will probably be favorably disposed. Sometimes the speaker will be wise to establish his own authority, his right to speak on the subject. This is best done indirectly or in a speech introducing the speaker. But if a speaker can begin an opening example by saying, "In my fifteen years as a high school teacher I never met a student quite like Johnny . . ." he may dispose a PTA group to respond more positively than they would if they did not know that he was an experienced teacher. The speaker might, in short, do anything which helps indicate to his audience that they share some common ground—common experiences, values, goals, affiliations; but he must take care not to bid too bluntly for favor.

CLARIFYING THE SUBJECT. Some of the examples already used indicated that the speaker can scarcely help clarifying the subject to some degree if he chooses carefully material to arouse the audience's interest. But he must decide how clear he wants to be! What if one were to choose to speak recommending the abolition of fraternities before an audience containing many whose pins indicate that they are a part of the "Greek system"? Would he be wise in his introduction to say, "Down with fraternities?" He might want to say something of the sort before the speech is over, but he might decide that he'll obtain a better hearing by using material that will indicate that he intends to discuss fraternities but which does not reveal his specific purpose immediately.

An audience will be satisfied not knowing specifically what the speech is about if it feels that the speaker knows and that he's unfolding gradually the material that will reveal his full thesis. But a listener is not apt to spend much time asking himself "What's this speech all about?" He'll probably turn his attention elsewhere. The beginner, especially, should be certain that he makes his subject clear.

Often a speaker will want to make an explicit statement of his thesis. If he has worded it carefully, this simple device may be abundantly sufficient. Often he can put his thesis as a question, or use a question or series of questions that suggests his thesis. If these questions are striking, they may well serve not only to clarify the undertaking but also to arouse the audience's interest. Avoid the lame, last minute attempt in which the unprepared speaker puts the topic flatly into question form, e.g., "Have you ever wondered about water conservation?" Often times the speaker may try to startle his audience with statements of opinion or fact. He may combine such statements with questions to arouse the audience and to give his listeners at least a glimpse of his subject. Consider this example:

Suppose that you had the responsibility of deciding whether or not the federal government were to continue farm price supports. Suppose you had the responsibility of determining the general policy that would govern our defense or the size of our budget or the conditions under which labor and business shall conduct negotiations. These would be a frighteningly difficult load to bear, wouldn't they? But you do have these responsibilities and I have them. If we don't, our government is a hollow farce.

But our birthright is on the auction block. It's about to be sold. I hear someone mutter, "Just what are you talking about? What's the problem? What do you want us to do?" These are legitimate questions. Let's try to find some answers. I propose that we start looking by examining a political campaign held in California in 1964.

The speaker has not yet stated his thesis, but the audience should have the feeling that they know in general what his subject is and that he is "going somewhere."

There is the oft-repeated story of the old preacher who explained in a single sentence the whole process of making a speech: "First I tell 'em what I'm going to tell 'em; then I tell 'em what I tell 'em; then I tell 'em what I told 'em." The preacher's first step, apparently, was to presummarize his development. Although a presummary is not always necessary or even advisable, we feel that it is much too seldom used by speakers. The development may be presummarized quite formally: "We should discontinue competition in intercollegiate football because, first, it is harmful to the participants; second, it is harmful to the nonparticipating student body; and third, it degrades our college as an institution of higher education." Or the development can be presummarized more casually: "If we are to assess the merit of our college's participation in intercollegiate football, we should ask what effect it has on the participant, on the student body generally, and on the college itself."

Good introductions take time and imagination to prepare. The speaker must remember, however, that they serve important purposes, which he can ill afford to neglect.

The purposes of an introduction are well exemplified in the opening of Arthur Larson's address for the Second Annual Law Day Observations of Harvard Law School. Certainly the speaker's words ought to have aroused interest and clarified his subject, but notice especially how he identified his interests with those of the audience by associating his goals with those of men his listeners should have known and respected.

Once in a great while we observe a phenomenon in the world of ideas which reminds us of what happens when the "critical mass" is achieved in an atomic reactor. An idea, which for many years has been gathering strength because of the efforts of a few lonely prophets, suddenly fires the imaginations of hundreds of thinkers and leaders at the same time. A sort of chain reaction sets in, and almost at once a tremendous amount of energy is released.

Something like this has happened to the idea that the rule of law must be achieved in relations between sovereign states. For many years pioneers in legal thought have been telling us that we must create a system of law between nations comparable to that between individuals—and this audience does not need to be reminded that an unusually large proportion of these pioneers were here at Harvard, including such men as Hanley Hudson and Dean Roscoe Pound.[4]

After developing his fundamental analogy in some detail, citing evidence of the "chain reaction" developing in international legal thought, Mr. Larson makes a formal division of his subject. We have called this procedure a presummary:

Let us begin by asking an elementary question: What is the total job to be done if we are to have a world legal system worthy of the name? What are the normal ingredients of a working system of law for the settlement of disputes? It seems to me that there are four: A body of law to apply; machinery to apply the law; acceptance of that law and that machinery by the persons affected; and compliance with the decisions after they are rendered.[5]

Conclusions

After a long and rather complex development, Arthur Larson concluded his speech in a manner that may well have helped some of his listeners recall his thought for some time to come:

[4] "Address by Arthur Larson, Director Duke University World Rule of Law Center and Special Consultant to the President [of the United States], on the Occasion of the Second Annual Law Day Observances of Harvard Law School, May 1, 1959," Mimeographed, World Rule of Law Center, Duke University, Durham, N.C.
[5] *Ibid.*

If [world law] appears to be expecting the impossible, let us remember that there is one force at work that has never existed before. The shadow of the hydrogen bomb is over us all. Perhaps the uncompromising necessity of finding an alternative to force will enable us to compress history and produce advances in international cooperation that normally would take many times as long.

Rousseau, in his book on education, *Emile*, wrote: "The best way to teach Emile not to lean out of the window is to let him fall out. Unfortunately, the defect of this system is that the pupil may not survive to profit by his experience."

The world has been learning about international relations for centuries by a process of periodically falling out of the window. The injuries have been serious, but never quite fatal. One more fall, however, will be our last. We must profit by our experiences of past international conflict, for we will not be given another chance.

I would like to close with a Brer Rabbit story on this theme of doing the seemingly impossible.

Uncle Remus was telling the little boy the story about the time Brer Rabbit climbed a tree. The little boy spoke up and said, "But Uncle Remus, you know that rabbits can't climb trees." Uncle Remus replied: "Yes, that's right, I know that rabbits can't climb trees. But Brer Fox was right behind Brer Rabbit, and Brer Rabbit just pleased to climb that tree."

In the same way, in the presence of appalling danger, we too can and must do the impossible and bring about that rule of law between nations which is the last, best hope of earth.[6]

Mr. Larson's long speech needed a long conclusion. A simple speech, which is clearly developed, may need almost no conclusion, for the purpose of a conclusion is to give the audience a feeling of completion, that things are done, and the speaker may well have done this as he utters the last word of the development. Stated a little more elaborately, the conclusion serves two possible functions:

1. The conclusion should restate briefly the substance of the speech.
2. The conclusion should focus the attention of the audience on the response the speaker desires.

These aims may be more or less important depending on the sort of development that has been made. Sometimes more than a simple restatement of the thesis will be superfluous.

Just as presummaries are sometimes useful, final summaries may help the speaker fulfill his purposes. His summary may be formal or casual.

Any piece of supporting material that the speaker feels will help obtain the responses he desires may be used. Detailed examples and testimony

[6] *Ibid.*

are often used in conclusions; analogies are less frequently found but may be useful.

Quite often in concluding a speaker will use a phrase, a sentence, a piece of material that he has used elsewhere in his speech. It is especially common, and often effective, to use material from the introduction. Consider the conclusion of the speech on highway safety, twice referred to, which began with the speaker displaying dummy dynamite and asking, "Would anyone care to light the fuse and put this stick of dynamite in his pocket?" At the end of the speech, he picked up the object once more.

This dynamite isn't really dangerous—but your car is. Treat it with as much caution as you'd treat a stick of dynamite.

I have a piece of dynamite fuse taped over the ignition switch of my car. I need a reminder of my responsibility to myself and to others. Maybe you don't need a reminder. But I have twenty-five pieces of fuse which I'll give to you in a minute. Take one and tape it over your ignition—or throw it away. But be careful—don't throw away your life.[7]

This conclusion is one that the speaker's audience is likely to remember.

If the speaker offers some sort of proposal, a solution, he might well want to visualize the effects of the proposal if put into operation, or he may want to visualize the lamentable state of affairs that will persist if it isn't, or he may want to do both, if he has time. In such visualization the speaker can make any number of abstract assertions, but if he is wise he will use supporting material to make the visualization clear, interesting, and impelling.

Like the introduction, the conclusion should be simple. It should be short. As with the introduction, the only sensible "rule" is to make it as short as possible while fulfilling its purposes.

MAKING OUTLINES

An outline is part of proper speech preparation. Therefore, the question students often ask, "Do I have to make an outline for this speech?" indicates a deficiency in their understanding of their task as speakers. This deficiency may arise from what they have learned from textbooks about speech outlines. But the moment the speaker puts pencil to paper to jot a phrase indicating his tentative thesis and, perhaps, several words to help him remember and consider a possible pattern of main heads, he has begun to outline. What he has made is a rough draft. He should make dozens of such drafts in preparing his speech. Some he will discard; some

[7] Adapted from a speech by Orrin Finch, University of Minnesota student, 1959.

he will modify. Eventually his outline will grow into a final, completed form.

Too often the student reads or hears advice like that just given and says, "A dozen outlines. Sounds like a needless drain on my time." So he works hard, gathers material, and sits down the night before he is to speak to plan his speech from beginning to end. In his effort to compose a polished speech, perhaps represented by a spic and span outline, at one sitting the student will probably spend more time than he would have had he followed the advice; and the product of his work will probably not measure up to what he is capable of doing. An early rough draft may take only a minute or two to jot down, and in making rough drafts, the student will form good habits: *plan, evaluate, modify.*

Outlines in process are not apt to be neat and attractive. As a speaker works on an outline it will become less and less neat until he is forced to recopy his modified version so he can continue building it toward its final form. In making a simple illustration used earlier in this chapter, one of your authors produced this:

> We must correct some common misunderstandings about fraternities.
> ~~The purpose of fraternities is misunderstood.~~ *The cinema stereotypes do not represent*
> I. ~~Common misunderstandings.~~ *the average fraternity.*
> II. The real aims of fraternities ~~are far different than many suppose.~~
> *serve legitimate individual needs.*

This is, of course, only the beginning of an outline.

What has been said ought not be taken to mean that complete, neatly written outlines have no value. The complete outline is simply the final step in a long series. It should be neatly done, of course, so that the speaker himself can see what he has and so that his instructor (or anyone who might help him) will be able to criticize it.

Even when the speaker feels that he has an outline completed, he will be wise to take it apart again. Make a list of the main heads. Are they divided properly? Patterned effectively? Stated effectively? Taken together do they satisfactorily express the thesis? Should the thesis be modified? Look at each main section. Are the subordinate heads well arranged? Are assertions supported? Are all the relationships clear? Have needed transitions been omitted? All of this is necessary because in building a more and more complex structure, the speaker may lose sight of some of the large patterns and relationships. But some of these questions touch on problems that have not yet been discussed.

Standard Symbols

Any system of outlining will be somewhat arbitrary and sometimes seem to be burdensome. The speaker may wish to disregard traditional practices at times, but when he does so, he should do so for good reason, taking care not simply to rationalize carelessness or laziness. Using symbols to indicate parts of the outline will help most speakers achieve an orderly structure. Here is a model to follow:

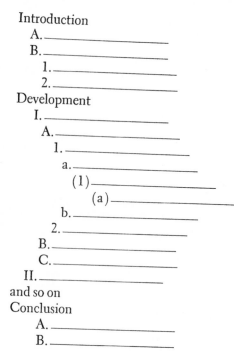

Introduction

   A._____

   B._____

     1._____

     2._____

Development

   I._____

    A._____

      1._____

        a._____

          (1)_____

            (a)_____

        b._____

      2._____

    B._____

    C._____

   II._____

and so on

Conclusion

   A._____

   B._____

Several explanations may be necessary. You may not need as many divisions as just indicated. In general, seek simplicity. You will notice that your authors prefer actually to write in "introduction," "development," and "conclusion." We feel that this is a simple but useful reminder. Finally, you will notice that we have used Roman numerals to indicate only main heads. This is arbitrary, but there may be some value in having a symbol that says "main head." Some authorities recommend repeating Roman numerals (as we have repeated capital letters, and so on) in each section of the outline; others carry the Roman numerals through from beginning to end.

Stating Assertions

Most textbook writers recommend that the beginner compose a complete sentence outline. We feel that it is unnecessary to indicate each minor detail by a complete sentence; often a phrase or a single word will suffice to indicate, for example, a piece of supporting material. There may even be disadvantages to a complete sentence outline, especially for

extemporaneous speaking.[8] Too often they become barely disguised manuscripts. If one wants to write a manuscript, one should do so and should
compose outlines in preparation for writing manuscripts. But a manuscript speech is a manuscript speech whether it is written in paragraphs
or in a number of lines with symbols before each.

What you have just read should not be taken to mean that the speaker
should not indicate each part of his speech carefully in outlining, nor
should it be taken to mean that no complete sentences should be written.
*The thesis and each main head must be written as a complete, declarative
sentence.* There is no other way of checking these important parts to make
certain that they are what one wants them to be. The speaker may write
such other complete sentences as may serve to help him compose critical
parts of the speech. Many speakers like to write out the first few sentences
of the introduction and the last few of the conclusion completely. Often
transitions should be written as complete sentences.

We discussed phrasing theses in Chapter 2. Like the thesis, the main
heads should be stated as concisely and vividly as possible. If possible, use
parallel sentence structure and repeat key words in phrasing main heads to
make them stand out boldly in the speech. Consider

> Thesis: D. H. Lawrence's novels are degrading.
> I. The intent of Lawrence's novels is to sensationalize sordid passions.
> II. The effect of Lawrence's novels is to encourage animalistic abandon.

or

> Thesis: D. H. Lawrence should be ranked among the world's great novelists.
> I. Lawrence is concerned with timeless problems of human values.
> II. Lawrence treats problems of human values in a frank but uniquely sensi-
> tive manner.

The speaker should examine quite carefully any main head he has stated
as a compound sentence. Such sentences usually indicate ideas that should
be treated in two (or more) main heads.

Ordinarily the beginning speaker should state his main heads explicitly at the beginning of the sections of the speech in which they are
developed. Sometimes, however, the statement of the main head may be
delayed or even left unstated, just as the statement of the thesis may be
delayed or left unstated. Often it is effective to introduce some material
and to draw the main head from it or to allow the audience to supply the
assertion. Inasmuch as the form of outlining requires assertions to be made
and development of material to follow in clear subordination, the beginning speaker is often perplexed in trying to indicate a delayed or im-

[8] Problems of delivering extemporaneous and manuscript speeches will be considered in Chapter 7.

plicit main head. The answer is to place in brackets, [   ], any assertion that is not actually to be stated at the point at which form requires it to appear in the outline:

I. [Public opinion engineers are usurping our rights of democratic free choice.]
   A. A political campaign in San Francisco in 1964.
   B. Experts in conducting campaigns testify concerning their methods.
I. Public opinion engineers are usurping our rights of democratic free choice.

Repeating the statement of the main head in the outline, with the Roman numeral, may seem strange at first, but the speaker's procedure is clear. Some speakers, probably those who cannot break old habits of outlining, make a note such as "state main head explicitly" at some subordinate point.

Transitions and Signposting

Careful attention to transitions is a sign differentiating the experienced from the inexperienced speaker. Transitions may be used between any major divisions in the speech, although usually they are thought of as being the bridge between the developments of two main heads. In a sense they serve as a conclusion to the point just finished and the introduction to the next. In simple, well-ordered speeches transitions may be unnecessary, but the speaker should make certain that this is the case before omitting transitions.

Restatement-forecast is the simplest method of transition: "But a lack of funds is only one of the problems we face; more serious is our lack of commitment to our ideals." "Not only must we hasten to meet this threat, but we must act upon a careful plan. This raises a natural question, 'What can be done quickly?' " As this last example indicates, rhetorical questions serve well as transitions. Often the question will be much like the main head, but it is not itself a main head and should not be mistaken for such. When a question is used as a transition, often the speaker will delay the explicit statement of the main head.

Pieces of supporting material, especially examples and testimony, may serve as transitions. The main problem, especially in short speeches, is to make such transitions quickly.

In the outline, transitions should be indicated by placing the statement or phrase indicating the transition in parentheses:

I._____
   A._____

(But there is another problem we must consider . . .)
II._____

Often a speaker will *signpost* to indicate a new idea, especially to indicate another main head. "In the first place . . ." "Secondly . . ." "My second point is . . ." "Finally we must consider . . ." Although this device may seem awkward, many great speakers have not hesitated to use it. With practice a speaker can signpost smoothly.

The student who has studied this chapter carefully ought to be ready to build rather carefully ordered speeches. He ought not be under the illusion that he will face no difficult problems, that secret doorways have been opened to him. But he should be able to proceed in his private learning process.

EXAMPLES

Study the following outlines. They are ones composed by college students in preparation for extemporaneous speeches. Very few modifications have been made in them for publication here. They are not perfect outlines; they could be improved as almost all outlines can be improved.[9] But they will indicate the form outlines take and ought to stimulate you to do at least as well.

You will notice that the speakers have maintained a labeling margin on the left-hand side. We recommend this practice for the beginning speaker. Taking stock of what you have done is one good method of laying a foundation for evaluating and improving specific speeches and thereby for becoming a more knowledgeable student of speech.

What sort of notes should you make in the labeling margin? Primarily you should be conscious of your methods of supporting ideas. When you have chosen a piece of material to make an assertion or implication clear, interesting, or acceptable, label the material. You should also be conscious of the organization of your speech. Label main points, transitions, summaries, and other efforts you make to give the sequence of ideas and materials clarity and impact.

Be imaginative in your use of the labeling margin. As a speaker analyzing his own work, you should see the particular procedures you are following and may need a unique word or phrase to describe them.

[9] Many textbook writers, as we have already indicated, would argue that the speaker, especially the beginner, should compose each entry in the outline in complete sentences. Because the following outlines are not composed in complete sentences, some entries will not be completely clear to the reader. Each speaker intends his outline primarily for his own use and must, of course, be able to complete the thoughts indicated at subordinate points in the outline by merely words or phrases.

Another Visit-Your-Dentist Speech?[10]

Discussion of purpose	Everyone is aware of his teeth and the care needed to preserve them. My audience knows what visits to the dentist are and has heard propaganda for the good sense of teeth care for years. Yet, I predict, most of my listeners do not follow the advice they know is sensible. Perhaps my ironic recommendation, "Have your teeth pulled now. You'll save money and look and feel better," will make them reconsider the discrepancy between their knowledge and their behavior.

INTRODUCTION

Story that sets the tone	A. My friend John visits the dentist.
Examples of vivid experiences I, at least, remember.	B. Other experiences with the dentist 　1. "The dentist is your friend"—your first visit with Mom. 　2. Drugs and shots 　3. Non high speed drills
THESIS is implicit: [Take care of your teeth!] Presummary	C. All your troubles can be ended if you will have your teeth removed and replaced with dentures. This should be done for three reasons: 　1. Financial 　2. Health 　3. Beauty
Transition Statistics Rhetorical question	(There are 50 million Americans wearing some sort of denture. Age 35, 1 in 5; age 45, 1 in 3; age 55, 1 in 2. Why are so many people wearing dentures? The answer is threefold.)

DEVELOPMENT

Main Point [Better go now!] Detailed example	I. We can save time as well as money from fewer dental appointments. 　A. No more waiting rooms. 　　1. Tedium and tension 　　2. Ancient magazines
Statistics More facts and figures!	B. No more worry about $25 to $50 dental bills. 　1. No more cavities 　2. Average tooth is filled two and a half times. 　3. But let drop the cost of typical dentures—

[10] Adapted from a speech outline prepared by Keith Engdahl, University of Minnesota student, 1965.

Main Point
[Maybe I do
need a checkup!]
Undetailed
  examples

II. Everyone should wear dentures to avoid the potential health hazards of teeth.
    A. Bad teeth—improper mastication
       1. Poor digestion
       2. Intestinal problems

Testimony

    B. Average teeth—some jagged edges, hence . . . Dr. Lester David has proved that the constant mouth irritation from jagged edges is highly associated with the development of cancer.
    C. Teeth can lead to trouble with the heart, blood, and liver.

Detailed example
Transition

       1. Aunt Sally's impacted wisdom tooth
(If Aunt Sally had only had dentures, she would have avoided this problem. Moreover, she would have looked better most of her life and Uncle Fred might not have left her.)

Main point
[But that's not
how your
Grandma
looked!]
Imply examples

III. With dentures you can have that beautiful, Hollywood look.
    A. Perhaps you had braces or wished you had.
       1. Remember those kids—or remember those days, kids?
    B. You can smile again without revealing ugly teeth —and, of course, bad breath!

Testimony
[Do we need
twenty years
taken off? How
do people get
that way?]

       1. Douglas W. Stephens, D.D.S., "Dentures can improve your looks by erasing old wrinkles and building up sunken faces. They can take twenty years off the wearer's age."

CONCLUSION

Rhetorical
  question
Testimony
Undetailed
  examples

    A. Are dentures practical? Of course!
       1. Dr. Peter C. Goulding.
       2. Don't worry about eating. Well—apples . . . or corn on the cob . . . or a good steak . . .
       3. Drop them? Well, parties need livening.

Rhetorical
  question

    B. Next time you go to your dentist, remember the three points I have made. Rather than go to him often, save pain, worry, and anxiety. Have some teeth made. Get those old ones out. Get three or four sets.

The Organization Man's Organization[11]

**Discussion
of purpose**

The purpose of this speech will be to convince the audience that bureaucratic organization is good.

The very mention of the word *bureaucracy* will elicit negative response from my audience. My listeners know a great deal about bureaucracy through personal experiences; they probably believe at best that it is a "necessary evil" and tend to regard it with something approaching hatred.

I would like to get my listeners to feel positively about bureaucracy. I don't expect them to wave flags proclaiming the death of small business and the birth of large-scale organization—"long live bureacracy"; but I would like to have them realize that it is an efficient, reliable, and necessary system. I will admit drawbacks rather than deny them but will try to strengthen the positive aspects of the system.

INTRODUCTION

**Focus attention:
Examples chosen
that involve
experience of
members of
this audience.**

A. [Each of us have experienced bureaucracy.]
   1. As college students
   2. A few housewives
   3. Several with business experience
   4. Remember basic training?
   5. Jerry was an officer-pilot.

THESIS

B. We wince, but in each of these instances, we were parts of the efficient, reliable, and necessary bureaucratic system that guarantees the security and opportunity which we all value.

DEVELOPMENT

**Main Point
May as well
recognize
negative
responses with
this testimony.**

I. Bureaucracy may be defined in many ways.
   A. William Buckley, Jr. in *National Review*
      1. Dreadful disease
      2. Causes one to become set in his ways.

   B. George Orwell in *1984*
      1. A law unto itself
      2. Defines its own truth
         a. A new day, a new truth
         b. Concealing the past.

---

[11] Adapted from a speech outline prepared by Arnold R. Enslin, University of Minnesota student, 1966.

Quote Whyte's "negative attributes"

C. William H. Whyte, Jr. in *The Organization Man*

A "neutral definition

D. Ely Chinoy in a sociology textbook, *Society*
"A formal, rationally organized social structure involving a group of people endeavoring to accomplish a common task."

Transition

(Certainly many folks don't like what Dr. Chinoy defines. I shall have a task supporting my assertion.)

Main Point

II. The bureaucratic system is efficient and reliable.

Subpoint

A. A bureaucracy contains a system of carefully defined positions or offices.

Undetailed examples

1. Military, government, education, or business

Explanation
Hopefully, this will remind listeners of examples.

2. Structure exists apart from the personnel.
  a. In case of a loss, the system continues and a replacement is installed.
  b. Slots can be filled with qualified individuals.
    1) Not relatives, friends, or neighbors
    2) Maximizes selection on basis of skills and knowledge.

Again, listeners may supply examples.

3. Every department in this college has experienced rapid turnover in the past few years. The departments carry on. You can complete your degrees.

Subpoint

B. A bureaucracy contains a hierarchial order of positions with clear-cut lines of authority and responsibility.

Example
Example

1. Archetype is the military.
2. A common mission doesn't always mean unanimous agreement on the means to that end.
3. Coordination and responsibility are needed.

Subpoint
Example
Testimony

C. A bureacracy has rules and regulations.
1. "Red Tape" is confusing, but without it, chaos.
2. Employee-employer relations are mutually agreed upon.

Testimony

D. A bureaucracy contains a security of tenure and possibility of career by promotion.

Undetailed examples

1. Our experience—military, work, university

Common values
Rhetorical questions

2. Do we not value the security and opportunity we have seen? See that others do?

Summarizes and makes transition.	(This "blue-print" bureaucratic system's characteristics are found in any bureaucratic organization today.)
Main point —implicit	III. [The bureaucratic system is necessary.]
Transition, con't.	(What accounts for the rise of bureaucracy?)
Subpoint Statistics and testimony Examples implied	A. Bureaucracy is correlated with a money economy. 1. Need to support the $700 billion Gross National Product predicted for 1966. 2. We are dependent on it for all the services we have come to expect from business and government.

Subpoint **Testimony Repetition** **Summary of Point "III"**	B. Bureaucracy reflects the values and attitudes of the society of which it is a part.
	1. Whyte
	  a. Security and opportunity
	  b. Calm and ordered
	2. These values are found in bureaucracy
	  a. Defined positions
	  b. Hierarchial advancement possible
	  c. Security, retirement, tenure

CONCLUSION

Rhetorical questions	A. Look at the world around you. Ask yourself: Do I really want it any other way? If it were suddenly wiped out, wouldn't I miss it? Wouldn't I work to rebuild it?
Admit limitations	B. The "congenital defects" are generally known and have been spelled out; however, they are tendencies we can guard against, not inherent qualities.
Final challenge	C. Until someone can show us an efficient and reliable system capable of producing and maintaining a standard of living comparable to that which we enjoy, we ought to accept the bureaucratic organization as a necessary and valuable part of living today.

Group Exercise

1. Divide the class into groups of about four students each.
2. Preliminary meeting. Each group should
   a. choose a subject for a speech.

b. discuss the purpose of the speech for the class-audience.

c. phrase a tentative thesis.

3. Each group member should work out an outline using the tentative thesis.

4. In group meetings, compare and discuss the outlines. Try to work out a "best" outline.

5. Optional: let each group discuss organizing a speech on its particular thesis, telling what they did and why.

Speaking Assignment

1. Choose a speech from *Vital Speeches.*
2. Describe the organization of the speech.
3. Criticize the organization using this question as a guide: "What could be done to improve the organization?"

5 ‖ Adjusting Ideas to Audiences

Speaking generally, we may say that the rhetorical function is the function of adjusting ideas to people and people to ideas.

DONALD C. BRYANT

The speaker's commitment to ideas and materials is a theme which we have constantly reiterated in this book. It is a theme that will be developed more deeply in Part II when we set forth a problem-centered system of analysis.

The inclination of good men to commit themselves to ideals, institutions, and programs is a major force in bringing progressive improvements into the life of man and in conserving past gains from the threat of corruption. But unless a man is inclined toward totalitarianism, he will recognize that such commitment is not enough. He must believe not only in a particular analysis of a problem and a plan or a program but also in the right and ability of others to assent or dissent intelligently.

The good speaker, in short, must temper his own convictions in the crucible of communication. As our metaphor suggests, the good speaker does not relinquish his commitments. Too often adjusting to audiences is taken to mean compromising in the negative sense that word often carries, or, to be even more pejorative, to "sell out" or to prostitute one's thought and effort.

Few feel admiration for the man whose opinions change with every breeze, but neither do we praise the man who may think critically on the problems he shares with his fellows but who can not or will not bring his thought in some way into the public forum. On the other extreme, we do often call the man who says, in effect, "Here are my ideas; I will not modify them to suit anyone!" a courageous man. Occasionally a man will be courageous and wise to forego the immediate prospect of appealing to a majority in order to serve more long-range convictions. Too often, however, the man we honor for the "courage of his convictions" may well simply be too stubborn or too lazy to take the responsibility of making his ideas as effective as possible for his contemporaries.

Ordinarily a sincere effort to make one's ideas effective, to adjust "ideas to people and people to ideas" in Donald C. Bryant's phrase,[1] takes more ability and courage than does striking the take-it-or-leave-it posture. One's thought may be tempered, as steel is tempered, in heat. Seldom, however, will the proper temperature be reached merely by the flash of hot proclamation. Much more often it is the friction of fine minds working to find an alloy that will suit the situation that brings the strongest fusion.

At this point a perceptive student may remark, "Yes, these arguments are obvious enough. They have, as a matter of fact, been present in the book from the beginning." He is quite right and might predict, further, that the task of adjusting ideas to audiences will be a major theme of most of the following chapters. The title we chose for this chapter would be descriptive of most speech textbooks, including this one. What we say in this chapter will be most useful if the student sees in it an opportunity to review Chapters 2, 3, and 4, especially, and recalls it in studying the problem-centered system of analysis set forth in Part II.

IDENTIFICATION—THE FUNDAMENTAL PROCESS

"To persuade a man is largely a matter of *identifying* the opinion or course you wish him to adopt with one or more of his established beliefs or customary courses of conduct,"[2] James A. Winans observed [italics, Winans']. Even the speech in which one sets as his basic task putting forth some body of information must relate somehow to the needs of auditors if it is to be attended to seriously; we may extend therefore Winans' remark to apply generally to the rhetorical function of adjusting ideas to an audience. (The student may wish to review our discussion of *purpose* in Chapter 2.)

In introductions, often, the effort of speakers to identify their interests with those of the audience is especially apparent. When places, occasions, and participants give speakers opportunities to refer to experiences, goals, or associations they hold in common with their listeners, many take ad-

---

[1] "Rhetoric: Its Functions and Its Scope," *The Quarterly Journal of Speech*, XXXIX, 4 (December 1953), p. 413.
[2] *Speech-Making*, New York, Appleton-Century-Crofts, 1938, p. 370.

vantage of the circumstances. Thus Grayson Kirk, President of Columbia University, addressing an audience at the University of Denver begins by referring to his experience as a faculty member at Denver: "It is a pleasure to be in Denver once more, to visit again this university where I taught one happy summer, and to have the opportunity to renew so many long-standing and precious friendships. Actually, I tend, in retrospect, to associate this institution with one of the major changes in the direction of my life."[3]

Whereas the identifying of interests in introductions may give us the quickest, most obvious examples, one should not expect to find the function fulfilled there and the matter put aside. Fundamental identifications should undergird the entire speech and will often appear only in subtle signs throughout. The basic nature of identification is neatly caught in the central metaphor of this statement of Kenneth Burke's:

True, the rhetorician may have to change an audience's opinion in one respect; but he can succeed only insofar as he yields to that audience's opinions in other respects. Some of their opinions are needed to support the fulcrum by which he would move other opinions. (Preferably he shares the fixed opinions himself since, "all other things being equal," the identifying of himself with his audience will be more effective if it is genuine.)[4]

Extending Burke's parenthetical remark, we must observe that if a speaker has reason to address an audience at all, he should be able to find some rather substantial grounds on which he might identify interests.

On what sorts of grounds may one identify with an audience? This question is natural enough. The answer will entail making a choice of a set of terms to guide the speaker's thought in preparing his speech. As we have said constantly in setting forth our nomenclature, other terms could be chosen, and whatever terms are chosen, they constitute merely points of departure for specific analysis.

Before discussing possible bases of identification, however, we shall suggest that the process of adjusting ideas to audiences, although it is a general process that may manifst itself in an infinite number of ways in speeches, may be given special focus if the speaker will concentrate on three elements of speech composition which we have already discussed.

Identifying in the Statement of Purpose

As we said in Chapter 2, the careful speaker composes for his own guidance a statement of the purpose which he wishes to accomplish.

[3] "Responsibilities of the Educated Man," *Contemporary American Speeches*, ed. Wil Linkugel, R. R. Allen, and Richard Johannessen, Belmont, California, Wadsworth Publishing Co., 1965, p. 166.
[4] *A Rhetoric of Motives*, New York, Prentice-Hall, Inc., 1950, p. 56.

Although he may be guided in forming his purpose by some traditional "ends" of speaking, his statement should be a unique one setting forth the specific response or group of interrelated responses he seeks to obtain from his audience.

The student who begins his statement of purpose with "I expect my audience to agree that a basic purpose of higher education is to enable us to learn to exercise free choice intelligently. In light of this belief, it is inconsistent for us to accept an administrative policy that limits strictly the political affiliations of speakers invited by student organizations to address them. Furthermore . . ." is probably seeing his purpose in the light of adjusting ideas and listeners. "It is the existence of some inconsistency within the microstructure of most auditors' opinions . . . that makes possible opinion change on controversial questions," Theodore Clevenger, Jr. has argued.[5] Whether or not the speaker highlights possible inconsistencies, and whether or not he is dealing with issues that are obviously controversial, he will be saying in some way or another, in effect, "These ideas are consistent with beliefs or behaviors which you already find important."

Because planning a statement of purpose should be a very early step in the preparation of a speech, and one which the speaker often reconsiders as his preparation continues, striving to include in it indications of the identifications on which he will work to accomplish his ends will help him fix sharply in his own mind the lines along which he must build his entire effort.

Identifying in the Key Assertions

In discussing organization, Chapter 4, we focused on arranging patterns of the statements of ideas directly supporting the thesis. These we called *main points*. The thesis, main points, and formal transitions are the key assertions to which the speaker may turn with profit in seeking to reflect fundamental identifications in the speech.

Abraham Lincoln's "First Inaugural Address" is a clear example of an effort to identify common interests in these key structural elements. Consider this major transition: "That there are persons in one section or another who seek to destroy the Union at all events and are glad of any pretext to do it I will neither affirm or deny; but if there be such, I need address no word to them. To those, however, who really love the Union may I not speak?"[6] The main points that follow this transition indicate

[5] *Audience Analysis*, Indianapolis, Indiana, The Bobbs-Merrill Co., 1966, p. 114.

[6] This speech is available in many anthologies. We are quoting from *Speeches for Illustration and Example*, ed. Goodwin F. Berquist, Jr., Chicago, Illinois, Scott, Foresman and Co., 1965, p. 136.

clearly the grounds on which the speaker hopes to identify his interests with those held by his auditors, e.g., "All profess to be content in the Union if all constitutional rights can be maintained."[7]

When he visited Russia in 1959, Vice-President Richard Nixon was invited to make a televised speech to the Russian people. Almost immediately he sought elements to identify with his audience, in this way building to a statement of thesis:

> These are some of the characteristics of the Soviet people which I particularly noted on this trip.
>
> First, their capacity for hard work, their vitality; their intense desire to improve their lot, to get ahead, is evident everywhere.
>
> There was another feature about the Soviet people which I noted which may surprise you and that is in how many respects you are like us Americans. We are similar in our love of humor—we laugh at the same jokes. The people of your frontier East have much the same spirit of what was our frontier West. We have a common love of sports; the name of Vasily Kuznetsov, your great decathlon champion, is known in the United States as well as in the Soviet Union. We are both a hospitable, friendly people. When we meet each other we tend to like each other personally, as so many of our soldiers who met during the last great war can attest.
>
> Above all the American people and the Soviet people are as one in their desire for peace. And our desire for peace is not because either of us is weak. On the contrary, each of us is strong and respects the strength the other possesses.[8]

Nixon's major concern throughout the speech was to make compelling with specific detail the interest in peace that he asserted Russians and Americans share.

Identifying in Supporting Materials

Quite often the identifications the speaker hopes to make with his auditors are reflected in the supporting materials. The experienced speaker will keep in mind the need to adjust ideas as he chooses and forms the supporting materials for his speech. The quotation from Richard Nixon's speech illustrates this contention.

As a senator from Massachusetts, John F. Kennedy addressed a Harvard University commencement on "The Intellectual and the Politician." It was mainly for those who thought that there was an antipathy between these roles that Kennedy spoke: "Authors, scholars and intellectuals can

---

[7] *Ibid.*, p. 137.

[8] "Address to the Russian People," *The Speaker's Resource Book*, ed. Carroll Arnold, Douglas Ehninger, and John Gerber, Chicago, Scott, Foresman and Company, 1961, p. 241.

praise every aspect of American society but the political. My desk is flooded with books, articles and pamphlets criticizing Congress. But, rarely if ever, have I seen any intellectual bestow praise on either the political profession or any political body for its accomplishments, its ability or its integrity—much less for its intelligence."[9] One can predict quite early that Kennedy will argue that in some way intelligence and politics are not mutually exclusive, but the genius of the identifications rests in the amazing quantity of specific supporting material, especially the examples, which reflect the speaker's thought. Consider just part of the development of one point:

First, I would ask both groups to recall that the American politician of today and the American intellectual of today are descended from a common ancestry. Our nation's first great politicians were also among the nation's first great writers and scholars. The founders of the American Constitution were also founders of American scholarship. The works of Jefferson, Madison, Hamilton, Franklin, Paine and John Adams—to name but a few—influenced the literature of the world as well as its geography. Books were their tools, not their enemies. Locke, Milton, Sydney, Montesquieu, Coke and Bolingbroke were among those widely read in political circles and frequently quoted in political pamphlets. Our political leaders traded in the free commerce of ideas with lasting results here and abroad.

In these golden years, our political leaders moved from one field to another with amazing versatility and vitality. Jefferson and Franklin still throw long shadows over many fields of learning. A contemporary described Jefferson, "A gentleman of thirty-two, who could calculate an eclipse, survey an estate, tie an artery, plan an edifice, try a cause, break a horse, dance a minuet, and play the violin."[10]

The Bases of Identification

Keeping in mind constantly the need to adjust his ideas and materials to his audience and focusing especially on his statement of purpose, key assertions, and supporting materials in making substantial his identifications of interest, the speaker may seek some guidelines in considering the nature of the audience to which he would adjust.

Probably no part of one's formal education and experience will be irrelevant to the task of gaining insight into the nature of man and his society. Every speaker will bring to bear the accumulation of his past on the tasks he shoulders at any moment. The division suggested here will serve as one rudimentary approach to the problem.

Most speakers will find it useful to consider the abilities and knowledge,

[9] See *Contemporary American Speeches*, p. 281.
[10] *Ibid.*, p. 282.

the physiopsychological needs, and the commitments of their listeners. We shall discuss each of these factors in turn.

The Abilities and Knowledge of the Audience

The class-audience that the beginning speaker faces is in many ways a difficult one. The speaker must realize that for his listeners he is not a special event. They are apt to be easily distracted from listening by the events of the day which have preceded and which will follow his speech. On the other hand, the student speaker has the advantage of speaking to a group of persons who have abilities and knowledge much like his own.

In general the speaker should ask himself two basic questions, each of which must be applied specifically to the subject with which he will deal: (1) "What is the educational level of my audience?" and (2) "What are the past experiences of my audience?" These questions will help the speaker determine whether the audience has special knowledge concerning his subject or whether it is markedly deficient in needed background, and whether his listeners will probably readily understand complex ideas or be easily perplexed by anything out of the ordinary. These inquiries will be especially useful to the speaker while he plans his statement of purpose.

James B. Conant's statements concerning his response to an invitation to speak indicate the importance of considering the abilities and knowledge of an audience:

When I was honored by the invitation to be the Bampton lecturer for 1952, President Eisenhower, then of Columbia, expressed on behalf of the committee the hope that I would undertake to provide "some understanding of the significance of recent developments in the physical sciences." On my inquiring as to the nature of the audience, I was assured professional philosophers and scientists would be conspicuous by their absence. My exposition, if not aimed at the proverbial man-on-the-street, was to be directed at the equally proverbial college graduate—the hypothetical individual whom college presidents welcome each commencement to the fellowship of educated men. Being thus assured that I was not expected either to give an appraisal of the impact of physics on metaphysics or a technical account of the inner workings of the atom, I gratefully accepted the privilege of being a guest lecturer at Columbia University.

After some further remarks on his subject matter, Conant shows clearly that his speech is founded on an appraisal of the sort of persons his listeners might be:

I wish to include in my survey the impact of modern science on the philosophic presuppositions of the average enlightened citizen of a modern democracy—on his ambitions, his hopes, his fears, his outlook on the world. So in a sense I shall relate physics to philosophy, but only by handling both subjects in a general fashion and viewing each from the point of view of a deeply troubled modern man.[11]

Conant's lectures are "popular" in the best sense of the word. They should be challenging to a well-educated audience. In judging the ability of an audience it is much better to overestimate than to underestimate. Nothing is as likely to irritate an audience as to be "talked down to." Whereas a listener may be perplexed or bored by intricate explanations for which he does not possess sufficient background, he may be outraged by elaborate explanations of what is immediately understandable.

The Needs of the Audience

The men and women who compose any audience will have basic needs. These needs grow out of their physiological nature but are considerably modified by the particular social context in which they live, as, indeed, the social context has in turn been molded by the needs of men and women. In large part, the study of speaking is the study of the needs of the persons addressed. The speaker should constantly seek different viewpoints from which to gain insight into the needs of men. His knowledge, gained from the study of many subjects—anthropology, sociology, and psychology in particular—should help him draw up some styles of thought that will be useful in determining how he might best adapt his ideas and materials to his specific audience.

The particular analysis we shall follow here is based on the work of Abraham H. Maslow.[12] Maslow classifies human needs into five categories:

1. Physiological needs
2. Safety needs
3. Belongingness and love needs
4. Esteem needs
5. The need for self-actualization

These human needs form a kind of ladder; it is necessary to climb the lower rungs in order to reach the higher rungs. The base of the ladder is composed of those needs that are necessary for life to exist at all. Unless the physiological needs are met we cannot reach the higher rungs of the ladder any more than a man who is being smothered can appreciate the most magnificent performance of Beethoven's Ninth Symphony. The physiological needs are those associated with hunger, thirst, elimination, balance of body temperature, and the like. We are seldom more than momentarily deprived of physiological satisfactions in our affluent society.

[11] *Modern Science and Modern Man*, New York, Columbia University Press, 1955, pp. 3 and 5.
[12] *Motivation and Personality*, New York, Harper and Brothers, 1954.

At the same time, some of our habits relating to these satisfactions may be interrupted and thereby cause tensions that will affect our behavior. We are used to certain foods on a certain schedule, for example, and if this schedule is interrupted, we may be affected. The speaker should sometimes consider potential tensions arising from physiological needs.

The next rung on the ladder is formed by the safety needs that emerge when the physiological needs are met. Security is apt to be a concern for any listener. He is driven by a sense of needing to provide security for himself, his family, and various groups—state, nation, political party, economic group, and so on. Simple self-preservation is apt to play a heavy role in the consideration of questions from traffic safety to safety from nuclear fallout. In general, we have learned (perhaps not always or even usually consciously) that the activities and institutions we have established provide safety or at least make us feel safe. Therefore, changes of any sort are apt to be threats.[13] The speaker should consider safety, especially as it is represented in established economic, social, political, religious, and educational institutions, when he chooses and states ideas for speeches.

The third rung is occupied by the need for love and belongingness. Belonging in and of itself is satisfying; therefore individuals will want to preserve those groups to which they belong and will want to establish, probably, groups in which they can satisfy their need for love and belongingness. Our increasingly complex, mobile society is making satisfaction of needs on this level more and more difficult. The family, for example, has been considerably weakened as a source of satisfaction for love and belongingness needs. One might speculate that the definite increase in church membership and attendance is due at least in part to an effort by great numbers to make identifications with groups that have traditionally helped satisfy belongingness needs.

The fourth rung on the ladder is the need for esteem. All men and women whom we call normal want a high evaluation of themselves—by themselves and by others. They are apt to undertake whatever modes of behavior they feel will help win this esteem and to avoid those which they feel will interfere with it. It is possible, of course, for demands for self-esteem to conflict with those for the esteem of others. But at the present moment, men and women in our society can be counted on to pursue external symbols to display as means of gaining esteem. The use of this tendency in advertising is too well known almost to bear mention. The alert reader will not be able to go through a day without finding a score of advertisements in newspapers and magazines or radio and television that offer some sort of promise of acquiring symbols the display of which will win the esteem of others.

[13] Eric Hoffer builds an entire book on this theme. His *The Ordeal of Change* (New York, Harper and Brothers, 1963) is instructive for the speaker.

Many of the words that indicate virtues we associate with our society have grown out of our particular sets towards the satisfaction of love and belongingness needs and esteem needs. We honor freedom, competition, curiosity, loyalty, and fair play. And these virtues are intimately associated with acceptable need satisfaction.

The highest rung on the ladder is occupied by the difficult concept of the need for self-actualization. It is a recognition of unique potentiality in every human. "What man *can* be, he *must* be."[14] Although the speaker will have more difficulty seeing the application of this level of needs, he ought recognize the inchoate yearning for "something higher" in most men, and the especially strong feelings of dissatisfaction in those who are observably well satisfied in all other needs. It is a uniquely human need that, in our society, has emerged with increasing strength.

A close study of the speeches of Martin Luther King, Jr. will reveal how much he depends on identifying his analysis of problems and his programs with the love and belongingness and the esteem needs of his audiences. In one speech, for example, he says typically: "But the Negro has a new sense of dignity, a new self respect, and new determination. He has re-evaluated his own intrinsic worth. Now this new sense of dignity on the part of the Negro grows out of the same longing for freedom and human dignity on the part of the oppressed people all over the world...."[15]

Almost any speech dealing with the current international tensions will illustrate how speakers build on safety needs. Regard for these needs are connected by speakers to wide varieties of proposed actions. This tendency is by no means a wholly recent phenomenon. In his famous "Quarantine" speech delivered in 1937, President Franklin D. Roosevelt, speaking to people who had been repeatedly exposed to the idea that the Atlantic was an effective barrier to involvement in European conflicts, laid the basis for a developing pre-World War II foreign policy on the need for security: "War is a contagion, whether it be declared or undeclared. It can engulf states and peoples remote from the original scene of hostilities. We are determined to keep out of war, yet we cannot insure ourselves against the disastrous effects of war and the dangers of involvement. We are adopting such measures as will minimize our risk of involvement, but we cannot have complete protection in a world of disorder in which confidence and security have broken down."[16]

Neither the beginning speaker nor anyone else should expect to be able to state immediately and precisely what needs are operating within his listeners. He should, however, begin to see potentialities in his own ideas

---

[14] Maslow, p. 91.
[15] "Love, Law, and Civil Disobedience," *Contemporary American Speeches*, p. 53.
[16] "The 'Quarantine' Speech," in Donald C. Bryant and Karl R. Wallace, *Fundamentals of Public Speaking*, New York, Appleton-Century-Crofts, 1960, p. 543.

for speeches that will be meaningful to particular audiences, and ways of selecting and handling his material.

The Commitments of the Audience

Just as the speaker will have his commitments to ideas, people, institutions, programs, and so on, so will his listeners. Sometimes looking for these commitments will give the speaker a clearer view of the nature of his audience than will anything else.

A person's commitments will tend to be shaped by his evaluation of their utility in satisfying his needs. Therefore, the lines of thought which we have suggested are scarcely independent. Whereas humans share the same basic needs, their commitments may differ widely and may be more immediately involved in responding to the ideas and materials of a speaker.

A speaker often makes the mistake of seeing an audience only in terms of the agreement or disagreement of its members with a basic commitment he holds dear. He ought to seek also other commitments which he might utilize in bringing about whatever changes in their alignments he would like

Adlai Stevenson worked adroitly to show a group of listeners that they were probably committed to two viewpoints that were less consistent with one another than one of their fundamental views would be with another that he recommended. The editors of an anthology, which includes the speech, "The City—A Cause for Statesmanship," write that "in his address he met with consummate skill the audience's desire that its own policies and objectives be rendered urgent and impressive through fresh, exhilarating restatement."[17] They are certainly correct. But Stevenson did more.

The group before which Stevenson spoke, ACTION (American Council to Improve Our Neighborhoods), was composed of eminent businessmen. These men were explicitly committed to programs of urban reconstruction, but on the other hand, they were probably also affiliated with political groups that mistrusted the participation of a strong, centralized, federal government in municipal affairs.

Throughout his speech, Stevenson identified himself with the goals of urban reconstruction to which the group was committed. Moreover, he warmly affirmed the proper role of profit-making private enterprise in such programs. But he pictured this role as interwoven with the participation of governmental agencies:

The problems of the American city will be met when, and not until, we recognize that they are already and inexorably committed to the *joint* [empha-

[17] *The Speaker's Resource Book,* p. 250.

sis Stevenson's] trusteeship of private enterprise and public responsibility; that they demand a shoulder-to-shoulder, two-fisted attack; that their solution depends entirely upon an alliance of private and public agencies—with each respecting its own limitations and the capacities of the other, and with each acting in support of the other.[18]

Later in the speech he was even more pointed, saying, "In the face of these great opportunities, I hope we are ready to stop the demagogic political debate which assumes that government and private enterprise are inherently antagonistic." This demand, politely put but a demand nonetheless, was well prepared for by a detailed consideration of the problem that identifies the speaker with goals and means to which the audience was probably strongly committed.

Summary

As we suggested at the outset, the basic concern of this chapter will scarcely be exhausted herein. We believe that the principles discussed will bear review as you prepare for your own speeches. Only as you try to state, support, and organize your own ideas will the problems of adjusting ideas to audiences and your ability to meet them become sharpened.

We believe that you will find the principles of this chapter reinforced and clarified as you study the second part of this textbook. The problem-centered system of analysis is one that constantly encourages speakers to become more deeply and intelligently committed to their own ideas and to see these ideas in relationship to patterns of thought that intelligent listeners are apt to manifest.

For Class Discussion

1. Prepare for a class discussion by collecting advertisements from popular magazines which you believe indicate clearly efforts to gain response based on some need discussed in this chapter. Probably several students will chose the same advertisement but will interpret it as involving different needs. What accounts for the difference in interpretation? What is the significance of the differences?

2. Prepare for a class discussion by collecting several letters to the editor of your local newspaper. What commitments to groups or programs are reflected by the letter writers? Do the writers simply stand for their commitments or against the commitments of others? Do the writers attempt to use some common commitment as the basis of gaining assent to an idea that may be fresh or unaccepted for potential readers?

[18] *Ibid.*, pp. 251–252.

3. In his book *Toward a Psychology of Being*,[19] Abraham H. Maslow argues that every person is torn between two sets of forces—those associated with security and those associated with growth. He presents this schema:

Enhance the dangers			*Enhance the attractions*
Safety	$\longrightarrow$	PERSON $\longleftarrow$	Growth
Minimize the attractions			*Minimize the dangers*

"Safety has both anxieties and delights; growth has both anxieties and delights. We grow forward when the delights of growth and anxieties of safety are greater than the anxieties of growth and the delights of safety." Do you agree with Maslow? Can you illustrate either your agreement or disagreement? What possible *anxieties* can be associated with safety? Will growth always be associated with danger? Are there any applications of Maslow's schema to the central concern of this chapter?

A Speaking Assignment

1. Choose a speech for analysis from *Vital Speeches* or from an anthology containing contemporary speeches.
2. Describe quickly the speaker's purpose and the audience from which he seeks response.
3. Using the principles discussed in this chapter as a guide, analyze the manner in which the speaker identifies his interests with those of the audience.
4. Try to discover opportunities for adjusting to the audience that the speaker did not choose. Would he have been wise or unwise to have chosen any of these?

[19] Princeton, New Jersey, D. Van Nostrand Company, 1962; see pp. 42–45.

6 ᶑ Developing
Confidence[1]

Hypnotized persons, when told that they are very strong, are able to perform feats that require nearly twice their ordinary strength. "You can, because you *think* you can," runs the adage. We have all experienced evidence for it: Your best theme may have been the one you dashed off quickly when you knew you could; your best game was the one you played when you were confident. Confidence is often a partial cause of success; it heightens and increases natural ability; it is a necessary ingredient of the champion.

The speaker, likewise, needs confidence if his skills are to have their maximum effect. The speaker needs confidence when he delivers his speech —or, at least, he must not be paralyzed by the audience. But the speaker also needs confidence while he *prepares* his speech. He needs to feel confident that he can find good supporting material, that he can discover the most significant ideas to develop, and that by somewhat systematic work, he can eventually evolve a speech that is worth hearing. The speaker

[1] This chapter originated with an article of the same title by Otis M. Walter, published in *Today's Speech*, II (September, 1954), pp. 2–7, and is here substantially revised.

needs the advantage that confidence gives at every point of the process of preparing a speech.

But the speaker must not be overconfident. Nor is confidence a substitute for skill. However confident the novice may be as he buys stock just before the market crashes, his confidence does not prevent the loss of his money. No amount of confidence can substitute for ability or for knowledge. Overconfidence can make the speaker look ridiculous, and can earn him the dislike of the audience. Yet, without developing a cheap overconfidence, the speaker must be free from unwarranted, neurotic, or depressive feelings that reduce his effectiveness.

The development of the kind of confidence that enables one to use his skills best does not come from easily stated nostrums; there are no cheap recipes for confidence. We can, however, achieve some understanding of confidence and, thereby gain some knowledge of how to develop it. Let us begin by trying to understand the opposite of confidence: stage fright.

Stage Fright

The ancients knew the discomforts of stage fright; even Cicero's contemporaries reported that he shook visibly before an audience. Although the ancients recognized the existence of stage fright, they knew little about reducing it. Even by the beginning of the twentieth century, students of the subject could do little more than produce a long list of the symptoms of stage fright. Although such a list was accurate, it was worse than useless, so far from suggesting treatments, the formidable list could induce additional symptoms in those already alarmed. Recommended treatments such as "Relax," "Breathe deeply," and "Think positively," were superficial and dubious at best, and at worst, harmful. Before the 1930's, few speech books discussed stage fright; because of our superficial knowledge of it, the best books on public speaking avoided the subject.

Today our knowledge of stage fright is still incomplete; by no means do we know enough to offer a guaranteed cure. Nevertheless, we understand much about the physiology and psychology, about the causes and treatment of stage fright, and today can help those for whom stage fright is a serious problem. The subject is especially interesting, moreover, because the causes of stage fright and its treatment are remarkably like the causes of maladjustment and its treatment. Inasmuch as the nature and treatment of stage fright are much like the nature and treatment of human maladjustment, insights into one may lead to insights into the other. The treatment of either may lead to the kind of confidence that enables a man to do his best. To begin, we must first have a brief understanding of the physiology of stage fright.

The Physiology of Stage Fright

The unfortunate speaker who is terrified by an audience, and the lucky speaker who is stimulated by one, undergo indistinguishably similar physiological responses. As far as we can determine today, the physiology of excitement and that of fear are the same. Nothing about this physiological response leads to discomfort; the discomfort is a psychological matter. The physiological response itself only readies one for action, for it performs the following function:

1. More blood sugar, which furnishes energy, is available.
2. Insulin, which increases the permeability of the membrane surrounding the cells to the blood sugar, is secreted, with the result that more food can get inside the cells.
3. Thyroxin, a catalyst that speeds the burning of sugar inside the cells, is added to the blood stream.
4. Blood pressure increases.
5. Respiration increases.
6. The conductivity of nerves increases slightly.
7. More oxygen is available so that more fuel is burned.
8. The poisons from metabolism are removed more speedily so that toxicity and fatigue are reduced.

Metaphorically, these changes simply add fuel to the furnace, increase the draft so that the fires can burn faster, and carry away the smoke from combustion at a more rapid rate. The energy from the reaction may be misdirected and may end in tensions and shaking, but the physiological reaction itself is not debilitating.

Experienced speakers, while undergoing this reaction, report that they think more rapidly in front of an audience than in the less stimulating comfort of their armchair. One study of stage fright among experienced speakers reports that 77 per cent of them had some stage fright before they began each speech; most of these speakers believed that a little stage fright helped one make a better speech.[2] The explanation may be that the stage fright of the experienced speaker is generally limited to *initial* fears that diminish as soon as the speaker begins talking; when speakers do not have this initial reaction, they lack the energy furnished by the reaction, and, consequently, they give a less effective speech. Not surprisingly, therefore, the presence of an audience may stimulate memory.[3] Although we

[2] Elma Dean Orr Wrenchey, *A Study of Stage Fright in a Selected Group of Experienced Speakers,* Unpublished M.A. Thesis, University of Denver, 1948, p. 37.

[3] N. G. Hanawalt and K. F. Butler, "The Effects of an Audience on Remembering," *Journal of Social Psychology,* XXIX (May 1944), pp. 359–272.

do not recommend it as a universal practice, especially to beginners, some experienced speakers report that they barely outline those parts of their speeches which they wish to be the most powerful, preferring to restrain their impulses toward final composition until they are standing before the audience where the physiological reaction will energize their thoughts and stimulate their imagination; in front of the audience, confident persons may be so energized that they will produce a better speech than they could without the presence of the audience. The physiological aspects of stage fright, therefore, do not commit one to discomfort, but they do ensure abundant energy, and reserve power. Insofar as we can tell, the physiological changes in stage fright are beneficial. Nevertheless, the speaker must prevent the conditions, often associated with these physiological changes, that produce anxiety, nervousness, and the resulting incapacity to think well. To understand how one may keep the effects of the physiological reaction and yet avoid anxiety, we must examine the psychology of stage fright.

The Psychology of Stage Fright: Stage Fright as Anxiety

Despite its name, stage fright is not limited to the stage, but is a rather common response experienced in a variety of "threatening" situations; this response goes under the name of *anxiety reaction*. We can see that stage fright and anxiety are the same, because the physiological reaction in each appears to be the same: each is characterized by increased heartbeat, increased tension, and increased metabolism. Moreover, the psychological reactions in stage fright and anxiety seem similar: both are characterized by dread and in both, the dread is not justified by the situation that produced it. The beginning speaker, for example, faces a classroom of students who are also beginners, who are friendly, who are pulling for him, and who may suffer with him. But the beginning speaker with stage fright often fails to perceive the situation for what it is, namely: a friendly situation in which mistakes are not only tolerated but expected. Rather than so perceiving the situation, he sees it as does the anxious person: as a fearful situation, full of threats and dangers.

Because stage fright is anxiety, if we can determine how to reduce anxiety, we can likewise know how to reduce stage fright. Let us examine the psychological causes of anxiety. *Anxiety occurs in people—and even, experimentally, in animals—whenever they are placed in an unresolved conflict situation.* The medieval donkey who starved to death between two stacks of hay because each stack was equally attractive, equally succulent, equally large and equally distant may serve as a paradigm of the unresolved conflict situation. Such conflict situations are the key to emotional responses that are disorganizing and tortuous; when one is in constant conflict, he is likely in a constant state of discomfort and disorganization.

A few examples will help us understand the nature of conflict. The mother who tells her child to go out and play, but not to get dirty, may place the child in a minor conflict situation: If the child plays with the roughness required to gain and keep the respect of his peers, he will get dirty; if he gets dirty, he will be punished. The normal child will resolve the conflict in some way, such as by playing just hard enough so that he isn't quite dirty enough to be punished. The less normal child may alternate between, at one moment, staying clean, and at the next moment playing hard. His energies will be divided, and he likely will meet neither the requirements of his peers nor of his mother. A young man who wishes to get married but who does not make enough money to support a wife may be in a perpetual conflict situation. If he does not marry the girl he loves, he risks losing her; if he does marry her, he cannot support her. This perpetually unresolved conflict situation batters his nervous system, and he may begin to respond in an undesirable way to situations not even remotely related to his conflicts: his employer may notice that he is less efficient at his job, and his girl friend may notice both a decrease in his capacity for warmth and an increase in his irritability. He is undergoing a reaction like that in stage fright, and exhibits tension, unhappiness, dread, and fear.

The speech situation is of the same sort; it is often a conflict situation: the speaker with stage fright is trying to speak well; yet he wishes he were not on the platform. He must continue the speech; yet he would like to run away or disappear. He is trying to earn a good grade; yet he is fearful that he will make a spectacle of himself. He must speak; but he doesn't want to. He is in conflict, and responds with the temporary anxiety that we call stage fright.

The Significance of Conflict

The intelligent resolution of conflict seems to be a key to a productive existence. Over twenty years ago, Symonds recognized that the resolution of conflict was necessary:

The happy man is one in whom conflicts are at a minimum of depth, frequency and intensity. His life is one that has a straightforward pattern. He can face outward, and meet with zeal and adequacy the situations that each day presents. The successful resolution of the conflicts, both major and minor, which beset one in daily living is the road to maturity. Integration depends upon the successful resolution of the conflicts inevitably met at all stages of development. A person's emotional stability is closely related to his conflicts. The stable person . . . is the person who has found a way through his conflicts. On the other hand, the person whose conflicts are intense gives way earlier to emotion and we recognize him as an emotionally unstable individual. . . .[4]

Gardner Murphy believes that most human unhappiness stems from conflicts that are not reconciled or that cannot be.

Tragedy falls upon King Lear because he is an old man who cannot discern truth from flattery, and upon Othello because he loves not wisely but too well, and upon Hamlet because he is divided himself. He will have his revenge, but he wants to delay; when the thought of suicide comes to him as a way out, he craves it and at the same time, fears it. Most tragedy, whether in the grand style or in the petty style . . . is a matter of a personality divided against itself. . . .[5]

To hide from one's conflicts, some people develop excessive shyness; others may turn to alcohol or narcotics to anesthetize themselves to an unresolved conflict; still others may blot out awareness of the world about them, as does the catatonic patient, who dares not respond to the world, and who sits motionless wherever he is placed, oblivious to the world and unmoved by it. When conflicts remain unresolved, they may tear powerfully and cause damage.

Maslow insists that the integration of conflicts may be a key to the superior adjustment of some exceptionally healthy people.

. . . What has been considered . . . to be polarities of opposites or dichotomies were so *only in unhealthy people*. In healthy people these dichotomies were resolved, the polarities disappeared, and many oppositions . . . coalesced with each other to form unities.

For example, the age-old opposition between heart and head, reason and instinct, or cognition and conation was seen to disappear in healthy people. . . . In these people, desires are in excellent accord with reason. St. Augustine's "Love God and do as you will" can easily be translated "Be healthy and then you may trust your impulses."

The dichotomy between selfishness and unselfishness disappears altogether in healthy people because in principle every act is *both* selfish and unselfish. Our subjects are simultaneously very spiritual and very pagan and sensual. Duty cannot be contrasted with pleasure nor work with play when duty *is* pleasure, when work *is* play, and the person doing his duty and being virtuous is simultaneously seeking his pleasure and being happy. If the most socially identified people are themselves also the most individualistic people, of what use is it to retain the polarity? If the most mature is the most childlike? If the most ethical and moral people are also the lustiest and most animal?[6]

Thus, the healthy person is not divided: what he wants to do, what he is doing and what he thinks he should do are the same. Because he is a

[4] Percival Symonds, *The Dynamics of Human Adjustment*, New York, Appleton-Century-Crofts, 1946, p. 360.

[5] Gardner Murphy, *Personality*, New York, Harper and Brothers, 1947, p. 296.

[6] A. H. Maslow, *Motivation and Personality*, New York, Harper and Brothers, 1954, p. 233.

"united" person, he plunges wholeheartedly into his activities, enjoys them more, and produces more than a person who is at war with himself.

Limitations of Integration

But is there not danger—to one's self, and to others—in being "too well" integrated? May not total integration produce a monomaniac—a man undivided, following a single unhealthy drive? The Hitlers, the Napoleons, the Joseph Stalins of the world seem at least on superficial evidence, to be "integrated." Yet these men probably were not: Each of them was known to have deep depressions that halted their activities; each made crucial and seriously mistaken judgments, trusting men who were untrustworthy, and supecting those who were trustworthy; each displayed symptoms of serious maladjustment, and at least one died insane. Their integration was not a general pattern of their existence, but a temporary state that permitted activity of such unusual and vigorous nature that it functioned to conceal their depressions and anxieties both from themselves and from others. The monomaniac does not display the kind of integration Maslow describes, in which the selfish and the altruistic blend together, in which the reasonable and emotional are one. We need not fear this latter sort of integration, for far from producing a monomaniac, such integration seems to produce people who have a great diversity of interests, and who, unlike the monomaniac, are closely in touch with reality.

In some ways, however, a civilized man is one who *will* experience conflict—the soldier who must kill when killing may be required, the judge whom the law requires to sentence the hapless product of a bad environment, the teacher who must fail the student, all probably should experience conflict and sense the tragedy of what they do. But their conflict, unlike that of the neurotic, remains tied *only* to the situation that warrants conflict, and does not permeate their life apart from that situation. Of course the well-integrated man has doubts, where doubts are warranted; he knows it is a mark of maturity to be unsure where no man can be sure. Probably some psychologists have overdone the idea that one must live a life without doubts and without uncertainty. After all, the hero in *Hamlet*, for all his uncertainty, is still the play's most civilized character, and among the most civilized in all dramatic literature.

The intelligent speaker, therefore, will have doubts. But he will have most of his doubts about whether or not he is giving the audience the right answer or for that matter whether or not he is asking the right question. His doubts are *subject-matter* centered, rather than *self-centered*. Has he read the best sources on the subject? Has he located the strongest supporting material? Is the theme of his speech important enough? Is his information accurate? Is his speech as clear as possible? These doubts an intelligent speaker will have over and over again.

But the healthy speaker will not have doubts when he delivers his speech—at least not doubts that are *ego-centered*. His energy, at the time of speaking, will be unified to communicate with as much vigor and power as wisdom allows—and he will not be divided because of unwarranted timidity or fear. His energy is expended in communicating, and not in restraining himself or in developing nervous tension. His doubts in preparation, moreover, are reconciled as time goes on, and drive him to prepare the speech so thoroughly that self-centered doubts will not arise during the delivery of the speech. Let us see some of the ways unjustified conflict may be treated to permit this kind of confidence.

The Influence of Personality on Stage Fright

Some types of personality can reduce conflict and, hence, overcome stage fright more easily than others. The development of confidence is easiest for those who lack shyness, who feel self-sufficient, who are somewhat uninhibited, who have relatively weak feelings of guilt, who have a sense of their own worth and who are socially active; stage fright is strongest in those who lack these qualities and who have a generalized sense of maladjustment.[7] So far as we know, however, even severe stage fright can be reduced, so that if you are among those who experience it, take heart. More than one superior speaker began his career terrified by audiences.

Those who have a sense of severe maladjustment and who have strong stage fright, however, should give their maladjustment serious attention and, perhaps, seek expert guidance. Severe conflict can reduce one's ability in solving problems and, as the conflict grows, one's ability to deal with it intelligently may decline. Some of Pavlov's famous dogs illustrate the debilitating effect of intense conflict: A dog can be taught to discriminate between a circle and an ellipse; the conditioned discrimination occurs if the dog is given food when the circle is flashed on a screen in front of the dog, but not given food when an ellipse is flashed on. After the dog had been conditioned so that he salivated whenever the circle was present, but not when the ellipse was present, the experimenter tested the dog's ability to discriminate between the circle and ellipse by making the ellipse more and more like a circle. When the axes of the ellipse were seven to eight, the dog could make the discrimination, but when they became eight to nine, which is quite close to the axes of a circle, the dog lost the ability to discriminate. Moreover, the dog *broke down:* he could no longer discriminate between the circle and the ellipse even when the axes of the ellipse

[7] See Stanley Ainsworth, *A Study of Fear, Nervousness and Anxiety in the Public Speaking Situation*, unpublished Ph.D. dissertation, Northwestern University, 1949, abstracted in *Speech Monographs*, XVI (August, 1950), p. 323. See also, William Hamilton, "A Review of Experimental Studies of Stage Fright," *Pennsylvania Speech Annual*, XVII (September, 1960), pp. 44–45.

were seven to eight. He had *lost* ability, and salivated indiscriminately for circles, ellipses, and even for the experimenter. He whined, barked, and tore at the harness, and henceforth was useless as an experimental animal. Serious maladjustments should not be ignored, for they may cause a reduction in the person's ability to tolerate conflict. The maladjusted person may be plagued by stage fright because he, too, has momentarily lost the ability to resolve conflict in other situations. With an increase in his ability to handle conflict in life, his ability to reduce stage fright will also increase. Therefore, those who are seriously upset by stage fright should consider seeking expert guidance to help them reconstruct their general state of adjustment; as this reconstruction is achieved, their stage fright will probably decrease readily.

The Treatment of Stage Fright

Because stage fright is caused by conflict, its solution lies in the reduction of conflict. *Conflicts are reduced by increasing some desires and by nullifying, preventing, or weakening desires that pull in other directions.* The medieval donkey need not have starved to death between the two stacks of hay had he reduced the desire for one of the stacks and increased the desire for the other. He might have remembered that he was a "left-footed" donkey and taken the stack of hay to the left, and thereby reduced the conflict sufficiently to permit his survival. The speaker is not given so simple a choice; on the other hand, so many possibilities for reinforcing the desire to speak and reducing the fear of speaking exist that he has a strong chance of reducing conflict in the speech situation. Look next at the ways in which he can unify himself so that when he *must* speak, he will *want* to.

Resolving Conflict: Some Automatic Treatments

There are some "instant" ways of reducing stage fright that can help a speaker once he knows of them. A speaker can take heart from the knowledge that if he has stage fright, the audience will not realize that fact. Experiments demonstrate that audiences—including even experienced speech instructors—are notoriously poor judges of the degree of stage fright experienced by a speaker. These observers, whether experts in speech or otherwise, *greatly* underrate the amount of stage fright they believe the speaker has.[8] When a speaker realizes that his stage fright will not be noticed, some of his apprehension may vanish.

A second bit of reassurance may come from the realization that stage

---

[8] See Theodore Clevenger, Jr., "A Synthesis of Experimental Research in Stage Fright," *Quarterly Journal of Speech*, XLV (April, 1959), p. 137.

fright decreases with age. Adolescents in the tenth grade experience less stage fright than those in grades below them, and by the time one reaches twenty, stage fright will have dropped even more. Inasmuch as time seems to decrease stage fright, you may trust that time will also help you to feel more confident.[9]

Thirdly, and far more importantly, experience in speaking reduces stage fright enormously. "All the investigations . . . showed that on the high school as well as on the college and adult level, practice was a significant factor in influencing gains in confidence."[10] Most students gain confidence as they proceed through a course in public speaking. Practice is so certain to reduce stage fright that it is the most frequently recommended treatment in textbooks,[11] and is recommended as a treatment by instructors more than any other single remedy.[12] The more frequently one speaks, the less will his stage fright be a problem. Especially does stage fright lessen in a classroom where the attitudes of the instructor and of the classmates are unthreatening, and when the student is taught so well that he receives genuine insight into the means of preparing and delivering fine speeches. In any event, students can expect a reduction in stage fright as a result of speaking frequently.

Finally, the student may take heart from realizing that nearly all beginners feel stage fright.[13] Inasmuch as his classmates have the same disadvantage, he need not feel upset.

These four automatic helps are at least reassuring: The speaker knows in advance that the audience can't recognize how much stage fright he has; as he grows older, his stage fright will lessen; experience in speaking will greatly reduce his fears; his classmates have the same difficulty that he does. These automatic helps will reduce the fear of speaking, but there is much more that the speaker can do to increase his desire to speak. Here are some further sources of reassurance.

Combating Unfortunate Previous Experiences Resolving Conflict

Some students may have had an alarming experience with speaking in which they may have felt publicly embarrassed. The fifth grader, who, on Parents' Night, was asked to recite a poem, but who, when he stood in front of his classmates, parents and teacher, couldn't remember the first line, may have become so frightened that he is afraid to get up in front of

[9] Clevenger, pp. 141–142.
[10] Hamilton, pp. 46–47.
[11] Edward R. Robinson, "What Can the Speech Teacher Do About Students' Stagefright?" *The Speech Teacher* VIII (January 1959) pp. 10–11.
[12] Lawrence Edward Cole, Jr., *A Critical Evaluation of Methods of Controlling Stage Fright*, Unpublished M.A. Thesis, Emerson College, 1964.
[13] Wrenchey, p. 37.

another audience. The young actor who accidentally stumbled against the canvas scenery during the class play and pushed his arm through the canvas "wall" may feel alarmed at the thought of being before people again. Usually such experiences are passed off lightly, but once in a while, the experience may cause undue stage fright. The student who has had such an experience should take the following steps to reduce or nullify the effect of it:

1. Recall the experience fully. The process of recalling may be temporarily painful, but to "forget" the experience may cause harm. Such "forgetting," which psychologists call *repression*, may be harmful and may continue to cause trouble. A standard treatment for phobias—unjustified fears—is to trace the origin of the phobia to the incident that caused it. This incident usually is painful to the person, and difficult to recall, because the experience makes him feel guilty. The guilty feelings, however, are unjustified, and as soon as the incident is fully recalled, the unjustified guilt feelings disappear, *as does the fear itself*. The best way, therefore, to reduce any feelings of anxiety caused by such an incident, is to recall the incident completely.

2. Discuss the experience with the instructor. The instructor will probably want to know if there are students who have been "traumatized" in front of an audience. Moreover, the act of talking over the experience with a sympathetic listener is, itself, therapeutic. Discussion of the episode with others not only reduces the repression further, but often helps one gain perspective about the situation so that one can realize its unimportance.

3. Above all, work as hard as possible to prepare fine speeches. One good speech given by a traumatized student may reassure him more than kind words from the class or from the instructor. As the student continues to give good speeches, his successes will nullify the old experience and begin to build strong feelings of confidence that will do more than merely heal the old scar.

The methods of reducing conflict suggested so far have been limited to a discussion of ways to *reduce the fear of speaking*. There are, however, ways to *increase the desire to speak*. These ways may be more important, for they tend to develop that kind of confidence that contributes to success, and that make the speaker, when he *should* speak, *want* to speak.

Resolving Conflict: Choice of Subject

A speaker can reinforce his desire to speak by choosing a subject that makes him want to speak. If he has a subject that he knows is interesting, important, or unusual, that subject will reinforce his desire to speak. However, if the speaker has chosen a banal, trite, superficial, or otherwise insignificant, subject, he will feel less impelled to speak; instead, he may be reluctant, fearing that the audience will recognize the shallowness of his ideas. Having reinforced his desire not to speak by choosing a poor subject, he will be more prone to suffer conflict.

Resolving Conflict: Preparation of the Materials of the Speech

Careful preparation can powerfully reinforce the desire to speak; lack of preparation will increase the fear of speaking. A speaker who has prepared his speech materials carefully, that is, who knows his subject well, who has vivid and valid supporting material which he knows will intrigue the audience, who knows that his speech is clear, and who has an introduction that is "sure fire" and a good conclusion, knows that he has little to fear. He will want to speak and can plunge into his speech wholeheartedly, with a minimum of conflict to disrupt him. But the speaker who suspects that his materials are dull, unclear, and who fears he knows less about the subject than he should, cannot help but be worried, and perhaps he should be. Unlike the speaker who is prepared, he cannot anticipate success; the unprepared speaker anticipates failure, and because he *must* speak, he will experience conflict and accompanying stage fright.

Confidence comes from competence. The well-prepared surgeon does not disintegrate at the sight of the operating table, nor does the competent boxer at the sight of his opponent. Nor does the speaker who has prepared his speech carefully disintegrate at the sight of his audience. None of these men need tricks of auto-suggestion or the other somewhat fraudulent devices sometimes advocated as "cures" for stage fright. Nor will these "cures" help those whose preparation is so poor that they are incompetent. If one thinks the speech is not worth listening to, reassurance will be hard to find. Even the beginning speaker, if he prepares his speech materials carefully, can feel competent when he gives the speech; more likely, his speech will be successful and his success will breed further confidence. Careful preparation will increase the comfort of the beginning—or advanced—speaker so that he will perceive the audience situation less fearfully and will be more comfortable than the unprepared speaker. Eventually, the speaker who prepares each speech thoroughly will begin to find an audience stimulating rather than frightening.

Reducing Conflict in the Moments Before Speaking

An inexperienced speaker may "work up" an unnecessarily strong case of stage fright by contemplating the blithering idiot that he thinks he is and by imagining the spectacle that he might make when he arrives at the platform. The student must avoid these thoughts. The moments just before the speech are not the moments to rehash the ideas of the speech nor to dwell upon one's ineptness. Rather, think about something else.

But it is not easy to "think about something else." One suggestion, however, may help. If you force yourself to concentrate intensely on whatever is being said just before you speak, you will probably be able to keep your mind off thoughts that are alarming. The more intensely you concentrate on the speeches that precede yours the less you can think about your plight. Moreover, you may find, in one or more of these speeches, some idea or fact to which you can refer in your own speech. (Classroom audiences listen closely when a student speaker refers to another student's speech.) Before you speak avoid thoughts about yourself and about your speech by listening carefully to whoever is speaking; try to find a way of referring to this speech when you give yours, and you will not only be more calm for having avoided unnecessary fears but will probably increase the attention the audience pays to your speech.

Resolving Conflict by Commitment to the Significance of One's Ideas

A beginning speaker may reduce the fear of speaking and reinforce the desire to speak by contemplating matters that are extrinsic to what he says: He may, for example, wish to give the speech "to get it over with." Or he may reinforce the desire to speak by remembering that by speaking he will have completed another requirement of the course, or by recognizing that he will gain more experience and expertise, or by contemplating that not to speak would be embarrassing. Although such reasons are extrinsic to the ideas and materials of the speech, they make a contribution to the wholeheartedness of the speaker. One should use these extrinsic reasons if they help.

One can better develop confidence, however, by reinforcing the desire to speak for reasons that are *intrinsic*, rather than extrinsic, to one's ideas. One should speak because one is committed to one's ideas, because one is alive with a crucial idea, because one feels he knows something that is important to the audience, because he understands or has clarified a significant problem, because he has found the right answers, or even the right questions.

To be driven to speak because of the importance of one's ideas is probably the best way to develop confidence. One who suffers stage fright is, literally, self-conscious, self-aware. "True neuroses are best defined," Gordon Allport says, "as stubborn self-centeredness."[14] The speaker, on the other hand, who speaks because he is committed to an idea, is not *self*-centered, but *idea*-centered. When a man is so committed to an idea

---

[14] *Personality and Social Encounter*, Boston, Beacon Press, 1960, p. 173.

that he has caught its fire, he will want to speak, and can do so whole-heartedly.

Most beginning speakers do not grasp the significance of their ideas, and their delivery reflects this lack by its timorousness, its lifelessness, and its ineffectiveness. The best reason to speak is for the intrinsic reason that one has found something worthwhile to say. Unless one's delivery reflects this perception of worth, it will be poor delivery. Good delivery has a lively reflection of the significance of one's ideas, and this reflection is the starting point of all good delivery. Without this reflection, instruction in delivery is of little avail, and with it most speakers have little need for further instruction. Moreover, the intensity that springs from speaking because one has a sense of the value of one's ideas is one of the roads to individuality in speaking. The speaker who reflects the spirit of his ideas will not be an imitation of his instructor or of any other speaker. He is more apt to be so immersed in his ideas that he is uniquely and fully himself. Therefore, one must work to grasp and reflect the significance of his ideas not only because such a grasp will help develop confidence, but because it will develop effective, individual delivery.

But how does one grasp the intrinsic significance of one's ideas? This grasp stems from depth of knowledge about one's ideas. In particular, the person who in a mature way recognizes this significance is one who has certain kinds of knowledge about his idea, suggested by answers to the following kinds of questions:

1. In what way are these ideas important today?
2. How do these ideas relate to the material needs of my audience? To their psychological needs? To their philosophic or spiritual needs?
3. In what ways might my ideas influence the attitudes and behavior of the audience?
4. Are there times in the past when these ideas have performed an especially useful service?
5. If these ideas are accepted, how might they change the course of events?

When one is vividly aware of answers to these questions about his subject, one will *want* to speak; moreover, he will have a deeper understanding of his subject, as well as of its importance, and will begin to develop the kind of attitude toward his ideas, toward himself and toward his audience that is in itself persuasive. The reflection of these ideas in his delivery will encourage the natural development of directness, variety, vitality, intensity, and poise that dedication to ideas brings. Thus, one will, through developing a deeper understanding of the significance of one's ideas, have also developed many of the skills of delivery.

The speaker who cannot answer at least some of these questions in such a way as to provide ideas that increase his desire to speak may have either a superficial understanding of his subject or may have chosen a poor subject. But if he has chosen a worthy subject, he must not fail to grasp its importance. To miss the power that can be derived from a significant idea is to miss one of the speaker's sources of strength. The power of a great idea is the source of strength that gave confidence—and much more—to men such as Socrates, Lincoln, Churchill, and others. Great ideas have inspired people and nations to wholehearted effort during times of danger. Men possessed by a great ideal seldom fear. Many such men have endured hunger, pain, persecution, and even torture or the threat of death with less terror than the neophyte giving his first speech. If the perception of a great truth can do so much to alleviate real tortures, it is not too much to expect that when a speaker begins to grasp the significance of an idea, he will reduce his weak-in-the-knees feeling on the occasion of a short speech in a beginning class.

There are some limits, however, that one should place upon commitment, inspiration, and the drive to accomplish. The person who seems to raise his aspirations too high may fall victim, by the very strength of his desire, to stage fright. The neurotic is often one whose aspirations are too great for his capacities. The student who expects to save the world by one speech is out of touch with both his own limitations and those of the classroom situation. But what constitutes too much commitment and what is too little is never easy to determine. The student himself is probably the best judge. Nevertheless, he should keep in mind that most students reflect the kind of delivery that is characterized too little by the life and fire of commitment, and that the student's spark would be increased by a deeper understanding of the significance of his ideas.

Because overcoming stage fright requires one to be idea-centered instead of self-centered, the real challenge to the student is one that calls him to stretch his mind. It is a challenge to recognize, appreciate, understand, and commit himself to ideas. The challenge calls one to discover ideas of worth and to turn his mind toward the significant. It calls one to bury self-centered ideas and to fix attention outside one's self. When one answers the challenge to stretch his mind around a great idea, he not only gains confidence, lays the foundation for good delivery, and begins to develop his own individuality, but he becomes a speaker deserving of the attention of the audience. Such a man is not only a more effective human being; he is likewise a more worthwhile one.

Resolving Conflict: Habit Formation[15]

Emotionally charged situations—those in which the rewards for success or the penalties for failure are great—do not always produce anxiety or breakdown *unless the situations are too complicated to be met skillfully.* Remember, for example, the first time you drove an automobile. Because you could have had an accident, the event was not only emotionally charged, but it was also too complicated for you: you had to manipulate the steering wheel, push down or let up on the accelerator and brake (and perhaps operate the gear shift and clutch pedal), and do these things not only in coordination with each other, but also in correspondence with what you saw through the windshield. You probably had anxiety—stage fright—and if a real emergency had occurred, you might have experienced breakdown, *e.g.,* stepped on the accelerator when you intended to stop the car, or thrown up your hands in horror. One experiences anxiety and breakdown in an emotionally charged situation that is too complicated for one to respond to ably.

Complexity produces a special form of conflict situation. The responses a beginning driver can make are, perhaps, infinite, and he doesn't quite know which response to make at a given time. He can speed up, remain at constant speed, lift his foot from the accelerator and slow down, touch the brake lightly or firmly, and make innumerable adjustments with the steering wheel (and perhaps add the clutch and gear shift or gear selector). These possibilities provide him with a multi-conflict situation; at the right time, each of these things must be done. The poor novice lacks the skill either to do these things well or to recognize when the right time is. He is, therefore, in a multi-conflict situation, and is apt to behave as many do in conflict: sometimes he will over-respond, sometimes under-respond, sometimes not respond at all and often respond the wrong way—and he is anxious most of the time.

But notice what happens to him: At first, these complexities required all of his attention, but he soon learned to make appropriate responses so that he could speed up or slow down with ease, turn corners without even slight difficulty, back up, park the car, and at the same time listen to the radio or carry on a conversation. He made *habits* of the skills of driving and therefore could respond easily and appropriately in a variety of situations. *Habits converted the previously complex situation into a simple one.*

Habits convert complex situations into simple ones because *habits are relatively independent of one's attention.* Note how habits are performed without much awareness: Putting on shoes is habitual; can you remember which shoe you put on first this morning? Or remember tying the shoes? Unless something unusual happened, unless one shoe was missing or you

[15] The writer is indebted to Professor Clarence T. Simon for his article, "Complexity and Breakdown in Speech Situations," *Journal of Speech Disorders,* X (September, 1941), pp. 199–203, and especially for the writer's interest in the psychological means of preventing stage fright, which received its first and greatest stimulus in Professor Simon's classes over a quarter of a century ago.

found a knotted shoe lace, the act was independent enough of your attention so that memory of it will be dim or, perhaps, nonexistent. Because habits do not require your full attention, they simplify complex situations for you. *The development of skills that are habitual may reduce the discomfort of anxiety-producing situations.*

Here are some examples of how habits may reduce anxiety. The good football player responds on the field (in front of perhaps a hundred thousand spectators) without disintegration because he has habituated techniques of passing, dodging, and running; because these techniques are habits, he is free to expend his attention and his energy searching for the pass-receiver or finding the hole through which he can plunge with all his strength. The complicated techniques of playing are made simple because they are independent of his attention, permitting him to play with courage and to put his full strength behind his skills. In the same way, the surgeon remains calm and in possession of his skills because he knows what to expect, and through practice knows what to do as he makes an incision. But place the surgeon, for a moment, in the huddle, or give the football star a scalpel, at the side of a patient, and neither star nor surgeon would display coolness or deftness. Confidence is born of competence. When one faces an emotionally charged situation for which he does *not* have habituated skills, he will lack the calm assurance of the star or the swift and quiet skill of the expert. To take another example, basic training in the armed forces, in some of its more worthwhile aspects, is an attempt to habituate certain skills of fighting. The soldier, properly trained, will know how to react when he faces the enemy, and instead of disintegrating, he will use his habitual fighting know-how. Because his habits of fighting will be semiautomatic, the soldier, instead of breaking down, fights. The seasoned Marine probably has an abundance of raw courage, but he *also* has habituated, through training, superior skills of combat; what would disintegrate other strong men will not do so to him. When the good airplane pilot is faced with an emergency he has a repertory of skills which he uses semiautomatically, and remains effective in a situation that would terrorize us. Teach us the same skills, and we might behave as well as he. Because habits can simplify a complex situation, they can help reduce anxiety and prevent breakdown. Confidence and courage are compounded, in part, out of knowing what to do.

The same principles apply to the speech situation. It, too, is a complicated situation: The beginning speaker must walk to the platform with ease and dignity, wonders how to stand when he gets there, worries about what to do with his hands, would like to loosen his collar, can't seem to use his voice normally, occasionally forgets items he intended to include, and cannot think well, or respond fully to communicating his thoughts. He has not yet formed habits that will free his attention from the more petty skills of delivery.

One reduces complexity in an audience situation in the same way that one does in driving, surgery, or fighting, for wherever complexity causes anxiety, habituating the required skills reduces that complexity. We can now see one reason that students who take a speech course experience a reduction in stage fright: In the process of giving several speeches they form habit patterns of the skills of delivery. (Some reductions in stage fright come from a different source: the student who speaks frequently before an audience not only forms habit patterns that reduce the complexity of speaking, but he also learns *what to expect* from an audience. Knowing what to expect often can help reduce anxiety; when the student finds the audience does not respond with catcalls or rotten eggs, but is mildly sympathetic, his anxiety lessens.) Experience not only builds habits that simplify the speech situation, but also gives one a healthy set of expectations that also help reduce anxiety.

The student should not rely only on the slow progress of the term to form habits that will build his confidence. He can speed the process of forming habits by practicing his speeches. Practice, however, does not make perfect; practice only makes more permanent. The wrong kind of practice may intensify the complexity. Therefore, the student should practice so as to incorporate the best skills of speaking in the easiest way. The following suggestions will help form habits of good speaking:

1. After the speech has been carefully outlined to include the best main points, subheads, supporting material and the like, memorize the outline. Memorize the outline so well that you *overlearn* it, for things that we overlearn are not forgotten, even under stress. (You have overlearned your name and address, and are not likely to forget them even before an audience.) A good test of a sufficient degree of overlearning is to see if, without reference to your outline, you can repeat it from the last line to the first. When you can recall it line by line from the bottom to the top, you know it so well that no audience will cause you to forget. Moreover, because your outline is well stamped in, you will feel more confident.

2. Practice the speech from this memorized image of the outline, until you can give the speech reasonably well. When a speech is delivered from the memorized image of an outline—without notes or a manuscript—it is called *extemporaneous* delivery. (See Chapter 7.) This sort of delivery is best for the beginner because it will help him learn to think before an audience. The speaker must think to recall his outline, and then must think to put it into words so that the thoughts are fuller than his sketchy outline. If, instead of delivering the speech extemporaneously, one memorizes the speech, he is not forced to think. Nor is he if he practices reading from a manuscript. Extemporaneous speaking, therefore, is preferable because it helps force a person to think while speaking.

3. Practice the speech as if presenting it to your class, imagining that

you are standing before it and looking at it. Such practice best habituates the skills you will use when you give the final presentation. If you practice sitting down, for example, you will reinforce habits that you can't use on the platform; such reinforcement may increase the complexity of your final performance, because the *wrong* rather than the *right* habits, are stamped in. Practice, therefore, as nearly as possible, in the same circumstances as those in which you will give the speech.

4. Practice the speech reflecting the significance of your ideas. (See pp. 116–118) It is especially important that the beginning speaker remind himself of the significance of his subject before he begins to practice the speech, and that he keep that significance before his mind throughout the speech. Especially, he should try to reflect the significance of each sentence and each idea. He should check himself occasionally and ask himself: "Did I say that so as to reflect its importance?" If he practices being idea-centered, he will be more apt to give the speech in such a way as to preserve the idea-centered attitudes of his practice session and be less self-centered in front of the audience.

With abundant extemporaneous practice, you will find that, inadvertently, you will memorize parts of the speech. But you will also, inadvertently, make habits of some of the skills of delivery. With practice, you can habituate good posture, responsive use of voice and body, and a strong spirit of communication. If you can stamp in these skills *before* you deliver the speech, the speech situation will be all the more simple. Because you know your speech and know that you can deliver it well, and you are quite certain to face the speech situation with less anxiety. You will be freer to think, to respond to your thoughts, and to speak in such a way that the audience catches and feels the same thoughts.

ON THE NATURE OF CONFIDENCE

Confidence springs not from a bag of tricks, but from two more difficult although more certain remedies: *competence and commitment.* To the extent that confidence and courage can be developed, they come from knowing what to do and from being dedicated. The speaker who knows how to prepare a speech, how to design it for his audience, and how to deliver it will feel the confidence that comes from competence. The speaker who, moreover, is committed to his ideas will feel the courage of one who is idea-centered instead of self-centered. Just as the surgeon whose skill enables him to operate without a tremor and the martyr whose commitment drives him on with no concern for himself, the speaker who is competent and committed possesses the confidence that enhances his success.

The problem in developing confidence is, first, to develop skill; that development is a function of the study of speech and of practice. Developing commitment is a longer process, involving a search for the ideas, movements, problems, and values. The study of speech, especially as it is presented in this book, will be of some help. Nevertheless, the student must search his heart, and look for help from whatever sustaining forces he can find. Perhaps his search through literature, history, philosophy, religion, science, or art will help him discover those things that merit dedication. Perhaps in one or more of the problems of the present age or the high values of the past he will find that which is worthy of commitment. At any rate, the kind of confidence that stems from competence and commitment is the kind that not only enhances success, but also makes one worth hearing and worthy to influence the lives of those who listen to him. Although there is no short way to develop competence and commitment, one can begin at any time, and in some ways, the college speech class is the best of places.

7 ❡ Delivering Ideas

"It's not what you say but how you say it!" This too-common remark is one of the most insidious catch-phrases ever invented. The serious student of speech should despise it, for it suggests that what is said is not important, that ideas which are frivolous and ill-supported can be "said well," and, worst of all, that the person who does say something well is to be suspected of being skillful but empty-headed.

In reacting strongly in opposition to those who consider delivery to be all there is to speechmaking, we ought not assume that delivery is without importance. A speech is not a speech until delivered to an audience. We have all listened to speakers who seemed to lack either the interest in what they were saying or the energy necessary to present their ideas vigorously. We have found our attention wandering and looked about us to see others in the audience meeting the apparently bored speaker with equal boredom. Often we have made an effort to listen and understand what the speaker was saying and found that intrinsically it was sometimes quite interesting and even vital. Yet the speaker's manner was such that instead of commanding attention he discouraged it. Such speakers are the opposites of the legendary "patent medicine man." Instead of making something worthless sound valuable, they make something valuable sound worthless.

124

On the other hand, we have heard speakers who live in auras of enthusiasm. Their eyes fix us; they point, they pound, they smile, they frown. But back of it all we sense an emptiness and are repelled by what seems to us to be a grotesque parody of what public speaking should be. These men really believe that "it's not what you say but how you say it."

We should not pretend that either of these sorts of speakers is always easily detected. The lackluster speaker is usually successful in concealing the value of what he has to say, and there are those who through knack and practice are experts at making vacuousness sound attractive. We assume that the student wishes to avoid being the former sort of speaker and has no interest in becoming the latter.

Good Delivery

We have not yet described with precision what good delivery is. Although it is unlikely that we shall be able to give a description that will satisfy every student, we must make a start toward helping the student set some standards. Absolute standards are impossible to set. The judgment, "That was well delivered," is at least partly a matter of taste. Individuals vary, often markedly, in what they like. Groups tend to vary also. In one set of circumstances at one time and before one group, what will seem quite proper and appropriate will seem not so appropriate to another group at another time. Recognizing these differences and without trying to account for them, we shall make some generalizations about delivery which we feel are basic to good public speaking.

From the point of view of the listener, delivery is good when it commands his attention and enables him to grasp the speaker's meaning. From the point of view of the speaker, delivery is good when it enables him to communicate what he intends. In general, good delivery is simple, lively, and emphatic.

The speaker should continually ask himself two questions: "Do I have the audience's attention?" and "Do my listeners grasp my meaning?" Although no speaker will probably ever be able to give an unqualified "yes" to each of these questions at every moment, they will direct his own attention toward that on which he must center it—the meaning he wishes to communicate.

Meaning is a broad word. We recognize that meaning in oral communication is dependent upon more than the sum of the dictionary definitions of the words uttered. The oral cues to meaning are many and often subtle, but any listener recognizes some obvious ones. A rising inflection indicates a question although the same words with a final falling inflection would indicate a declarative sentence. Thus we readily distinguish, "I am?" from "I am." We recognize that different meanings arise when different words in a sentence are emphasized. "*I* am going shopping," carries a different meaning from "I *am* going shopping." Or consider these statements: "I believe that I shall go home." and, "I believe that I shall go [long pause] home." These are different statements; although they are in no context, we can safely assert that they carry different meanings.

The oral communication of a message, furthermore, gives the audience some cues about the person communicating the message. The attitudes the speaker suggests are an important part of the meaning. What about, for example, the attitude of the speaker toward his subject matter? Toward his audience? Is he matter-of-fact or impassioned? Is he pleased or angry? Is he antagonistic or conciliatory? The person's manner of speaking helps convey meaning in this broader sense. The speaker who wishes to conciliate his audience will probably fail if he sounds as though he's antagonized. The speaker who believes that his ideas are vital to the welfare of his listeners ought not sound as though he is making polite conversation at an afternoon tea. In short, the audience should feel that the delivery is appropriate—appropriate to the speaker, to the ideas, and to the situation.

ATTAINING GOOD DELIVERY

Paradoxically, the best way to attain good delivery is *not* to attend to it, that is not to attend to it directly. The speaker should give his attention to his message and to the audience to whom he wishes to communicate that message. The best foundation for a well-delivered speech that the beginner can lay is the well-prepared speech, one that contains ideas to which he feels committed, one with a purpose that he wants to accomplish.

Our statement that oral cues are important in indicating meaning, that changes in inflection, in rate, in loudness indicate to a listener changes in meaning, does not mean that the speaker ought try to plan such changes consciously. To plan every inflection, pause, change in loudness, or gesture is probably impossible; to plan many will consume time heavily. For most speakers planning any of these details of delivery will probably result in observable artificialities that will distract the audience and interfere with the communication of the intended meaning. One of the authors remembers listening to what he considered to be an excellent speech by a college student in a contest. At a critical point near the end the speaker stepped stiffly backward and placed his hand over his heart. At that moment worthwhile ideas became ludicrous. The speaker was embarrassed, and so were many of his listeners. Except for that false note, his speech was well delivered. His mind had seemed to be on the ideas of the speech in which he was vitally interested and about which he wished his listeners to feel just as strongly, but at the climax he withdrew his attention from the thought of his speech and made a studied gesture.

The point is not to avoid pointing, or shouting, or whispering, or speaking more loudly or less rapidly. The speaker referred to had gestured time and again during his speech. He had made many changes in his vocal pattern, some subtle, some quite marked, but these had seemed to arise spontaneously from the ideas. The problem is to get and retain *spontaneous* delivery.

Watch people in conversation. Most of them without conscious attention to voice and body respond quite vigorously when they speak. They gesture; their facial expression changes; they modify intensity, rate, and inflection. Think of speaking as a conversation, a rather advantageous conversation for a speaker in which he may think and talk with little interruption from his polite listeners.

Even though the speaker will have to be somewhat more intense, more vigorous simply to make himself heard because he talks to an audience rather than a few, conversation makes a good model. To gain the natural responses of conversation, Richard Whately gave this sound advice well over a hundred years ago: "The practical rule then to be adopted . . . is, not only to pay no studied attention to the voice, but studiously to *withdraw* the thoughts from it, and to dwell as intently as possible on the Sense; trusting to nature to suggest spontaneously the proper emphasis and tones."[1] What is needed is, in James Winans' memorable phrase, "the full realization of the content of your words as you utter them. . . ."[2]

Much of the speaker's success in concentrating on ideas, not on manner, and thereby increasing the effectiveness of his delivery, will depend upon his rehearsal, a topic we shall discuss presently. Some difficulty may arise for the beginner simply because he feels awkward speaking before an audience. In Chapter 6 we discussed reducing tensions, and, quite obviously, the problems are closely related. The beginning speaker should expect to feel awkward when talking to an audience, just as he would if he were to undertake any other activity to which he is not accustomed— skiing, bicycling, golfing, or swimming. Your first kiss was probably rather clumsily executed, but you learned.

Individual Problems in Delivery

Each speaker will meet many problems in developing an effective delivery. He must come to recognize them, large and small, and seek to overcome them. There is little sense in trying to predict what these problems will be or to try to meet them in advance; the best advice is to concentrate on ideas and to follow some positive directions that will help fix good

[1] *Elements of Rhetoric*, London, B. Fellowes, 1836, Pt. IV, ch. II, Sec. 3.
[2] *Speech Making*, New York, Appleton-Century-Crofts, 1938, p. 25.

habits of delivery. A friendly listener, preferably one whose experience in speaking is quite broad, can help each learner identify and meet individual problems as they arise. In the speech classroom, the instructor will probably take this advisory responsibility.

What do we mean when we talk about individual problems in delivery? Take one general example—the problem of distracting mannerisms. Every speaker, even the very experienced, is in a state of tension in speaking. This is natural and it is, in normal degree, desirable. This tension may manifest itself in many ways, some of which will tend to make the delivery of the speech more effective, some of which will help release tension in ways that are not apt to draw the audience's conscious attention, but some manifestations of tension are intrusive and distract the audience. A speaker may pick up a pencil, move it from hand to hand, put it down, pick it up, shake it, and put it down again. This sort of activity is apt to distract the audience's attention from the ideas that the speaker wants to communicate.

The problem of distracting mannerisms may seem petty, and in a sense it is. The friendly critic ought not be too quick to call them to the attention of the speaker. A mannerism may be a good releaser of tension, and be at most minimally distracting. Often as the speaker becomes used to the public speaking situation, much of his tension will flow into useful bodily and vocal activity. On the other hand, if the mannerism persists and seems likely to interfere with communication, the speaker should be told about it and urged to make an effort to eradicate the tendency. Sometimes negative practice will help, that is, in rehearsal to rattle loose change, or pace, or scratch, or do with conscious exaggeration whatever is interfering with communication. The main point is, however, that individual problems ought to be met as they arise with the help of a friendly, knowledgeable observer.

FORMING SOME POSITIVE HABITS

Beginning speakers raise all sorts of questions about how they should conduct themselves before an audience. They ask, for example, "What should I do with my hands?" The answer, of course, is "Do what you feel like doing (unless a friendly observer has urged you to concentrate on removing some distracting mannerism), but don't think about it. Concentrate on your ideas and let your hands do what they will. Chances are that you will find yourself gesturing to reinforce your meanings." In general, this is good advice, but still there are some positive habits that the beginner can cultivate that will make him a little more at ease, probably, and which will help him concentrate on communicating ideas to his listeners.

As simple as it might seem, the beginner would do well to concentrate a little practice on posture. Sit in a chair near the back of a room. Stand up, walk quickly and firmly to the front, turn around purposefully and face an imaginary audience. Do this until you start to become accustomed to "rising to speak." Stand erect before your imaginary audience, your weight distributed about equally upon each foot. Starting with your left foot, move a few steps to your left. Starting with your right foot, move a few steps to your right. When you move, move firmly. When you stand, stand erect. You will soon start to feel comfortable, and, although you are doing only what is natural for you to do, most natural activity feels awkward at first. Give yourself a chance to become used to facing an audience. Practicing facing an imaginary audience will help you develop these helpful rudimentary habits.

Ordinarily in conversation you look at those to whom you are talking. Do this also in speaking to larger groups. There are two reasons for this advice: listeners, consciously or unconsciously, expect you to look at them and become uneasy or distracted if you do not, and you will probably find it easier to keep your mind on communicating your ideas if you will fix your eyes on your audience. This suggestion does not mean that you must never glance away to check your notes or simply to rest for a moment, but it does mean that you should not bury yourself in your notes or fix your attention more than momentarily anywhere except upon your audience. You probably cannot see everyone at once, but you can look at one portion of your audience, and then another, and another, giving all about equal attention. Do not shift your gaze constantly, but do distribute your attention to all parts of your audience. Forget any tricks you might have heard about how to appear as though you are looking at your audience. These tricks are of dubious merit. See your listeners, watch them react; although now and again a listener may disconcert you, usually the audience will serve as a stimulus to a positive, effective manner.

Finally, you should realize that delivering a speech is a physical activity. You must work—your vocal mechanism works; your body works. You should consciously exert yourself. Be vigorous. You need not rant and shout. Far from it. A normally quiet person can be energetic; if he is not to seem vapid, the quiet person must be energetic. It may be well to overreact to ideas in practicing, to be too energetic. Overdo gesturing in practice. Few speakers are too energetic before an audience so there is little cause to worry about carrying too much activity with you from your practice sessions.

The speaker needs to develop a sense of communication. He must feel that he is conversing directly with listeners who, although they remain silent for the most part, are actively engaged in the communication process. If the listeners are to be actively engaged, the speaker must be actively engaged. A speaker who rises and faces an audience purposefully,

who stands erect, gives his attention to the audience, and speaks energet-
ically will find that he has the power to develop a strong sense of communication.

MODES OF DELIVERY

A speaker may speak impromptu or extemporaneously; he may write a
manuscript and then either memorize it or read it. Each of these modes of
delivery creates special problems.

An impromptu speech is one for which the speaker has made no specific
preparation. Ordinarily, the impromptu speaker is moved by specific circumstances to deal with ideas and materials with which he is familiar. A
courtroom lawyer, for example, may engage in a good deal of impromptu
speaking simply because he must meet ideas as they arise. He will, however, be dealing with a case for which he has made a thorough general
preparation and will speak in familiar surroundings. Furthermore, insofar
as possible he will prepare specifically. The congressman in a debate will
speak impromptu, but, like the lawyer, he will draw from ideas, materials,
and procedures with which he is familiar. He may, indeed, have discussed
the issues involved again and again even though he has not specifically
prepared a particular speech. You have done and will probably do some
impromptu speaking. In general, preparing specific speeches will give you
the sort of experience that will be useful when circumstances demanding
impromptu speech arise.

In speech classes, probably, most if not all of the speaking you do will be
extemporaneous. Extemporaneous speeches are prepared in advance. The
speaker plans his purpose, his thesis, a pattern of main heads and subordinate heads; he chooses supporting material to make ideas clear, interesting,
and impelling, but he does not set the language of the speech specifically.
He lets his words come to him as they do in conversation. He might, as
we indicated in discussing outlines, phrase some critical statements precisely, but he will not compose a manuscript.

If the speaker writes a manuscript, he can either memorize it or read it.
Although some authorities argue otherwise, we can see little merit in
memorizing speeches. The time spent in memorizing could be more profitably spent in composing and rehearsing the speech. Reading a manuscript
is difficult, but some occasions demand a speech that is carefully phrased
in detail. The best advice is to learn to speak well extemporaneously before
undertaking to compose and deliver manuscript speeches. With a thorough
grounding in extemporaneous speaking, you will be better equipped to
deliver speeches in a direct, communicative manner.

Before discussing the rehearsal of extemporaneous and manuscript
speeches, there is one other remark about manuscript speeches that should

be made. Too many beginners are tempted to write out speeches in full immediately thinking that having ideas written verbatim will help them. Almost universally, however, this hinders the development of a speech; it tends to become a final draft immediately. In composing a manuscript speech, the speaker should proceed as he would for an extemporaneous speech. He should plan large units, outline, and revise. He might even practice the speech extemporaneously as a further check on the appropriateness of his plans. Finally he should phrase the ideas specifically. Unfortunately, many speakers treat the manuscript as a short cut. The manuscript speech has the advantage of allowing the speaker to choose words carefully. This advantage is wasted, however, unless the ideas and their support are carefully crystallized first.

Rehearsing

The speaker cannot be told too often that he must practice his speech. If he is to practice, he must prepare far enough in advance to give himself adequate rehearsal time. Only by rehearsal will the speaker gain the familiarity with his ideas and materials necessary to enable him to deliver the speech in a clear, interesting, and impelling manner.

You may take advantage of all sorts of odd moments in preparing and rehearsing speeches. Riding a bus, or walking across campus, or waiting for a meal in a busy restaurant, you may turn over in your mind ideas for a speech you are preparing, or you can even engage in silent rehearsal of a speech that has been thoroughly planned. But even though such efforts may be quite useful, they should not be considered as substitutes for careful preparation with paper and pencil resulting in a series of outlines leading to the final plan, nor should silent rehearsal be thought to obviate any need for oral rehearsal.

Repeated oral rehearsal is necessary. A ten-minute speech could be practiced a half dozen times in an hour's time. You are unlikely to spend an hour of preparation more profitably. Actually, however, it is unwise to practice several times consecutively. It is better to practice and revise; then practice again. Or if you feel that little revision is necessary, to wait a short while before practicing again. If at all possible, spread your rehearsals over several days.

Oral rehearsal is difficult. At first it will seem utterly ridiculous to stand talking in an empty room. As a matter of fact, it is easier and better for most speakers to recruit a few friends to listen. Unfortunately friends are not always available, so you must get used to imagining an audience in an empty room.

There is another reason why oral rehearsal is difficult. Except in those rare instances when every turn of fortune is good, speeches, the first few times they are delivered, are apt to be much less than adequate. It can be a rather trying experience to make a good speech, even before an imaginary audience. Quite obviously, however, it makes more sense to try the speech out orally, to revise it, and to bring it under control before facing a real audience.

As we have suggested, a primary reason for practicing orally is to lay a basis for revision. Most speakers do not begin practicing soon enough. They feel that rehearsal is to be undertaken only after the speech is finished. By this attitude they lose a potent instrument of composition. A good deal of the composition of an extemporaneous speech can be oral. Mark Twain is supposed to have commented that he sometimes practiced stories (detailed examples) as many as a hundred times "before I got them the way I wanted them." Whereas most speakers will not go to this extreme, Mark Twain's example is worth emulating. By practicing orally you will be able to discover what parts of your speech need more support, need rearrangement, or perhaps can be omitted. Having a friend listen to rehearsals, especially one who is willing to react in detail to the speech, will help in deciding upon revisions. You ought to question anyone you get to listen to you practice in order to find out what is clear and what is not, what is interesting, and what is impelling to that particular listener. But with or without the help of a friendly critic, you must practice and revise repeatedly.

Another function of oral practice is to help fix the speech in your mind. You should not try to memorize the speech, but as the ideas are developed and refined and practiced repeatedly, you will find yourself choosing without effort words that you have used before. Ordinarily it is better to practice the speech from beginning to end without stopping to repeat or to correct.

In practicing, you should use your outline. Many speakers find that the complete outline they have planned, as necessary as it is, is not a good outline to speak from. The detail distracts them. You should try preparing a vastly simplified outline after you have prepared thoroughly and rehearsed a few times. Cut down words. Use a few key terms to indicate ideas; the key word outline will resemble an early draft, but it will represent careful and complete preparation. On the other hand, some speakers work well from rather complete outlines. You should find out what works best for you; whatever sort of outline you use to speak from should help you be a direct, energetic speaker.

Some speech instructors request that for short classroom speeches students use no notes at all, except perhaps a few cards for complex statistical material or direct quotations. In this case, careful rehearsal is essential. A clear, simple outline, perhaps one that has been reduced from the full outline to a key word outline for initial rehearsals, will help you hold the sequence of your ideas and your materials in mind.

In practicing orally, try to simulate as closely as you can the surroundings in which you will finally speak. If you will have a speaker's stand, practice with one even though it may have to be a makeshift. Try to find a room approximately the size of the one you will speak in. If you can, go to the room itself and practice.

For the overwhelming majority, direct, energetic manuscript reading is much more difficult than good extemporaneous delivery. Part of the problem lies in the fact that too many speakers feel that once the manuscript is written, the job is done. Not only do they often fail to prepare a good manuscript, as we have already mentioned, but they fail to practice what they have prepared.

In general, the procedure for practicing a manuscript is like that for practicing an extemporaneous speech. But the speaker will have more difficulty in concentrating on ideas because his impulse will be to read words. The first step in solving his problem lies in having a good manuscript, one that is well organized. The speaker should study his outline; he should repeat his pattern of assertions without the detail of support. It is often helpful to practice the speech as if it were extemporaneous, using different material even to develop the ideas. In this way the speaker becomes familiar with the ideas so that his mind can fasten on the ideas while he is reading the words.

The speaker must practice reading the manuscript repeatedly no less often than he would practice an extemporaneous speech. He should not try to memorize the speech, but as he practices he will find himself becoming freer and freer from his manuscript. The speaker's goal should be to be able to look at his listeners while he reads. A well-delivered manuscript speech can be nearly as direct as a good extemporaneous speech.

The speaker should prepare a clean manuscript. If he has pencilled in many changes, he should recopy the pages on which they occur. Recopying takes time, but a legible manuscript is necessary if it is to be read well. Some speakers like to mark cues on the manuscript—perhaps underlining an emphatic word or writing a note, "slow down," and so on. Quite frankly we do not think that this is advisable. It may indicate simply that the speaker is not familiar enough with the pattern of his own ideas or with his manuscript. If you feel impelled to indicate such cues, however, keep them simple and hold them to a minimum.

Actually delivery is not a separate topic. It is a part of the speech. Rehearsing for a speech is not so much a time set aside as part of the preparation, the very composition, of a speech. The speaker who develops a sense of communicating to an audience will probably carry this sense over into his choice of material and his patterning of ideas. The speaker who chooses material and patterns ideas carefully will probably lay the basis for and be impelled to deliver his speech in a direct, energetic manner. The result should be a speech that is clear, interesting, and impelling.

8 | Listening Analytically

It does not take a particularly alert student to conclude quickly that the attitudes and skills we have recommended that the speaker study and apply can be turned to good use by the listener. Quite obviously as a listener you have asked yourself such questions as: "Just what is he driving at?" "Is this his point?" "Is that example relevant?" "I wonder if he'll advocate this as a solution?" You have raised such questions for two reasons: (1) to learn more about speaking, and (2) to help determine the merits of the ideas that the speaker has recommended to you. If you already listen analytically, why bother with a chapter on the subject?

Undoubtedly you have learned some attitudes and skills which you can turn to excellent use as a listener. You probably had some good habits of listening before you ever opened this book. But on the other hand, all of us probably assume much too readily that listening is no problem for us. Paradoxically, we know all too well how easy it is to fail to listen analytically, or to listen at all for that matter. We have sat too often in an audience and suddenly realized that our minds have wandered off. We have been given directions, often important directions, and discovered to our dismay that although we thought we knew what we were to do and how we were to do it, we did not know. How many times has each of us taken an action on someone else's advice and said later, "I wish I'd listened more carefully." We are not much different from the average person. Ralph G. Nichols, who has been in charge of testing the listening of thousands of students, writes:

These extensive tests have led us to this general conclusion: Immediately after the average person has listened to someone talk, he remembers only about half of what he has heard—no matter how carefully he thought he listened. What happens as time passes? My own testing shows—and it has been substantiated by research at Florida State University, Michigan State College, The Methods Engineering Council, and elsewhere—that a few weeks after listening to a person talk, the average listener will remember only about 25 per cent of what was said.[1]

Too often we blame the speaker for our lapses. "What a boring sermon," we say as we drowse in our pews. "If that professor could only make an idea clear . . ." as we find ourselves unable to reproduce the ideas in writing an essay in an examination. "That glib devil tricked me," when we find ourselves the possessors of an inferior product or find a belief hollow. There can be no doubt that there are uninteresting, unclear, and unethical speakers in the world, but too often our judgments are simply excuses for our own inadequacies. And even when such judgments are accurate, they should be the spur to better, not less analytic listening. Whereas the brilliant speaker who is interesting, clear, and ethical may be able to carry even poor listeners along, the poor speaker must have fine listeners.

WANT TO LISTEN

"I can listen well when I want to." This statement tends to represent our attitude toward listening. In one way it's a good attitude; in another way it is not. We should not forget that the students Professor Nichols tested probably *wanted* to listen well, and still they did not listen well enough.

To say, "I can listen well when I want to," is to imply, "but I may not want to." Herein lies the problem. We live in a society that has learned to shift the responsibilities from listeners to speakers. We say, "Make me want to listen. I dare you." If we are distracted, it's not our fault but the speaker's. As speakers, we ought to recognize this common attitude and try to meet it. But we cannot expect the impossible from ourselves nor from others and, try as we might, we shall not always be perfectly clear and interesting. To use an analogy that's at least as old as Plutarch, one

[1] "This Business of Listening," *American Trade Association Executive Journal*, January, 1956. Anyone who writes about listening must acknowledge a debt to Professor Nichols' extensive work. The authors have drawn stimulation and many ideas from his research and writing.

may throw a ball, but another must catch it. Even with the best of pitchers, a catcher will have to move off his haunches once in a while. Poor listeners tend to dwell on the responsibilities and the disabilities of speakers. The only person who has a right to say, "That was a boring sermon," is the person who has listened as closely as possible to it. And the only person who has a right to say, "He certainly didn't make that point clear," is the person who has made the utmost effort to ferret out the idea.

On the other hand, the person who says, "I can listen well when I want to," may make the statement a resolution to listen well. Motivation, wanting to listen well, is the starting point. It is possible to give many detailed reasons to anyone who asks, "Why should I want to listen?" But we shall give only three general ones.

1. *Personal integrity.* We inevitably make judgments concerning the value of speeches and speakers. Even an almost unconscious turning of the mind from the speaker to other matters is a kind of judgment. Sometimes we communicate these judgments to others, perhaps at length verbally after the speech, or during the speech by merely raising our eyebrows. Sometimes we keep the judgments private. In either case, to be honest we must listen carefully. An irate student once brought a term paper to one of the authors. The paper had just been returned to him by another professor. It was neatly typed, well written, and had an "A" marked boldly upon it. Why was the student angry? Buried in a long paragraph in the middle of the paper was a sentence much like this, "I'll bet you didn't read this, you. . . ." There was a similar message at another place in the paper. Although the student did not mind getting "A's," he did resent deeply the apparent lack of effort on the professor's part to evaluate the paper meaningfully. Not long ago a housewife asked in exasperation after the assessor had just left her home, "How could he assess our property? He didn't get out of the living room." We recognize that the professor and the assessor had no right to make evaluations in these cases, but how many evaluations of speeches, of ideas, of materials, of motives, do we make that are essentially dishonest ones?

2. *Personal profit.* The reader of this book is no ordinary listener; he is a student of speech. He can learn about speaking in no better way than by listening carefully to speakers. It is not enough for him to say that a speech is effective or that it is not. He must try to analyze just what it is that prompts his judgment. The student of speech, then, will be an especially busy listener and must be an especially alert listener. We have discussed, for example, the necessity of good organization, but nothing will drive the lessons home more quickly than to hear some poorly organized speeches. The student may learn to handle supporting material adroitly by listening to speakers who do so. The possible lessons are too numerous to mention, and the possible benefit too great to overemphasize.

Even if we were not trying to learn more about speaking, we should, as intelligent persons, resolve to listen carefully to speakers. What are the ideas in the speech? On what materials do these ideas rest? Herein lie high potential profits. We should resolve to find as much as possible in any speech out of sheer acquisitiveness. We are inclined much too quickly to say, "There's nothing here for me." If we were wise, we would turn our attention away from a speaker only when we could use our time profitably for some other activity, but this is almost never possible. If for no reason than to make the best out of a bad situation, we should listen carefully; and quite often we shall find that the situation is not so bad after all.

3. *Simple courtesy.* Even if we could turn profitably to something else, we probably should not do so. As speakers we should be interested in creating the kinds of listening situations in which decent communications can prosper. As human beings we should be interested in creating a social situation in which all of us can respond intelligently to one another. If a speaker takes the time to prepare a speech for an audience, that audience owes him the courtesy of listening carefully. What if the speaker does not take the responsibility of preparing carefully? No doubt we hear too many speakers who do not make honest efforts to prepare, but on the other hand, as listeners we should assume that speakers have taken the time. If there is blame that can be attached to a failure in communication, we should take care that as listeners we do not deserve that blame.

The person who resolves to listen carefully will take the first step toward being a good listener. Although this resolution by itself is not enough, without consciously convincing himself that he should listen and that he wants to listen, no one is likely to become a good listener.

Declare a Truce with Bias and Emotion

One of the authors happened to be in the home of a friend at presidential election time a few years ago. The television set was on. As the announcer informed us in ringing tones that we were about to hear a speech by one of the candidates, the set owner turned vigorously to another channel, snapping, "We don't want to listen to that guy. He won't do anything but tell a lot of lies anyway." We would be safe in saying that even if this man had not tuned out the candidate he would not have listened, not listened well at any rate, to the speech.

We tend to concentrate on those things we like and to turn away from those things we dislike. Our existing attitudes—towards ideas, toward people, toward groups—shape what we hear, until, at times, we hear only the weird phantoms of what is said if we hear at all. Consider this hypothetical example:

The firm's accountant goes to the general manager and says: "I have just heard from the Bureau of Internal Revenue, and . . . " The general manager suddenly breathes harder as he thinks, "That blasted bureau! Can't they leave me alone? Every year the government milks my profits to a point where . . ." Red in the face, he whirls and stares out the window. The label "Bureau of Internal Revenue" cuts loose emotions that stop the general manager's listening.

In the meantime the accountant may go on to say "here is a chance to save $3,000 this year" if the general manager will take few simple steps. The fuming general manager may hear this—if the accountant presses hard enough —but the chances are he will fail to comprehend it.[2]

We could cast this hypothetical case in a hundred different forms; and, if we try, we can probably remember ourselves in the role of a listener who let his emotional responses keep from understanding what was said.

Our problems are not new ones. Among other pieces of advice which he gave his own contemporaries in regard to listening, Plutarch declared, "He therefore who comes to hear must for the time come to a kind of truce and accommodation with vainglory. . . ."[3] Although there are a few who may be so impressed with their own powers as a speaker that they cannot listen carefully to others, this feeling is probably not going to be a principal problem with most of us. Still Plutarch's advice is apt; we do need to come to a truce. Whenever we sense the tug of our own strong feelings on a subject, we must be cautious. This is not to say that we must forget our own beliefs. Far from it. We must remember them; but in remembering them, we must recognize our inclination to tune out, to distort, to forget conveniently those ideas and materials that do not fit our prevailing attitudes.

When we listen to ideas to which we are opposed, our inclination is to start to compose rebuttals. In so doing, we turn our attention from the speaker to another task and so are apt not to hear much of what he has to say. We have all had the experience of attending a lecture to hear afterwards someone ask a question, probably one framed to embarrass or expose the speaker, which indicated that the listener had tuned out at some point to work on his own composition because the speaker had quite clearly (we thought) answered the question in his speech. If you are actually debating and must refute what is said, you will be faced with an extremely difficult task of combined listening and composition. You should be well prepared in advance, but even so you will need to make sure that you hear and understand the entire argument if you are to respond to it intelligently.

Learn to set aside your judgments temporarily. "Hear me out," a speaker may answer a questioner who interrupts him, and he makes a fair request. We must wait for the speaker to complete each idea, and we must wait to see the relationship of one idea to the next. Only if we are willing to wait

[2] Ralph G. Nichols and Leonard A. Stevens, "Listening to People," *Harvard Business Review*, September–October, 1957, pp. 88–89.

[3] Plutarch, "On Hearing," sect. 6.

and listen can we decide on the basis of what is said whether the material is clear or the requests are reasonable. It may be well for us to bring our own beliefs and the basis of these beliefs forward, to compare what we have heard with what we already believe, but if we let our beliefs step in too soon we may be doing ourselves and the speaker a disservice by taking our attention from him. Final comparisons and decisions will take time; we do not have the time during another's speech for careful, final decision making.

It will not be easy to declare a truce with each speaker, but if you make a conscious effort to do so, to keep your attitudes from interfering with your comprehension of what is said, you will begin to build a habit of listening that will serve you well. If you respond fully to speakers, you will be fairer to your own beliefs in the long run.

LISTEN ANALYTICALLY

What we have discussed thus far is, in a sense, preliminary to listening. The listener is not inactive. He does not sit back like a blotter ready to absorb everything that comes along. He has a mind and his mind works, and herein, strangely enough, lies the problem.

Although the listener does not have time to make detailed comparisons, evaluations, decision, and refutations, he does have time to do more than listen to each word the speaker utters. The average person will speak from 125 to 150 words per minute, but the average person can think at a much more rapid rate. Most persons reading this book can read at least 300 words per minute. Who has not, in his impatience, taken a magazine away from a friend who was reading some tidbit aloud in order to get through the material at a much faster rate? The average listener, then, has spare time. The question is, how will he use that time?

Too often we use our spare time for nonlistening activity. While the speaker is poking along at 125 words per minute, we compose a grocery list. We return to the speaker satisfied that we have missed nothing and soon dart away to ponder some tangential thought the speaker has raised in our minds. "When was it that I heard Archibald MacLeish lecture? Oh, yes . . . It was . . ." By the time we return we may well have missed some critical detail. The good listener learns how to turn his spare time to use as a listener; a few suggestions for the use of "spare time" follow.

Search for Ideas

As students of speech, you know that speaking is a purposive activity, that the speaker has a pattern of ideas that he wants to communicate to his listeners. As a listener you should search for the speaker's ideas. This must be a conscious and diligent search. We cannot expect every speaker to be efficient enough to make us recognize his ideas with little or no effort on our part. Try to find his thesis. Try to determine the main points upon which the thesis rests and the ideas subordinate to the main points. In so doing, remember three key words: *anticipate, verify,* and *review.*

Try to predict from the outset what the speaker's thesis will be, and what each succeeding point will be. This is one way to use your spare listening time constructively. Some speakers may unwittingly mislead you, so you ought to make your decisions tentative. You know, as a speaker, that ideas are not always stated explicitly; you must, therefore, search for unstated ideas.

Try to verify your predictions about the ideas underlying the speech. Search for statements and materials that would lead you to reject or modify your interpretations. Do not be easily satisfied that you know what the speech is all about. If a speaker is good, even an idea explicitly stated and recognized will be made increasingly clear and meaningful to you as he speaks.

Take Notes

You will try to make a pattern of the ideas as the speech unfolds. In so doing you will be tempted to make notes. This is a good impulse. You have a record of what you have heard and making notes often helps you sharpen your understanding, that is, your own interpretations of what you are hearing. But making notes can be hazardous. It is easy to become too involved in the note making process and thereby to lose the thread of the speaker's thought. Keep your notes brief, and do not start making them immediately. Think and rethink an idea and then jot it down. Do not try to set it down in elaborate detail. The most useful notes, the notes that will indicate most accurately what was said, will be just a few reminders from which you can rework ideas carefully at your leisure later if you feel that the ideas are important ones to record. You'll probably understand better what is said and remember longer if you make few notes as you anticipate, verify your anticipations, and review the speaker's ideas.

Reviewing is important. Use your excess listening time to recapitulate for the speaker, even as he should review occasionally for you. A review will help you anticipate new ideas and make a pattern of the whole. You will be better able to discover how ideas fit together or fail to fit together. A final review should summarize your search for the ideas of a speech.

Find the Basis of Ideas

As a student of speech, you should recognize examples, statistics, analogies, and testimony. When you recognize pieces of supporting material you should be looking for the relationship between them and the ideas which they are purported to support. Finding an example may help you recognize an idea or understand it more clearly; it will also help you determine whether or not the idea is founded upon substantial material. This is not to say that you can immediately judge the quality of ideas. You should be willing to delay that judgment, but you should also note the material upon which the ideas rest and make some tentative estimates to which you may return.

Lay the Groundwork for Analyzing the Quality of Ideas

Your aim in searching for the speaker's ideas and the materials upon which these ideas are based ought to be to establish a basis upon which to analyze the worth of those ideas. As we have indicated consistently, this final analysis will be the result of painstaking listening during the speech and careful thought after the speech is over. A final analysis will ordinarily not be reached through a quick flash in which all truth is made clear. Accept or reject ideas tentatively, but be sure you understand what those ideas are. Continually analyze and check the ideas from a speech as you understand them. As far as the speech itself is concerned, you will often be made uneasy by an assertion or the relation of one assertion to another or to the material the speaker uses to establish its worth. When you find symptoms of something amiss in thought, you should seek out the causes. You may not decide finally that the speaker's ideas or materials are deficient. If you do decide that the speaker's beliefs do not merit acceptance, be sure that you are not being blinded by your own biases and emotions. Remember, you are interested in judging not simply the speaker's ideas, but your own as well.

In judging the acceptability of claims made, the material which we have already discussed especially in Chapter 3 should be of use to you. Even more, you will find the material in the second part of this book useful. Listeners as well as speakers analyze social problems, causes, solutions, and values. You should study the material in these later chapters; they will provide an introduction to the sort of analytic activity you must carry on in order to listen intelligently to others.

Be Alert for the Signs of Poor Listening

No matter how well intentioned we may be as we begin to listen, we shall be prone to lapse into inefficiency in this activity just as we may in any other. We should, therefore, be alert for the signs of our poor listening. We have mentioned the principal signs already, but we shall review them briefly.

Beware of negative evaluations of the speaker, especially of the small matters of delivery. If you find yourself beginning to dwell on these, you are probably not searching for ideas. It would be a shame, for example, to have heard Einstein speak and to have come away only with the impression that he had a pronounced foreign accent. Negative evaluations are often the beginning of a rationalization for not listening. If, in the classroom situation, you wish to make a friendly suggestion to the speaker concerning some distracting mannerism, note it briefly and turn your attention to ideas and the material upon which those ideas are based. There will be plenty of time later to list and consider in detail negative evaluations of the speaker himself if you are really inclined to do so after you have exhausted the potential worth of what he has to say.

If you find yourself composing rebuttals to what the speaker is saying, resist this impulse temporarily. Be sure you have heard and understood what he has to say first. Often the tendency to make rebuttals is a sign that our attitudes are interfering with our listening. We should resolve to hold our truce until we have heard the speaker out.

Check your note taking, If you find yourself trying to copy in detail what is being said, you should remember that you are taking on a task that will probably prove impossible. Make only a few notes to help you remember. Expand and organize these notes later. Concentrate on ideas; anticipate, verify, and review them. With such concentration and a few jottings, you will understand and remember more of what the speaker has to say.

LISTENING TO CLASSROOM LECTURES

We have been discussing listening to speeches in general. Whereas most of what we have said will apply to the special case of listening to classroom lectures, the college student may need to make some special adjustments to his particular circumstances which he would not necessarily make if he were listening to a political campaign speech or to a speech after a dinner. Most especially, he must adjust his note taking habits. Inasmuch as classroom lectures are undoubtedly the listening situation most frequently encountered by users of this book, we ought consider their special circumstances briefly.

A college lecture has been defined, not always inaccurately, as a device for getting notes from the notebook of the professor to the notebook of the student without going through the head of either. We discussed the listener's motivation earlier; remember two assertions in relation to your motivation: (1) Intend to remember. You cannot listen passively to a lecturer and expect to retain much; you must listen actively intending to understand and to remember. (2) Do not always expect to understand the importance of what you hear immediately. Often one must submit frequently to a great deal of preliminary data before one can start to see connections between ideas and the value of the material presented.

Although students will vary in the amount and sorts of notes they take, we can generalize somewhat about taking lecture notes. Our generalizations will differ somewhat from those we made before concerning note taking. It is, of course, possible to try to take too many lecture notes just as it is quite possible to try to take too many notes in other situations. The graduate student who writes down everything the professor says, including "Good morning," probably takes too many; but the average college freshman takes too few. His sketchy notes may fail to record many of the lecturer's subordinate ideas, the limitations the speaker puts on his own general statements, and the support given for these ideas. The poor student's notes are thus oversimplified to the point that even if he learns all that he has recorded, he cannot hope to perform well in an examination, much less have a thorough knowledge of the subject he has studied. *One should take as many notes as one can while still comprehending the relation of what is being said to what has been said.* One should, therefore, try to record the speaker's main themes, his subordinate ideas, and his support of them as accurately as possible.

Again we should warn the student that he may not be able to make a perfect record as he listens. He should be willing to invest a few minutes after the lecture in reorganizing his notes, perhaps filling out in more detail some of the items; he may even have to rework and recopy everything he has jotted down during the lecture.

Reworking lecture notes will not only create a more orderly record, but it will strengthen your memory considerably. Most forgetting occurs immediately after learning. Thus after hearing a lecture, we forget more during the first five minutes than we forget in any subsequent five minutes. We can slow the curve of forgetting and further stamp in the lecturer's ideas and materials by spending even five minutes reviewing immediately following the lecture. When one reviews lecture notes immediately following a lecture, he remembers six months later twice as much as he would had he not spent this time in review.

Good listening is especially valuable in a speech class. A class discussion after speeches, which concentrates on the speaker's ideas and upon the basis of those ideas, will probably reveal how difficult it is to communicate accurately one person's thoughts to others. As a speaker, such discussion should stimulate you to plan your purpose and thesis carefully, to pattern ideas simply, and to find a variety of concrete supporting materials to help make your ideas clear, interesting, and impelling. Such discussion can give you an insight into your listeners and into the general problems of communicating to an audience.

We have, of course, given you only a few simple guidelines to good listening. We believe that the admonitions, if followed, will help you form good listening habits. Forming these habits is not a matter of applying a set of absolutely dependable rules; such rules do not exist. Skillful listening can only be built slowly and consciously by each individual.

Listening Assignments

FOR CLASS SPEECHES

1. After each speech, write quickly on a piece of paper the speaker's thesis and his main ideas. You might make brief notes during the speech, but do not try to make final, full statements of the ideas until the speaker has finished.
2. Give the notes to the speakers. Each speaker should summarize the statements, noting agreements and disagreements.
3. At the next class period, the speaker should report to the class the apparent accuracies and inaccuracies in his effort to communicate.
4. Discuss possible reasons for significant disagreements among the listeners and lack of understanding. Do not assume that all difficulties lie within the speeches.

A REPORT ON A SPEECH HEARD OUTSIDE CLASS

1. Choose a speech (or more than one speech if it is impossible for the entire class to schedule one speech to listen to) for the class to hear. If possible, find a speech that is likely to be controversial, one toward which the members of the class are likely to respond differently in terms of their beliefs.
2. Each person should write a report of what he hears, stating the speaker's thesis, summarizing his major ideas, and indicating briefly the supporting material upon which each idea is based.
3. Each person may write several paragraphs responding to the worth of the speech in general and any of the ideas in particular on which he wishes to comment.
4. In class discussion, compare what the listeners heard. Concentrate, especially at first, on item two. Are there significant differences in the reports? Can these differences be accounted for by differences in the beliefs held by the listeners?

Part II | Working with Ideas

9 ∥ Thinking and Speaking About Problems

Great speeches have only one characteristic in common: *each great speech is concerned with a great problem.* The kinds of problems may vary, the manner of the speaker may vary, but a brief glance at some great speeches shows that they never vary from their concern with a great problem. The first great speech of which we have record was the announcement by Moses of the Ten Commandments; this speech was generated by moral problems that were destroying the Children of Israel. The speaking of Socrates was of a different sort; Socrates gave no speeches, but rather, asked questions. The questions were of such decisive brilliance that they performed two great functions. First, Socrates' questions revealed the unintelligent ethical base of Athenian life with such brilliance that some Athenians knew that they must either change their way of life or destroy Socrates. These people regrettably took the easy way; Socrates' death marks the end of the Golden Age of Greece. Nevertheless, even after death, the speaking of Socrates performed its second function, namely, generating dozens of schools of philosophy. There is no philosophy originating in the Western world that does not claim Socrates as its founder; he may well be the greatest Founding Father of all time. Different problems generated the speaking of Pericles and Demosthenes: their speeches were fired by the necessity of understanding and preserving the first free society. The speaking of Jesus also arose from problems; one need not be a convinced Christian to recognize that the Sermon on the Mount is one of the great speeches, and that it was generated by the problems of the artificial ritualism into which religion had fallen, and by the desperate need of religion, and of man himself, for a transformation.

In modern times as well, great speeches come about only when they are generated by a great problem. From the speaking of Moses to that of Abraham Lincoln and on to that of Franklin Roosevelt and John F. Kennedy, only problems of significance generate speaking of genuine excellence.

And so will it always be. There is no possibility of writing a great speech, or even a significant one, unless in some way, the speech is a response to a significant problem. Nor can a great speech be understood apart from its concern with the problem that sparked it.

Great speeches are generated only by great problems and this reason is sufficient for devoting the rest of this book to the study of problems. Nevertheless, additional and compelling reasons justify a strong concern with problems in a book about speaking.

THE VALUE OF PROBLEMS

The ideal world, we might think, would be a place without any problems; indeed, Valhalla, Nirvana, and Heaven seem to be places where problems cannot exist. But on earth, the situation is different, because *when man responds to certain kinds of problems with great intelligence, and at the same time, with great vigor, he often rises to a higher level.* Some examples show the way problems help man develop: When man responded intelligently and vigorously to the problem of disease, he ended the great plagues, learned to restore the sick, and found ways to maintain good health until advanced age. When, at long last, man reacted intelligently and vigorously to the problem of poverty, he created scientific agriculture and invented means of producing great abundance. So successful has the industrial-scientific revolution been that it suggests that, at last, man can create enough goods to free himself from want. At any rate, for the first time in history, in some countries, surpluses are a "problem." The same growth from intelligent and vigorous responses to problems develops not only great civilizations, but great nations as well: England solved the problem of being a small island that could not be self-sufficient by developing the most far-flung Empire in history. Holland, even though a tiny country, has at times led the world in art, philosophy, and in per capita wealth; even today she responds so intelligently and vigorously to the problem of land scarcity that if we managed all arable lands on earth as efficiently and productively as those in Holland, our planet could support a population of ten times those now alive. America responded to the challenge of an almost perpetual labor shortage—which we still occasionally experience—not only by the tragic and cruel importation of slaves but also by becoming the most industrialized country on earth. Thus do intelligent reactions to problems raise one to a higher level.

Not only does this principle of growth apply to civilizations and nations, but also to cities: Pittsburgh was infamous for being the world's smokiest city; today it is probably the cleanest of the Northern metropolises. The same law applies to individuals: perhaps it is not an accident that the greatest orator of antiquity, Demosthenes, was a stutterer, or that the greatest composer in history, Beethoven, was deaf, or that Milton, who could see so many things so clearly, was blind, or that the most active United States President up to his time was a cripple. When men react intelligently and vigorously to certain kinds of problems, they reduce human misery, create new sources of strength, and present themselves and those influenced by them with fresh possibilities for humane fulfillment. Problems, then, are like Mephistopheles in Goethe's *Faust:* They may "try" to do evil work, but in the end, they increase—instead of stultify—growth, provided, of course, that they are reacted to with both great intelligence and great vigor.

Why do problems—certain kinds, anyway—seem to bring out the best in man? At least six major reasons suggest that much of man's speaking—as well as much of his education—ought to direct itself to means of locating and solving the great problems that beset him.

Thought

First, as John Dewey discovered, a problem is necessary to start thought. We do not think about our feet until the shoe pinches, nor about our health until we get sick, nor, perhaps, about achieving a genuine education until we realize we are dangerously ignorant. No man, said Dewey, even begins to think until he first notes a perplexity, a need, or as he put it, a "felt difficulty."[1] Because thought does not begin without a problem, a corollary is that when we are absorbed in petty problems, our thoughts are correspondingly petty. The suburbanite who believes his greatest problem is crab grass is not apt to reach great heights, except in lawn growing. The challenge of a significant problem may stimulate the best thinking, and with it, the best speaking.

[1] *How We Think*, New York, D. C. Heath and Co., 1910, p. 9. Perhaps the discovery that thought proceeds from problems—rather than from syllogisms—may turn out to be Dewey's gretatest contribution to philosophy.

Civilization

Secondly, problems bring out man's best—provided, again, that he responds intelligently and vigorously—because certain problems are the generating force behind all civilizations. Arnold Toynbee showed that each civilization of the past arose, not because the living was easy and man had time to think, but because the living was extremely difficult and *to survive, man was jolted into the necessity of thought.* To use his own words, civilizations arose as a result of a "challenge followed by a hitherto unprecedented effort."[2] Those societies that have remained primitive, Henri Bergson pointed out, are probably those in which the living was too easy and which were never required to stretch their minds by solving demanding problems.[3] Problems not only provide the necessary jolt to get a civilization going, but they seem to be the generating force behind the continued growth of civilizations. Whether or not a civilization continues to grow depends on the ability of a culture to respond to further problems—not merely problems of creating wealth, although wealth is needed, but also problems in philosophy, government, the arts, economics, science, law, and religion. The failure of a culture to recognize such problems can cause the stultification and eventually the death of that culture. Problems are necessary not only to generate a civilization, but also to ensure its continued growth.

Motivation

Problems are, likewise, the starting point of human motivation. All motives begin with a need, a desire, or with a lack, a deficiency. Just as we are not motivated to eat unless we are hungry, neither can a horse led to water be made to drink until it feels thirsty. Problems are, under certain circumstances, energizing forces that can stimulate activity and drive man on to greater achievement.

Creativity

Fourthly, problems are the prerequisite for creativity. "Necessity is the mother of invention," rightly runs the old adage. Inventions may not always come when they are needed, but they will not likely come and will

[2] Students interested in the study of civilizations will be stimulated by reading *A Study of History*, abr. by D. C. Sommervell, New York, Oxford University Press, 1946. The writer acknowledges that although he cannot accept the work of the later Toynbee, he is still grateful to Toynbee, for his *Study* provided one of the major stimulants that helped lead to the approach to speech here presented. Especially significant are Parts II, III, and IV.

[3] See *Two Sources of Morality and Religion*, Garden City, New York, Doubleday Anchor Books, 1954, p. 172.

not be adopted until a need for them is perceived. Creativity in art, likewise, springs from a problem, although the problem may be merely the artist's wish to express something in a way different from the current style. Nevertheless, with no problems, there would be no creativity.

Democracy

Fifthly, problems are especially important in a democratic state, for only a democratic state has institutionalized the possibility of locating and solving problems. Only a democratic state is persistently responsive to the problems of people, and only such a state offers the possibility of continued growth through perpetual problem solving.

Thus, problems, which often enough are a curse to mankind, still, when responded to with intelligence and vigor, can raise man to a higher level. Nor is there much mystery why, for when something is the starting point for thought, the generating force behind civilization, the basis for human motivation, and consequently, for human energy, the source of creativity, and the spark behind democratic government, that thing, indeed, could raise man to heights he could not otherwise reach. Problems are, therefore, the great dynamos behind the development of man and his society.

Speeches that point out the great problems and, in a burst of intellectual vigor, help point to the solution of these problems, are of incalculable value to man. The rest of this book is devoted to helping you speak about problems in such a way that you may convert problems from forces that deprive and plague man to forces that will raise him to a higher level.

THE DANGER OF PROBLEMS

Suffering and Degradation

But when problems are not responded to with a combination of intelligence and vigor, or when people, because of weakness or lack of knowledge fail so to respond to them, problems do not invigorate, but only enervate. The history of problems is also the history of man's suffering and degradation. In our rich and free country, it is hard for us to conceive of what life was like for the more than seventy billion people estimated to have lived on earth before us. These people were plagued by disease, stunted by starvation, cursed by flood and famine, only to die an early death and to leave little record of their pains, sorrows, and fears. These men, who lived in hovels sometimes made of no more than grass and mud, yet were forced to build great palaces and tombs for the tyrants who enslaved them. These men died chained to the oars of sinking galleys, or were abandoned to rot on thousands of half-forgotten battlefields, or

were strangled by a disease that no one understood. Their survivors drew
no welfare checks, and soon followed them to the grave. For billions
of people, the problems of war, poverty, caste, tyranny, and disease
brought suffering and degradation of a type which we are poorly equipped
to imagine.

Destruction of Civilizations

In addition to heaping pains and sorrows upon mankind, unsolved
problems are the cancers that weaken and destroy civilizations. The unsolved problem of fratricidal wars fought by the city-states of ancient
Greece wasted the vigor and wealth of the Greeks, and helped kill, too
soon, the first free civilization of the world. In India, caste systems
strangled large masses of men who, had they been freer, might have added
strength to the civilization. The problem of disease, virtually unsolved
until a hundred years ago, brought plagues that dealt the final death blow
to defeated Athens, later smothered dying Rome, and nearly destroyed
Europe in the Middle Ages; in each of these cases, a plague put at least
a third of the populace in a hastily dug and unmarked grave, and left
millions more permanently enfeebled. Declining Rome reminds us that
ethical and moral blight can weaken a great culture. The value of the
great institutions of Rome was destroyed because these institutions were
perverted into devices that filled the vaults of the corrupt with gold,
which they used to purchase power over more deserving men. The unsolved problems of war, poverty, caste, disease, political immorality, and
tyranny have obliterated every civilization created by man, except as yet,
our own.

CURRENT PROBLEMS

The wealth of our country often leads some to think that these problems are in the past, but they are not, for problems have caused more
intense suffering in our century to more people than in any other era.
Poverty in the world at large is as great as ever, and more people are alive
to suffer it. The average person in the world, despite the wealth of a
few countries, has an income of about $130 per year. In India, the average
income is $75 a year, and it is still lower for perhaps a billion more
people. However low the cost of living is in countries having so low an
income, no man can come near to achieving his potential on such income.

For at least a century, five to eight million Asians have starved to death
each year. The problem of poverty is with us, and is a constant source
of weakness to the world, as well as a source of danger to the wealthy
countries.

Nor must we think that only others have these problems. Even in some highly civilized countries, systems of caste and prejudice dangerously weaken large populations so that the total strength of a country that tolerates a caste system (or its milder form, prejudice) is much less than it might have been had the nation developed the strengths of all its people. Nor are the problems restricted to underdeveloped countries; some of the worst problems are found only in the wealthy countries. In the more developed countries, the rate of crime, divorce, suicide, and insanity seems to soar each year. And especially only in the most civilized countries is the problem of war one that can bring instant devastation. Our wealth and many comforts must not blind us to the fact that this century is the bloodiest in history. More have died from war in the twentieth century, and more have been killed in pogroms—particularly in Germany, Russia, and China, than lived on earth in the fifth century, B.C. The destructive power available in the form of atomic fission is such that we could destroy Russia nineteen times—and she could destroy us only twelve times. There is enough nuclear power available to give the equivalent of one-half ton of TNT to every man, woman, and child on earth. The great problems are not from the past, but exist here and now; they are problems for you and me, and will decide much of our destiny. These problems must not be forgotten, for Western civilization seems to have at least started down the same road that has taken all previous cultures to their funeral pyre. A failure to study these problems may not only increase human misery and human degradation, but it could blast the last remaining civilization from the earth, and with it the best creations of man—his philosophy and his wisdom, his art and science, his freedom, his religion, and perhaps even his existence. If, perhaps, our last chance is at hand, it is well that we learn all we can about problems.

SPEAKING AND PROBLEMS

Speaking, one of the great drive-shafts that transmits the power to propel man's civilizations, likewise acts as a rudder that steers. The course and speed are set in part—in large part—by what speakers say. Therefore, *the aim of speaking ought to be to direct us toward the solution of our problems with the greatest possible speed.* The speaker must awaken those who sleep or who are indifferent; he must help others see the unnoticed danger, and understand it; he must direct us away from the false and petty problems that set us off course. The focus on problems, which is primary in the rest of this book, is important if we are to improve the quality of our civilization, and perhaps, if we are to survive at all.

Some think one should not speak of a nation's problems, and that to do so is unpatriotic. To such people, we should point out that one of the

highest forms of patriotism is to study the problems of one's people so
that the problems might be solved; such problem solving can insure the
permanence and well-being of a nation, whereas constant super-adoration
of the nation cannot. The Golden Age of Augustus was the best attempt
to save a nation by praising it: Augustus paid poets, artists, and architects
to sing the glory of Rome and greatness of the Roman gods. Such praise
did not save Rome, and the Empire grew weak even as the choruses of
praise grew louder. In the end, the problems destroyed the City.

Among our greatest needs is to develop speakers who can help direct
us toward the solution of our problems. No society can move forward—
or long exist—when its speakers lull people to sleep, or when they lead
people to believe that there are no significant problems, or when speakers
produce no more than interesting but superficial trivia.

In the present age, the task of speaking so as to solve problems is
greater than in all previous ages, because the problems themselves are
greater in magnitude, if not also in number. Perhaps the results will be
more gratifying than in past eras, for we know more about solving the
problems of war, poverty, caste, disease, and tyranny than in any previous
age. The task is worth the unprecedented effort that will be required, for
there are signs that we stand on the threshold of a new world in which
man will rise to a higher level or plunge to destruction.

DISCOVERING PROBLEMS

If our speakers are to direct us to solutions, they must first search for
whatever gnaws at the human spirit, they must find the sicknesses of our
age, and they must discover the forces that may be weakening the last
remaining great culture. Speakers, however, often have not performed
these crucial functions. One could cite illustrations from Rome where
speakers (as well as poets and dramatists) never discussed the grimy
poverty of most Romans, or contemporary Russia where speakers cannot
discuss all the Soviet Union's policies, but let us take an American
example, for the failure to discuss problems sometimes happens in democracies as well. In 1932, the life savings of millions of Americans were
wiped out as banks closed, and the income of millions more was stopped
as businesses and industries shut down. Mass starvation was prevented
only by setting up bread lines and soup kitchens. Yet in the presidential
election of that year, one of the two principle political parties of the
country tried to make it appear that the real issue of the election was not
the depression, but prohibition. Party speakers insisted that "Prosperity
is just around the corner," and proceeded to discuss the evils of Demon
Rum. These speakers who tried to divert attention to prohibition failed

to grasp the central problem of the people, but the voters did not. The party that ignored the important problem of that day was not returned to the nation's highest office for twenty years. The penalties for failing to treat great problems are often not so mild as this.

Intelligent speaking about problems is not easy, and requires special study. One cannot learn much about attacking the problems of the world by speaking about "How I spent my summer vacation"—unless, perhaps, it was in the Peace Corps—or by speaking about "How to hold a golf club," or on "My most embarrassing moment." Just as bad are those speech topics that are selected to develop confidence (but that do nothing to foster competence and hence, do not work) and that aim at making the speaker merely a skillful or even deceitful salesman. Such speaking encourages the least possible growth in both the speaker and his audience.

Criteria for Selecting Problems

But what is a "significant" problem? To offer pontifically a succinct definition might be to omit some problems of importance. We cannot say, for example, that a significant problem is one that influences a large number of people—a national or international problem, for example. For local, even personal problems that occur in the classroom, the college, or the community likewise take their toll and should be recognized and solved. We will, therefore, offer some criteria, and if a problem meets any one of these, it may be worth speaking about:

1. A significant problem may be one that has caused the decline of a previous civilization. The problems of war, poverty, caste, tyranny, and disease are the classic problems of humanity, and wherever one finds civilizations in decline, one or more of these problems was a significant part of the cause.
2. A significant problem is one that has caused or causes human suffering.
3. A significant problem is one that limits human achievement.
4. A significant problem is one that, when solved, releases new energy.
5. A significant problem is one that prevents growth and development.
6. A significant problem is one that forces on us an important choice.

In any event, the kinds of problems that are worth solving vary from personal to international, from agricultural to zoological, from economic to spiritual, from political to religious. The array is vast, but the rewards for selecting the most significant problems are great, and the penalties for failing to do so are terrifying.

A classification of these problems will help point out their variety and thus, perhaps, encourage better choices. Problems may be classified as

(1) timely or timeless, (2) conscious or unconscious, and as (3) survival or growth problems.

Timely and Timeless Problems

The kinds of problems one reads about in the newspapers and magazines are, generally, timely problems—problems of shortages and surpluses, floods and famines, strikes and lockouts, accidents and wars. These problems are urgent problems, but they are problems that change, disappear, or increase. In 1932, for example, the timely problems were how to prevent banks from closing, how to restore employment, and how to increase purchasing power. By 1942, the timely problems had changed drastically: They were how to win the war against Germany and Japan, how to keep prices down, and how to prevent strikes in defense industries. By 1952, the problems had again changed: They were how to reduce agricultural surpluses, how to make the world secure against the aggression of our former ally, the Soviet Union, and how to win the war in Korea. In 1962, the problems again changed so that they were how to restore full employment, how to desegregate the schools, how to get the Soviet missiles out of Cuba, and how to land the first man on the moon. In a few years, they will have changed again. But although these problems change quickly, there is no reason to disregard them. Nor is there the slightest reason to think, if we ignored them, that they would go away. Soviet missiles in Cuba are no longer a problem—they have been removed—but if we had ignored them they would not have been. So is it with timely problems. They demand our attention, and unless we give it, these problems can become chronic. By quick recognition, careful diagnosis, and a bit of luck, we can render these problems short-lived.

Some problems, however, are and will be present in any age. They are problems such as "How should a man live?" or "What are the potentials and limitations of the human being?" or "What is a just society?" or "What is the significance of art?" or "How can a society provide for the individuality of its members, and yet maintain order?" These are questions each generation must answer, and does answer, although the answers are usually not carefully thought out. These questions were also asked 2,000 or more years ago; the Egyptians answered the same questions as did the Greeks and Aztecs after them.

Timeless problems are thought, in our culture, to be "impractical." Timeless questions are ignored by the super-practical man, because like philosophy, "they bake no bread." In other words, they do not tell us what to do in a specific situation, they do not increase our earning power, nor do they usually contribute to our prestige, at least not until recently. The practical man doesn't know it, but he has already made up his mind about the timeless problems—and has done so without the careful scrutiny he would give a business deal. Although timeless problems have been thought of as unessential in our culture, the relative interest in timely and timeless problems is reversed in a few oriental cultures. In our own culture, the timeless is not studied in school, although bookkeeping is and so, too, is cooking. For these reasons, Western peoples have more difficulty understanding and discussing timeless problems.

Nevertheless, timeless problems are extremely important, because underlying each timely problem are one or more timeless problems. "How much should the city spend on the art museum?" is a timely question. But the answer must—or should, at any rate—depend on an answer to the question, "What is the significance of art in human life?" If art is merely a means for momentary escape, for a bit of variety or for amusement only, then perhaps we should not spent so much as if art is a means of symbolizing ideas that cannot be put in words but that can be communicated through color and form. "How much should we tax people to support the schools?" is another practical question, but underlying the various answers is the timeless problem of "What is the significance of education?" "What should our foreign policy be?" is a timely problem, but underlying it are questions such as "What are our responsibilities to the rest of humanity?" and "How may we guarantee the responsibilities of others toward us?"

The timeless problems of living have generally been neglected by our culture. College students will find it easier to prepare a speech on a timely problem, yet we hope that these more neglected permanent problems will prompt some to speak about them. Each age gives new answers and re-examines old answers. A speaker who would speak well in the twentieth century must be informed about timeless questions and the answers given by different ages. If our speakers will impress on our people the significance of these timeless problems, perhaps education will respond by helping our people understand the often unnoticed but, nevertheless, demanding timeless problems; for these, too, determine our successes and failures.

Conscious and Unconscious Problems

We are relatively aware that war is a problem, that education can be improved, that periodic inflation and deflation pose threats to our economy, that medical care is not always so good nor so universally available as it should be, and that our air and rivers are polluted. We are conscious of these problems, for they are discussed in our newspapers, over radio and television, and sometimes even from the pulpit. They rightly deserve our attention, and we must work toward solutions of them.

Some problems, however, are not so clearly seen as these; they are problems of which humanity does not seem aware. Sometimes it takes centuries to bring one of these problems to consciousness. Slavery did not seem to be a problem to the Greeks; Aristotle avowed that some men were destined to servitude, and that destiny seemed perfectly natural to him. But by the 1860's in the United States, through the influence of the abolitionists and with the effect of *Uncle Tom's Cabin*, slavery became a significant enough problem so that thousands enlisted in the Union Army to end the problem. Cruel and inhuman treatment of children seemed no problem early in the nineteenth century, but with the novels of Charles Dickens portraying the plight of the child, legislation was soon enacted to ensure the safety of children.

We are made conscious of problems, not so much, at first, by writers of polemics, but often by artists, sculptors, poets, and novelists. Much later, do these problems receive consideration from philosophers, and long after the sensitive artist has tried to symbolize the problem, psychologists, sociologists, and news commentators take up the problem. To take an example, the idea that life is becoming mechanized and therefore somewhat subhuman seems first to have been reflected by cubist painters and musical composers about the turn of the century. (Soren Kierkegaard, the Danish philosopher, had anticipated the problem, but he was largely ignored, suggesting perhaps that unconscious problems are best first depicted by less discursive forms than philosophy until the people have been prepared by poets, artists, and musicians for discursive consideration.) After 1900, ten or more years elapsed, during which time artists were depicting the mechanization of life; then, novelists such as Franz Kafka and H. G. Wells, wrote about how life was becoming more and more meaningless and increasingly more dehumanized, despite our proudly proclaimed progress and, indeed, precisely because of this progress. Still later, by the middle of the century, certain philosophers—usually existentialists and phenomenologists—began to find a growing sense of alienation, loneliness, and futility in modern life. Eventually, psychologists and sociologists brought the skills of their professional orientation to the problem. Today, among educated people, the problem is well known. Thus, unconscious problems are recognized slowly, and usually noted first by the artist, the poet, the novelist, and only later by politicians, editorial writers, and polemicists.

To discover problems that exist but of which we are unconscious, the speaker must cultivate the study of art, music, and of contemporary writing other than that found in news magazines and even in the best idea magazines. He should try to discover what men are trying to reflect or symbolize in art and music; he should read the most advanced contemporary writers, especially those who are men of uncommon sensitivity. Perhaps through these media, he will learn to look at our society more clearly and will be able to keep in mind that there are problems of which we are not yet aware that must, one day, be the subject for discursive discourse.

Survival and Growth Problems

Certain kinds of problems must be solved in some degree if we are to live at all. The problem of obtaining safe and clean food in adequate amounts to support life is a "survival" problem. The dangers of food contaminated by poor handling and by super-pesticides, of polluted water and air, of dangers from home accidents, and of automobile and industrial accidents constitute survival problems. The classic problems that seem to have destroyed all previous civilizations—war, poverty, caste, disease, and tyranny—are survival problems and are of enormous significance. In our own times, these problems seem to increase in number, and they must be met if we are to survive and to live securely.

Yet even if we were to solve *all* these problems, if we were all to have full—and even overfull—stomachs, and to be as safe as a baby in his crib, we would still find life unsatisfying, for when our survival needs are reasonably well met, a new set of needs arise. These needs we will call *growth* problems, as does A. H. Maslow.[4] These problems are unique to human beings, for no cat or dog, nor even the highest of the apes, seem to encounter them. To man, life must offer more than a full stomach, or be unsatisfying and uninteresting. According to Maslow, once man has enough to eat and can live with security, he begins to feel the need for more than food and security; the next step in the ladder of growing needs is that, after experiencing reasonable security in his survival needs, he then feels the need for love, for affection, and for admiration from others. But once this need is reasonably well met, still another set of growth needs emerge; he then feels the call of more "higher" needs: perhaps he wishes to make sense out of his world, or wishes to interpret the world in art, music, or literature. At any rate, when certain basic needs are met, man begins to feel the pressure to create, to build, to grow, to understand, to symbolize, to compose; the call of the trinity of Western culture—the good, the true, and the beautiful—is most fully manifest in those whose needs for survival and whose needs for others have been somewhat gratified. The higher, more philosophic needs permit man to rise to new levels, and lead man to evolve in directions impossible for other animals. These growth needs offer man the possibility of continuing the transformation of himself and his society beyond any known limit.

But the growth problems of an individual or of a society are not easy to

[4] *Motivation and Personality*, New York, Harper and Brothers, 1954, Chapter 8.

locate. A frustration of growth needs does not cause the same kind of pain that a frustration of the lower needs does. When a man is thirsty, his nervous system leaves no doubt in his consciousness that he needs water. When he is in pain, the nervous system can usually help tell him what is wrong. But a frustration of a higher need is often ambiguous, and may result in behavior that does not solve the growth problem. When, for example, a man suffers from being misunderstood, or when he suffers from not being accepted and liked by others, there is no specific set of nerve endings that make this need clear to him. Even though his greatest need is for acceptance by others, he may become antisocial and behave as if friends were the last thing he wanted. Higher growth problems are even less possible to feel than this psychological problem, and are harder to diagnose. Yet their vague call is powerful, especially today. Today we have full stomachs, and grow richer every year, but we hunger for a vague something, and life is somehow boring. Our growth needs, today, are at their all-time high. If we locate and gratify them, we can create, build, understand, and thus transform ourselves into something uniquely and grandly human. Despite the press of our survival problems, let us try to locate some of the needs we have that will lead us to new levels of existence.

Education and the Location of Problems

An intelligent speaker must be on the outlook for significant problems —whether they are timely or timeless, conscious or unconscious, survival or growth problems. He must constantly consult the best thinking of the best minds both in our age and in the past. He must read widely, wisely, and well; he must observe and feel; and he must think about what he has read, observed, and felt. He should study problems in his college work, and can find valuable information about economic, political, social, and international problems in his courses. He should study literature, at least because it abounds in reactions to problems, particularly to philosophical and ethical problems. He should study history and anthropology to discover how other peoples have responded to their problems or failed to respond. At all events, he must learn much, for only if he does will he be able to speak intelligently about the problems that confront us and that might, one day, destroy us.

Thus the starting point of good speaking must be the speaker's own education, and not a search for some magic formula of rhetoric, for some trick that will make people listen, or for some device that will persuade. If the speaker, instead, speaks from his deep understanding of problems, he will find his speech colored by the sense of values he is developing in a way that no bag of tricks nor cheap attention-getting devices can earn for him. Rather, the audience will listen because they perceive the significance of his ideas and not because he has tricked them into listening. Thus the starting point for good speaking springs from intelligent choice of ideas, from careful reading and study, and from a constant willingness to search for the significant.

PRESENTING PROBLEMS TO AUDIENCES

Once a speaker has decided to speak on a certain problem, he must search for ways of leading an audience to grasp the importance of that problem. Certain general ideas will enable an audience to recognize and feel the significance of a problem.[5] The speaker should try to use each of the lines of argument to see which units work best for his speech. Quite obviously he will find that some applications of a particular line of argument will be fruitless, but he will also find those lines of argument that *do* yield usable discourse and that will help him to compose some effective units. The speaker must, however, be selective. He should *use as few of the lines of argument as possible,* because he can gain impact from selecting the best ideas if he supports these intensively with statistics, examples, testimony, and the like. Therefore, the speaker should select the best and most effective methods of leading the audience to accept his problem as important and supply a barrage of support for them.

To locate the one or two lines of argument that are best to use, the speaker should attempt to select those that are *most appropriate to the problem, to the audience, to the occasion on which the speech will be given, and to the speaker himself.* These four aspects of the speech situation should govern his choice of the following lines of argument:

1. *Show that the problem is a source of danger, suffering, or degradation to those who experience it.* If your problem is the world food supply, you can help us feel its importance if you illustrate it by showing what it is like to be a member of a starving family in India, or by giving statistics about the shortage of food throughout the world, or by supplying the testimony of experts on the shortage of food. We recognize a problem as important when we know that it is hurting others. *But we recognize the problem even more clearly when we understand that these people who suffer are like ourselves.* Speakers must remind us that the sufferers have some of the same aims, hopes, fears, and troubles that we do, that they are hurt by

[5] The reader who is rhetorically sophisticated will recognize in these general ideas, a remnant of the old idea of *topoi,* which, when used in moderation, will help the student direct his energy and will suggest ideas he might not otherwise have thought of using.

the same things, or that they make the same mistakes that we do. If then, you can show that the problem causes suffering, and can show that the sufferers' goals, aspirations, and needs are like our own, you may tend to lead the audience to recognize the problem.

2. *Show that the problem, directly or indirectly, injures the audience.* Most of the great problems of other people do influence us because our world is tied together by communication, transportation, and commerce. When a man anywhere in the world is poor, he cannot buy from our industries and thus cannot help keep our own people employed. When a man anywhere in the world is degraded to the extent that his abilities cannot function, the world, although it may never be aware of it, has lost those abilities. When suffering embitters men, the world loses those who might influence their associates to be more understanding and more compassionate. Sometimes we have not understood our relatedness to others. In the 1920's some people considered it humorous to joke about the starving Chinese on the other side of the earth. Some of those who joked lived to see their sons die in Korea and Vietnam fighting those embittered by starvation.

The intelligent speaker must find support for the idea that the problems of others are the problems of us all. He must locate the facts and let his imagination work to see the relation between others and his audience. It may not be easy to show a comfortably seated audience that the pains of others are the problems of each of us, but it is one of the surest ways to arouse interest in a problem.

3. *Show that the problem prevents the operation of an ideal and growth toward it.* In these days of two cars in many garages and a sirloin on every barbecue grill, we yet sense that something is lacking in our lives. Life is more than riding in a big car, more than overeating, and more than gratifying the obvious natural urges. We have spoken of these "higher" needs previously. Life is unsatisfying when we cannot create and feel creative, when we cannot make sense out of the multiplicity and chaos of the universe, or when contentment with physical comforts begins to breed boredom and emptiness of soul. The man with the full stomach recognizes, vaguely, that he is still empty, and if his stomach is not too full, he will begin the search anew. But as we have seen, these uniquely human desires are not easy to recognize because there is no sense organ connected with them to bring specific pain. The hungry man feels hunger pangs, but the uncreative man feels no specific pain, and is more like an unfeeling apple that rots while still hanging on the tree. Yet everywhere, even in the savage state, man will still invent art if it is absent. Men blocked from creativity in their jobs will find an outlet, however distorted, in their family, in their sports, or in their hobbies until, when age takes its toll, their creativity is permanently smothered. Somehow, in the late

twentieth century, we begin to realize that man does not live by bread alone. Today books about ideals, philosophy, religion, art, ethics, and values are selling better than ever before; presumably, some of these books are being read. One can notice a hunger in audiences for intelligent consideration of values and ideals. If the speaker can locate the ideals that have potency in our time and show that a problem prevents the operation of these values, audiences will listen. This process requires maturity and intelligence, but it is an effective one.

4. *Show that the problem is a fundamental one.* If you can show us that the problem is fundamental because it causes other problems, we will listen. Poverty, war, caste, disease, and tyranny have destroyed whole civilizations in the past; yet perhaps these problems are not *fundamental.* A religious leader can insist that they are manifestations of the failure to be our brother's keeper. A scientist may insist that they are all the result of failure to use intelligent sources of investigation to find the facts. A politician may insist that they are the result of the wrong economic system, and a good democrat might insist that if the democratic system were practiced, the people might solve their own problems. All of these are attempts to show that some other formulation is more fundamental. We will listen if we think a particular problem is more fundamental in the sense that it may engender other problems.

5. *Show that the problem is recognized by others.* Many experiments in psychology and sociology show how we are influenced by the opinions of others. Sherif has done some of the most clever work on this matter with what he calls the "auto-kinetic" effect.[6] If you are in a totally dark room, and a tiny light the size of a grain of wheat is turned on, the light will seem to move. The light, of course, is stationary, but the uncontrollably jerky movements of one's eyes make it seem to move. Because the room is so dark, no one can tell how far the light "moves." Now suppose a group of five are put into the room, and four of them are told to say that they believe that the light moves about two feet, but the fifth man is unaware of this deception. Generally, on hearing the responses of the other four, this fifth man will also report that the light moves about two feet. We tend to recognize things in the way that those about us recognize them. Thus if we can show that others recognize a problem, we can be more certain of convincing an audience of its importance.

But there are sound and unsound, ethical and unethical ways of using this technique. Audiences are not influenced by everyone who recognizes a problem. An audience may be influenced, however, if those who recognize the problem are highly regarded by that audience. In a famous speech at

[6] Muzafer Sherif, *An Outline of Social Psychology,* New York, Harper and Brothers, 1948, p. 266.

Cooper Union, Abraham Lincoln argued that the federal government had a right to control slavery in federal territory. Lincoln demonstrated that "our fathers who framed the Constitution" understood the problem as he interpreted it; he did so with thorough research into the actions the signers of the Constitution took on slavery in specific cases; inasmuch as the majority of the signers acted to limit the extension of slavery in some way or another, his argument showed that those the audience admired disapproved of slavery. Lincoln's appeal was more elaborate and painstaking than the hackneyed appeal to "the founding fathers" by the Fourth-of-July orator or the office seeker. Audiences are not much impressed by an attempt to show that "experts"—unnamed and unqualified —endorse a certain program of action or a certain brand of toothpaste. Use of such techniques merits the cool reception that an intelligent audience will give the sophistic speaker. Thus this method of bringing an audience to recognize what others have recognized, in the hands of the TV announcer or the ward-heeling politician, may not represent the application of intelligence to speaking. Yet men such as Abraham Lincoln could use it intelligently, effectively, and with originality. Try it, but use it well.

6. *Show that the problem makes our society or the institutions in it operate less effectively than they should.* We often recognize the importance of a problem by realizing that it causes our government, educational system, family system, or businesses to function poorly. These kinds of problems are called *dysfunctional* problems because they pervert, render ineffective, or slow down the operation of needed institutions. Thus one can show how corruption in government delivers power to those who should not have power, or how the rising divorce rate threatens children who ought to be free from the neurotic manifestations of insecurity. This method, of course, requires knowledge of how our institutions work. No simple, unsupported assertion that a problem may bring about a malfunction of an institution will be effective. The student must corroborate the assertion with examples, testimony, and other support to show that the problem causes a maladjustment of one or more of our institutions. When carefully substantiated, the method can be convincing, but the student who is unable to develop such support should not use this method.

7. *Other methods.* One can show that a problem interferes with certain goals of the audience, or that the audience itself has once before been harmed by the problem, or that the removal of the problem would produce a better life, or that the problem is increasing. We have not exhausted the methods by which people come to recognize problems, and in the last analysis the speaker must select and tailor the method he uses so that it fits *himself,* his *audience,* his *problem,* and the *situation* in which he gives his speech. An experienced speaker will prefer to avoid formulas, and will select the method of making audiences recognize problems by

searching his audience, himself, the problem, and the occasion to find that which fits all four most appropriately.

A free society probably has the best chance to select the most important problems. Problems, in such a society, are chosen by voters who have heard many speakers on many sides talking about many problems. In such a milieu, we are more apt to make an intelligent selection of the most important problems and to come to recognize the superficial and false problems. Thus a free people can define and select for themselves the problems they feel are the most pressing. Herein lies one of the great strengths of a democratic society over an authoritarian society. But the intelligent choice of problems demands intelligent speakers and intelligent listeners. It demands that speakers occasionally be willing to risk a stand for unpopular causes. It demands an electorate willing to listen even to ideas to which they are opposed. It demands that speakers frequently become teachers rather than mere persuaders. But the rewards are worth it, both in achievement and in one's personal satisfaction.

Problems and the Future

We have seen that problems cause suffering, degradation, and decay. But we have also seen that intelligent solutions to problems may bring a new burst of energy and a new level of life. If, in our time, speakers can help channel the energy of the people of Western culture behind the solution of these problems, the quality of our civilization may make unprecedented improvements. The great problems of our time would then be met by a people who are rich, powerful, free, and gifted; the problems might not only be removed so that our survival may be ensured, and better ensured than ever before, but it may also be that we shall have created a new society—one, and perhaps the only one in history, that deserved survival. The attempt is worth the effort.

Problem Speech Assignment

Introduction

Problems cause human suffering, the degradation of human beings, and the stultification and decay of civilizations. But an intelligent and vigorous attempt to solve problems stimulates thought, reduces the threat of a problem, creates new energy, and permits life to begin at a new level. It is imperative that we recognize problems and their importance. We will not solve our problems unless our speakers can help direct our energy toward these problems. The aim of this assignment is to enable a speaker to recognize a significant problem and to lead an audience to understand its importance.

Assignment

Give a four- to six-minute speech in which you select a significant problem and make the significance of this problem clear and vivid to the audience.

At the conclusion of the speech, there will be a question period. To be sure that there is at least one question for you, arrange with a member of the audience to ask you one.

Note: No solution is required for this speech. The solution should be omitted in most cases. Sometimes, however, the solution may be so obvious that it would be inappropriate to omit stating it. In such cases, you may present a one-sentence solution at the end of the speech. No further development than that involved in a single sentence, however, is acceptable, because most of the time should be spent on the techniques of presenting the problem. Nor should the causes of the problem be discussed. The only objective is to make the problem clear, vivid, and important to the audience.

Technique of Presenting Problems

You should select those methods of leading an audience to understand the urgency of a problem that are most appropriate to you, to your problem, to your audience, and to the occasion on which you speak. *You should select only a few of the most important methods, and support each intensively.* Among these techniques are the following:

1. Show that the problem is a source of danger, suffering, or degradation to those who experience it.
2. Show that the problem, directly or indirectly, injures the audience.
3. Show that the problem prevents the operation of an ideal and growth toward it.
4. Show that the problem is a fundamental one.
5. Show that the problem is recognized by others.
6. Show that the problem makes society or its institutions operate less effectively than they should.
7. Use whatever other methods are appropriate to the speaker, the audience, the problem, or the occasion on which the speech is to be given.

Subjects

One of the functions of a course in speech is to help you make your own decisions about which problems are most important. Therefore, no list of subjects is presented. One's judgment of which problems are the most important should be the outcome of intelligent study, of discussion, and of debate. The subjects a speaker considers important should evolve gradually, and as the speaker becomes wiser, should change. Moreover, as the speaker himself reads and listens to other speakers, he will be in a better position to select that which is important and to recognize false or less important problems. Hence, a list of what the authors consider the important problems would defeat this purpose of developing a sense of values in the student.

10 | Thinking and Speaking About Causes[1]

Consider a typical, though hypothetical, suburbanite trying to start his gasoline-powered lawn mower. At first, he thinks causally. After turning the engine over several times without starting it, he uses his knowledge of possible causes by looking into the gasoline tank to see if there is fuel. Then he turns the engine over several more times. He still is causally oriented, for then he checks to see if the wire is attached to the spark plug. It is. He turns the engine over and over again without getting so much as a "pop" from it. But depending on his mental state at the time and the heat of the day, he now begins to drop good causal analysis and indiscriminately pushes and pulls various levers or adjusts fuel valves in an attempt to try anything. But with each failure, his actions become less intelligent. At last, he addresses the machine with special epithets reserved for such situations, but his language has no effect, except on the passersby. Finally, he gives the machine a swift kick of exasperation, and surrenders by calling the repair man. The repair man behaves differently; because his living depends on his ability to locate causes, he follows a systematic procedure

[1] This chapter was previously published in a different form by Otis M. Walter in *Today's Speech*, IX (September, 1961) pp. 12–14; 31 and (November, 1961), pp. 20–21; 29, and is presented here by permission of the editor.

for doing so until he discovers that the magneto points are corroded and therefore, the engine cannot produce a spark. The solution is simple: replace the points, and the engine will start at once. *Solutions often require that one locate the cause; when the cause of a problem is discovered, its solution often becomes obvious.*

Although the analysis of causes is indispensable to problem solving, we often behave toward the problems of our day as does the suburbanite. Instead of using careful causal analysis, we fail to understand the causes of inflation and deflation, or to understand how to help underdeveloped nations make their country economically strong, or the causes of crime, of school drop-outs, and similar problems. Legislators fail to grasp the causes of the problems for which they propose bills, teachers forget to analyze the causes of their students' failures, and students, likewise, are less apt to respond to a poor grade by a searching causal analysis than by anger or by feelings of defeat. Too frequently, when the causes of a problem are not understood and removed, the problems stubbornly remain.[2] If we are to solve our problems, we must learn (1) to discover the causes of our problems, (2) to look habitually and automatically for causes, and (3) to lead an audience to understand these causes. Only when we do these things can we speak intelligently about problems. Not without reason did Aristotle avow that the test of one's wisdom is whether or not one can understand the causes of events.

Methods of Analyzing Causes

There are two basic approaches to the analysis of causes, and each type can be broken into various subtypes:

1. Explaining *how or why* a cause operates *by describing the conditions that produce an effect.*
2. Demonstrating *that* a cause operates *by showing that a cause and effect are associated.*

One might, for example, explain that insulin causes a reduction of diabetic symptoms by either of the two methods. To use the first method, one might describe the chain of conditions that the injection of insulin produces:

1. The injection of insulin into the blood stream increases the permeability of the body cells to blood sugar.

[2] Sometimes problems can be solved by treating the symptoms of the problem, as we will see in the next chapter. But we can best judge whether we must treat symptoms or the causes of a problem *after* the causes have been discovered. Hence, good problem solving usually requires that we try to locate the causes of the problem.

2. Because more blood sugar can permeate these cells, it is removed from the blood stream where it can cause damage.
3. Once the blood sugar is inside the cells, it can be oxidized.
4. When blood sugar is oxidized, it becomes carbon dioxide and water, which the system can remove easily.

Thus we have explained *how* insulin operates to reduce diabetic symptoms by describing the conditions that produce the effect.

We could also use the second method, showing that a cause and effect are associated: we would have to present evidence to show that whenever diabetics take insulin, their symptoms decrease. In so doing, we would not show *why* the symptoms decreased, but we would be certain still, *that* insulin can reduce them. Thus the second method does not tell us *why* the symptoms decreased, but only *that* they did. Either method is convincing, and both together are especially strong.

Let us examine another illustration of these two contrasting methods. In the famous, and perhaps legendary, experiment at the Leaning Tower of Pisa, Galileo refuted the notion that gravity causes bodies to fall with a speed proportional to their weight. Which method of causal analysis was he using? In dropping the weights over the side of the Tower he showed that bodies of different weight *did* hit the ground at the same time, but he did not show *why*. Thus he was clearly using the second method. To understand *why* they fall at the same speed, one must remember that heavy weights have more inertia than light ones—it takes more energy to move a heavy load than a light one. As the heavy weight falls, it has a greater pull of gravity on it, but because it has more inertia, it takes more pull to get it moving. The greater inertia of the heavier body exactly balances the greater pull of gravity. Inasmuch as the heavier body's greater inertia exactly balances its greater pull, it falls no faster than the light weight.

The student should try to find additional illustrations of each of the two methods. If he can do so, he is more apt to understand them and to see that both are useful and both have limitations. Each of these methods now requires a closer examination.

Methods of Describing Conditions that Produce an Effect

There are two variations of our first method of demonstrating a cause. These two should be clearly understood and will be of use to speakers who wish to show an audience the causes of certain problems.

THE CHAIN OF CAUSES

In some cases, a cause will produce a chain reaction. In our previous illustration of how insulin reduces diabetic symptoms, we used a four-step chain inaugurated by the increased permeability of cell membranes to sugar, leading to the result that diabetic symptoms were reduced. We might use a similar chain to explain why carbon monoxide causes death:

1. Carbon monoxide, when inhaled, reaches the lungs where it forms a compound with hemoglobin.
2. This compound makes it impossible for the hemoglobin to absorb free oxygen.
3. Because the hemoglobin cannot carry oxygen to the tissues, the organism dies of asphyxia.

Such a chain of reasoning shows how a cause leads to a result by breaking the cause into discrete units that form a series of causes, as depicted in the following diagram.

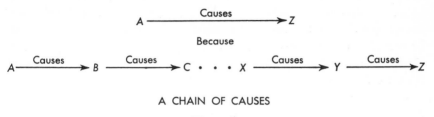

A CHAIN OF CAUSES

Figure 5.

Thus, the chain of causes can be used to show an audience how one factor may cause another in a relatively simple and understandable series of steps.

LISTING MULTIPLE CAUSES

Not all phenomena in human affairs can be easily explained by a simple chain of causes because in some problems many causes may operate to produce an effect. In describing the downfall of Greek civilization, for example, one cannot single out one supremely important factor because many factors operated to produce downfall. (Fig. 6.) Among the forces

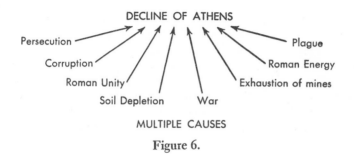

MULTIPLE CAUSES

Figure 6.

that led to the weakening of Greek culture are the following: the Greeks persecuted their best thinkers; the Peloponnesian Wars wasted the vitality and manhood of Greece; a plague destroyed at least one third of Athens' population; the soil became depleted; the silver mines at Laurium became exhausted; the Greeks were confronted with a physically more energetic and more unified people; political corruption dissipated Athens' strength; and so on. Thus multiple causes instead of a simple chain produced the result.

Many contemporary problems have multiple causes. Juvenile crime, for example, has several causes, some of which operate in one particular juvenile delinquent, and some of which do not. Thus the tension produced by broken homes or poverty, the lack of socially acceptable ways of finding adventure, serious psychological maladjustment in the parents or the juvenile, the lack of an acceptable adult model for the juvenile, the influence of the juvenile gang, and an unchallenging school environment, may all operate in various ways to encourage delinquent behavior. In such cases, the speaker should be aware of the many factors that produce the effect; *he should mention that there are many* to the audience, but *he need not present each one* and probably *should confine his speech to one or two of the most significant causes.*

After mentioning a cause, the speaker may have to explain it. For example, one might sketch the ways in which the depletion of the silver mines at Laurium contributed to the decline of Athens:

A medium of exchange greatly increases the possibilities for creating wealth. Money is necessary to make money. Several reasons account for this fact: First, the nation without a medium of exchange must do its business by barter; that is, it must trade, for example, grain for wine. When it barters, it must buy and sell *in the same place*. But with a money economy, one may sell where the price is highest and may buy where the price is lowest. Thus nations using a medium of exchange can become richer nations than those who only barter. When Athens exhausted her silver mines, she exhausted her best single source for the coinage of money; money was hard to get and trade suffered.

But a medium of exchange has other ways of increasing the wealth of a nation. Wealth is not only the value of all goods and services in the country, but is also in part dependent upon the *number of times* the wealth changes hands. It is easier for wealth to change hands in a money economy than in a barter economy. More goods can be bought and sold in a money economy, and therefore, more people can be employed; the employed people will, themselves, spend more money, which will further increase the turnover of wealth. With the exhaustion of the mines that produced her medium of exchange, the ability of Athens to reap the benefits of a thriving business life were more limited than before. She was not so rich, and she would suffer for it.

CLARITY

Whether one is using a chain of causes or listing multiple causes, he must take care to be clear. In order to be clear to an audience, the speaker must first order his own thoughts; only then can he clearly explain causes to his audience. This clarity can be achieved, in part, by *stating each causal element in a separate sentence.* Thus, if one is using a chain of causes, or a list of multiple causes, each factor should be stated in a carefully phrased sentence so that the audience can understand that factor with the least effort.

Moreover, understanding will more likely be achieved if the speaker, while stating a sentence that gives the cause of something, *watches his listeners carefully* for cues indicating that he may have failed to communicate. If he senses that several listeners have not grasped the idea, he may wish to repeat it or to restate it in different words.

Finally, realizing that even strongly motivated, intelligent listeners appreciate occasional reiterations, the speaker who has a complicated chain of causes or a long list of multiple factors should *summarize frequently enough so that the audience will be able to keep the formulations clearly in mind.*

SUPPORT OF ALLEGED CAUSES

Any statement of a cause is a generalization, and generalizations are generally dull. Moreover, generalizations depend for validity on the evidence that can be marshalled to support them. (There are a few exceptions, but they are not very important in speaking.) The mere assertion of a cause is generally not sufficient to convince or interest an audience. Especially when the audience is dubious of an alleged cause, must that causal statement be supported by a barrage of convincing material.

Review the methods of support, as treated in Chapter 3; nearly all these methods can be used to support causal statements. Here are some of them.

The *detailed example* can be used. If you wish to support the idea that psychotherapy can treat alcoholism effectively, you might support this causal idea with an example of an alcoholic who underwent a full course of treatment: tell us of his state before treatment, of his gradually increasing insight into the causes of his drinking, of his ability to remove or control these causes as treatment progressed, and of his final release from the problem.

Undetailed examples can be used to support causal generalizations. If you wish to refute the idea that socialism causes a country to become communistic, you might use undetailed examples as follows:

If socialism leads to communism, why are the countries that seem the least in danger of becoming communistic Norway, Sweden, Denmark, The Netherlands, Belgium, England, Canada, Australia, and New Zealand? All these countries are socialistic, and not one of them is in danger of becoming communistic.

But most of the nations that have become communistic—Estonia, Latvia, Lithuania, Poland, Czechoslovakia, Hungary, Roumania, Yugoslavia, Bulgaria, and Albania—all were once capitalistic. Only two—Russia and China—were not, and they were feudal states. If so many socialist nations are safe from communism and so many capitalistic nations are now communistic, where do we get the idea that socialism leads to communism?

Sometimes an audience can be led to accept an alleged cause by means of an *hypothetical example*. For instance, one might explain how the lack of a satisfactory adult model could contribute to delinquency:

Consider the kinds of adults that delinquents know. Take Johnny, who is an adolescent of the Lower Hill district. The adults who Johnny knew were, first, his father who was too tired, too bored, too worried, and too often drunk to serve as a model. The second was his mother, understandably a drudge and too bitter to be attractive. In addition, he knew his teachers who were, for the most part, harassed maiden-ladies whose prime concerns were the prevention of disciplinary problems. Finally, the only other adult he knew was the policeman on the corner whose restrictive arm was a barrier to the boy's antisocial expressions of freedom. These represented the mature adult world to Johnny. He does not want to be like them, and he will not be. And we shall pay the price.

Hypothetical examples can be found in good drama or good novels, or can be constructed by the speaker himself.

Statistics can also be used to support causal statements. If one asserts that more policemen on the beat can reduce the crime rate, he can use the statistics from an experiment in police protection in New York City.[3]

In a tenement district with a high crime rate, the number of policemen was increased from 248 to 613 for three months. During that time serious crime dropped from 1,102 in the same four months the previous year, to a low of 448—a decrease of 55 per cent. Muggings were nearly stopped, and the tough 25th Precinct became one of the most orderly areas in New York City.

Testimony can, of course, be used to support a cause. Whenever experts know and understand causes, use their testimony. In using testimony, explain exactly why the authority is to be believed, for his qualifications

[3] Taken from an article by Richard Dougherty, "The Case for the Cop," *Harper's Magazine*, CCXXVII (April, 1964), pp. 129–132.

help make his testimony believable. Wring all the deserved authority possible out of an expert by explaining the experiences he has had that make him an expert.

Both *literal and figurative analogies* can be used to support causes. The literal analogy can be used when the situations are basically similar. If, in England, socialized medicine causes an increase in good health—or doesn't —one may argue that it would do the same here. If a course in speed reading increases the academic ability of thirty college students who took the course, one may argue that it might benefit you. But so can the figurative analogy be used. James Jeans in *Philosophy and Physics* explained why the sky is blue by using an analogy with waves.

When you stand at the shore of an ocean and watch the waves come in, you notice that the small waves, when they hit a post in the water or a large rock, are bounced back, and reflected from the obstacle. The larger ones, on the other hand, roll over the object and continue their course. Light, too, can be thought of as consisting of wave motion. The long waves—those at the red end of the spectrum—"roll" over the obstacles they encounter. But the shorter waves—at the blue end of the spectrum—are reflected by the tiny dust particles that fill the atmosphere. From these dust particles, only the blue light is reflected so that it enters our eyes from every angle of the sky and makes the sky look blue.

The Method of Consequences

One of the more complicated ways of supporting a chain of causes is by the *method of consequences*. The method of consequences requires that one support a given causal statement by finding additional consequences of cause. One looks for signs of the cause operating. Thus one might believe that someone caused the murder of another person, and he would look for signs—additional consequences. The alleged murderer would have to have been present; he would have no alibi that could be supported; he would have left clues to his presence. The following is a detailed example of the method of consequences. A recent theory of the origin of ice ages, devised by Maurice Ewing and William Donn,[4] leads to the surprising conclusion that ice ages are not caused by an increase in cold weather, but instead by warm weather. The theory first of all involves the assertion of a chain of causes:

1. As the great glaciers have been melting for 11,000 years, they add more water to the slowly rising ocean.
2. As the oceans rise, the shallow shelf between Greenland and Europe

---

[4] An interesting popular account of the theory can be found in "The Coming Ice Age," *Harper's Magazine*, CCVII (December, 1958), pp. 39–45, by Betty Friedan.

becomes deeper, permitting the Gulf Stream to flow into the Arctic Ocean. The warm Gulf Stream slowly melts the Arctic ice cap.

3. Once the ice cap is melted, water from the Arctic Ocean can be evaporated into the earth's atmosphere and more precipitation falls all over the earth.

4. Some of this precipitation falls in the form of snow in the Northern Hemisphere where it accumulates faster than it can melt.

5. As snow accumulates, the level of the ocean falls to the point where the Gulf Stream can no longer flow into the Arctic and the Ocean freezes over. Less precipitation falls all over the earth.

6. Because less snow falls than can be melted, the glaciers melt with the result that the level of the oceans slowly begins to rise, and the cycle starts over.

Support for this theory is hard to find because direct observations of what happened in the past several thousand years are not possible. But the theory can be supported by looking for *consequences* that we would *expect* to find, if the theory were correct. If link number one were true, we would expect that the oceans would have been much lower 11,000 years ago than they are now. Geologists tell us, that at that time, the earth's oceans were 300 to 400 feet below their present level, thus supporting this link. If link number two were correct, we would expect that the ice cap over the Arctic would be getting thinner all the time; measurements, in fact, indicate that the cap is the thinnest it has been since man has begun measuring it. If link number three is correct, we would predict that much more rain would have fallen 11,000 years ago than falls now. What do we find? We find that at that time, *even the Sahara was a grassland*, again supporting the theory. Additional consequences that might be expected are strongly supportive: The snows that cover northern North America, northern Europe, and northern Asia are ancient in origin, and little fresh snow has fallen there in recent centuries. In addition, it is clear that the oceans have suddenly become warm, as is indicated by pink layers of tiny warm-water animals—as one would expect if the Arctic became a warm ocean; about 11,000 years ago the oceans entered their present cool cycle.

Such evidence supplied by the method of consequences, strongly supports the theory, but the method is not completely safe. For example, although the oceans became warm 11,000 years ago, nothing in that fact indicates that some other cause, such as an increase in radiation from the sun, might not have produced the effect. As with all other evidence, particularly in human affairs, the results are only probable, and the method of consequences can provide us with only an educated guess that may help us reduce the number of errors we make.

Thus the speaker may support alleged causes with detailed and undetailed examples, hypothetical examples, statistics, testimony, literal or figurative analogies, and by the method of consequences. In addition, the speaker will find the Canons of Causation, to be discussed later in this chapter, of help.

LIMITING THE NUMBER OF CAUSES

In a short speech no speaker should present an audience with a long chain of causes or give too many causes that are unsupported. In order to have time to use supporting material, he must limit the number of causes he uses, making each clear and supporting fully those that require support. To give a speech on "the causes of crime" including every conceivable cause in ten minutes would be ineffectual and, probably, quite dull. Moreover, the audience will not retain long and complicated iterations of causes. If the speaker covers too many causes, he might as well not have given the speech; indeed, he will have done the audience a disservice, because he will have bored them on a subject in which their interest should have been increased. On the other hand, to take one factor in the cause of crime and explain it carefully with an abundance of testimony, examples, statistics, and other forms of support would be to perform a genuine service in aiding the audience to understand the significance of at least one causal factor. Therefore, the speaker who is restricted to a short speech should select the fewest number of causes possible, and support each fully.

Which causes he selects will depend on his purpose. He may wish to select a cause that is not commonly accepted or one not well understood, or one that he considers the most important, but he must select the smallest feasible number of causes to present to an audience. In doing so, he should acknowledge the existence of other causes, and perhaps mention them or explain why he has selected the ones he discusses. Thus by limitation of the number of causes he presents, and by careful explanation and support of each, he will give a more effective speech.

METHODS OF SHOWING THAT A CAUSE AND EFFECT ARE RELATED

Just as there were two variations to our first method of demonstrating a cause, there are several possible variations to our second method, which shows that a cause and effect are associated. Under various conditions, each of these will enable a speaker to show an audience the causes of certain kinds of problems.

The Method of Agreement

John Stuart Mill, writing in the last century, developed five "Canons of Causation." We shall present a simplified version of Mill's analysis, which will be of help to speakers. The first and easiest is the method of agreement. We might illustrate it by the following:

Suppose seven men living in a dormitory are sick to their stomachs. To locate the cause of their illness, we would try to find something common in their experience that might have caused their difficulty. We would inquire of them where they ate, and would not be surprised to find that they had eaten in the same restaurant. Then we would try to find if they had eaten the same thing, and might be at a loss if we found that some ate hamburger and that some had eaten ham. But we would, probably, have located the cause of their illness when we discover that they had *all* eaten mustard. We might then form a tentative hypothesis that something in the mustard had caused their plight. In forming this hypothesis, we would have found a common element in their experience—something in which their experience agrees—that may be the cause of the illness.

The method of agreement may be stated as follows: *Whenever an alleged cause is present, a related effect must occur.*[5] This method requires a speaker to accumulate examples and statistics to show that the cause and effect are associated in a convincing number of instances. If we used the method of agreement to demonstrate that a certain factor caused crime, we would accumulate cases showing that when the factor was present, crime resulted. If we used the method to show that reducing the work load of teachers resulted in better teaching, we would find examples and compile statistics to show that whenever the teaching load was reduced, measurably better teaching resulted. Or we might support the idea that economic aid to depressed countries reduces the danger of communism by statistics showing that membership in the communist party in these countries was reduced as economic conditions became better. Again, we might try to show that a certain factor causes the decline of civilization by pointing out that whenever that factor was present, civilizations in the past have declined. Thus the method of agreement is one that requires that we accumulate instances and statistics to show that when the alleged cause was present, the expected effect also occurred.

The method has, however, some difficulties. In the following diagram,

---

[5] Once you become familiar with our simple statement about the Canons of Causation, you may want to read the original by John Stuart Mill in his A *System of Logic, Ratiocinative and Inductive*, New York, 1859, Chapter VII. He states his Canon of Agreement as follows: "If two or more instances of the phenomenon have only one circumstance in common, the circumstance in which alone all the instances agree, is the cause (or effect) of the given phenomenon."

we might, if we were untutored in such matters, draw the wrong conclusion about the cause.

$$Whiskey + H_2O \longrightarrow Intoxication$$
$$Gin + H_2O \longrightarrow Intoxication$$
$$Scotch + H_2O \longrightarrow Intoxication$$
$$Rye + H_2O \longrightarrow Intoxication$$
$$Vodka + H_2O \longrightarrow Intoxication$$
$$Wine + H_2O \longrightarrow Intoxication$$
$$Brandy + H_2O \longrightarrow Intoxication$$

Figure 7.

The Method of Difference

We could easily test whether the water is the cause of intoxication by redoing the experiment with one difference: leaving out the water, for example. If, then, intoxication still resulted, we would be convinced that it was not the water that caused the result, but some unnamed common element in the wine, brandy, and gin. The method of difference might be stated as follows: *When the cause is not present, the effect should not be; and when the effect is not present, the cause should not be.*[6] The method of difference, which must always be preceded by the method of agreement, is, in effect, a further test of the hypotheses suggested by the method of agreement. Let us take some further illustrations.

At one time, physiologists were convinced by their use of the method of agreement that the cause of hunger was the stomach contractions that occurred when a person was hungry. A tube with a balloon at the end of it was inserted into a subject's stomach and inflated. This tube was attached to a pressure gauge that, whenever the subject felt hungry, showed increased pressure resulting from the contraction of the stomach walls. In every case tested, when the subject reported that he was hungry, contractions were present. If the method of agreement were perfect, we could be sure that these contractions were an indispensable part of the

[6] Mill's second Canon of Causation is here combined with his third. His original statement of these two is as follows:

Second Canon: "If an instance in which the phenomenon under investigation occurs, and an instance in which it does not occur, have every circumstance save one in common, that one occurring only in the former; the circumstance in which alone the two instances differ is the effect, or the cause, or a necessary part of the cause, of the phenomenon."

Third Canon: "If two or more instances in which the phenomenon occurs have only one circumstance in common, while two or more instances in which it does not occur have nothing in common save the absence of that circumstance; the circumstance in which alone the two sets of instances always differ is the effect, or the cause, or an indispensable part of the cause, of the phenomenon."

cause of hunger. But there are no "perfect" methods of analyzing causes. Several years later, the method of difference was used to overthrow the older theory. This method requires that we find people who are hungry, but who have no stomach contractions. But where can we find such people? There are at least two kinds: those born without stomachs and those who, for one reason or another, have had their stomachs removed. We have found that people without stomachs—and hence, without stomach contractions—still experience hunger. Therefore, this method has shown us that the conclusion suggested by the method of agreement is wrong.

The method of difference can be used to help establish hypotheses as well as to reject them. In the previous illustration of the men in the dormitory who were ill from eating mustard, we might use the method of difference to confirm our hypothesis. How could this be done? We could supply hamburgers and ham from the same restaurant to several subjects, but not permit them to use mustard. If these people did not become ill, we would be more certain about the hypothesis that the mustard was the cause of the illness. Better yet, simply inquire among those who ate at the restaurant, and if we find that those who ate there but did not have mustard remained well, we would have strengthened our hypothesis.

Thus the method of difference removes the alleged cause to see what effect is produced. It is the method used by careful experimentalists. If one wishes to test the effects of a given drug on influenza, one will use the method of agreement and give the drug to a number of patients. But one will also give a placebo—a drug known to have no effect—to other patients to rule out psychological effects of receiving treatment and, thus, create a difference in which the alleged cause is not present.

The Method of Correlation

The method of correlation is not unlike the previous methods and may be stated as follows: *If a large amount of the cause is present, there should be a large amount of the effect; if a small amount of the cause is present, there should be a small amount of the effect.*[7] Thus we might find that

---

[7] Mill's statement of this Canon is as follows: "Whatever phenomenon varies in some particular manner, is either a cause or an effect of that phenomenon, or it is connected with it through some fact of causation." He also included another Canon, which though useful, has too often been misused: "Subtract from any phenomenon such part as is known by previous inductions to be the effect of certain causes, and the residue of the phenomenon is the effect of the remaining causes." In human affairs, it is nearly always impossible to be sure that one has all the causes, and, consequently, this "Method of Residues" is not particularly useful. Nevertheless, the student is urged to read Mill on the subject of the Canons of Causation. He is still the best single source, and although his Canons will not prevent every error that can be made in causal thinking, they will prevent many.

when the economic conditions of a European country are very bad, there are also many members of the communist party, but as the economic conditions of that country improve, there are fewer members of the same party, and as conditions become more productive and wealth increases, the number of communists becomes negligible. Or to return to our illustration of the men in the dormitory who were ill: those who ate a large amount of mustard should be very ill whereas those who ate only a small amount should be only slightly ill. We might, again, find the effects of good grades on later earning capacity. A careful study would reveal that generally students with "C" grades in college receive lower incomes than students with "B" grades, and those with "A" grades receive the highest incomes; in fact, so high that in the course of a lifetime, they will make over $100,000 more than the "C" student, or $25,000 a year for each of four years of study!

Dangers Inherent in the Canons of Causation

There are dangers in the Canons of Causation just as there are dangers inherent in every other form of reasoning. At least three of these dangers should be noted. First of all, *two things may be closely associated without being related to each other causally* when both things are caused by some other factor. Two clocks, for example, may be perfectly related in that each moves at the same speed; yet it could not be argued that one causes the other. The two clocks, of course, move together because they both have the same construction.

A second error often made in interpreting correlated phenomena is to *mistake the cause for the effect*. The rooster may think that it brings the sun up when it crows, but, of course, the sun gets the rooster up. In a like manner, some sociologists believe that it is not the comic books that cause a tendency toward socially undesirable behavior, but rather that the tendencies toward such behavior may cause the reading of comic books.

Thirdly, a mistake in the analysis of correlated factors may occur because *the relation may be accidental*. If one takes too seriously the following associations, he would assume that there is something about twenty-year cycles that seem to result in the death of Presidents of the United States. The presidents elected to office in the following years died in office:

1860: Abraham Lincoln
1880: James Garfield
1900: William McKinley
1920: Warren Harding
1940: Franklin Roosevelt
1960: John Kennedy

Accidental associations are difficult to distinguish from casual associations, and one must take care to be as certain as possible.

LEARNING TO USE CAUSAL REASONING

The student must learn to look for causes habitually. When he faces a problem, one of his first responses ought to be to look for the cause, and then check carefully to be certain that what he thinks causes the phenomenon really does so. To learn to use casual thinking habitually, we suggest the following procedure:

1. First be certain that you understand the forms of causal reasoning. You should be able to duplicate the following outline of them:
    I. Explaining *how* or *why* a cause operates by *describing the conditions that produce the effect*
       A. Chain of Causes
       B. Multiple Causes
       C. Method of Consequences
    II. Explaining *that* a cause operates by *showing that a cause and effect are associated.*
       A. Method of Agreement: When an alleged cause is present, a related effect must occur.
       B. Method of Difference: When the cause is not present, the effect should not be; and when the effect is not present, the cause should not be.
       C. Method of Correlation: If a large amount of the cause is present, there should be a large amount of the effect; if a small amount of the cause is present, there should be a small amount of the effect.
2. Find your own illustrations of each of these kinds of causes—good and bad—and analyze each illustration. Books on the sciences, psychology, history, and literature abound with illustrations of these causes.
3. You should try to examine the causes of phenomena in your own life and maintain a curiosity about the causes of things you observe daily.
4. Most important, you should try to discover the causes of the problems that confront us locally, nationally, and internationally.
   Habitual causal thinking is not common, but it can be valuable when we try to understand and solve our problems.

SUFFICIENT CAUSES

A complicating feature makes the analysis of causes particularly difficult: *Many kinds of causes may produce the same effect.* I may cause myself to be transported across the country by automobile, train, plane, or bus. Any one of these causes is *sufficient* to get me to my destination. In the same sense, there are many sufficient causes of delinquency, each of which can produce, under certain conditions, delinquent behavior. In investigating, however, the relation between broken homes and crime, we will find many cases in which individuals from broken homes have *not* engaged in criminal activity. Could one then assume that divorce is not a partial cause of delinquency? This conclusion might be as unsound as saying that death could hardly be caused by a bullet in the head because so many people have died without such a wound. We must not let the Canons blind us to the fact that there are some causes that will operate under some conditions, but not under others. What we need to do is *to specify the conditions under which a sufficient cause will operate.* Thus our causal statement should take the form, "Broken homes predispose children to juvenile delinquency when . . . ." Until we can make more careful statements of conditions under which certain causal factors operate, we must be careful about permanently abandoning an alleged cause that is not immediately confirmed by the methods of difference or correlation.

There are no sure methods for discovering causes, and in human affairs we must use faulty methods to make decisions. Our decisions will always be based on probable rather than certain evidence. There is no road to certainty, no perfect rule for thought and analysis, and no formula for problem solving that does not have limitations. Our methods are admittedly imperfect, but these methods will help us make fewer errors than we might without them.

The function of these methods is to come as close as possible to demonstrating that an alleged cause produces an effect. The Scotch philosopher, David Hume, pointed out, in the eighteenth century, that causes were never observed, but only inferred. No cause can be seen. All we can see is the conjunction of two events. To use his own illustration, when billiard ball "A" strikes billiard ball "B" and sets "B" in motion, all we can observe is that "A" moves forward until it strikes "B" and stops, and "B" begins motion. The conjunction of these events is as far as we can go in discovering a cause. The Canons of Causation help us to analyze such conjunctions. They are not perfect, however, and the intelligent student will always be willing to test further his hypotheses about causes.

SPEECH ANALYZING CAUSES

Sometimes societies have been destroyed because they failed to analyze the causes of their problems and failed to provide solutions that removed these causes. Too frequently we try to solve a problem by treating the symptoms of the problem; but when only the symptoms are treated, the original cause of the problem may still operate and the problem may continue. We must learn, in these cases, to find and remove the cause of a problem. Moreover, even when we decide (as sometimes we should) to treat the symptoms of a problem, we cannot make such a choice intelligently unless we first know the causes, and after knowing them, recognize that the causes cannot or should not be removed. Therefore, intelligent problem solving demands that we analyze causes.

Assignment

Prepare a five- to seven-minute speech in which you present a phenomenon of significance and show that one or more causes are responsible for it. In cases where many causes are responsible, select only one cause or very few causes.

Techniques of Demonstrating Causes

Use any of the following techniques to make your cause clear. See the text to be sure you have used them properly.

I. Describing the conditions that produce an effect
  A. Chain of causes
  B. Multiple causes
  C. Methods of consequence
II. Showing that a cause and effect are related
  A. Method of agreement
  B. Method of difference
  C. Method of correlation

Subjects

The cause of any phenomenon in economics, government, psychology, science, or other area is acceptable, provided the phenomenon is sufficiently *important, and the cause is sufficiently unknown to the audience* to merit a speech.

Analyze the causes (or the most important cause) of any of the following: price changes, inflation, depression, warm or cold fronts, absenteeism, fluctuations in the stock market, forgetting, crime, dreams, evolution of any part of the body, the decline of civilization, disease, prejudice, good grades, safe driving, maladjustment, corrupt government, old age, rapid learning, headaches, monopolies, war, genius, happiness, dope addiction, or any other subject worth the time of the audience.

11 ▯ Thinking and
Speaking About
Solutions

THE IMPORTANCE OF SOLUTIONS

Problems must be solved because each problem represents a source of
danger to a civilization. Each problem is like a physical ailment—it
weakens, degenerates, or destroys whatever it seizes. On the other hand,
each problem solved adds strength, health, and vigor to the culture. Problems must be solved, then, because each of them represents a source of
potential weakness and because each problem solved contributes strength.

But in our times, there is a far more important reason for trying to
solve problems. The final test of any society is whether or not it can
solve its problems. All societies before us have failed that test. Egyptian,
Greek, Persian, Roman, the ancient Indian and Chinese cultures all have
died. Western culture is the only remaining civilization and at this
moment it faces the same problems of war, poverty, caste, tyranny, and
disease that destroyed every previous civilization. Oswald Spengler
examined Western culture in his famous *Decline of the West* and produced evidence to show that our culture has every characteristic that is
found in civilizations as they enter their last period of existence. Albert
Schweitzer said:

It is clear now to everyone that the suicide of civilization is in progress. What yet remains of it is no longer safe. It is still standing, indeed . . . but like the rest it is built upon rubble, and the next landslide will very likely carry it away.[1]

Our own survival depends on our ability to solve our problems. Our progress in technology has exceeded that of any previous civilization, but our progress in solving the classical problems that have destroyed previous civilizations is not noteworthy. The problem of war today is more dangerous than ever before. The two greatest nations in the world could now obliterate each other many times over, and there is no foreseeable end to the danger. Now that other countries have the same kinds of weapons, war is so great a danger that it could not only obliterate our country, but could possibly destroy Western civilization, and perhaps, even the human race. The problem of poverty is so great that one billion people have an annual income of less than one hundred dollars. Caste and prejudice weaken millions in the United States, Africa, and India; these millions might have developed skills and then contributed their skills and strength to the general welfare. Tyranny in this century reached an all-time outrageous peak as Stalin, Hitler, and dozens of lesser dictators poured out their insane venom on their own people and half the world. Except for a few countries, the problem of disease rages the world over. Let not the condition of our two hundred million citizens blind us to the danger that for 1,500 times as many people, life is a dangerous misery. Western culture faces the same threats that have annihilated every previous civilization.

But Western culture has some hope. In contrast to all other cultures, we have so great a burst of knowledge that *we may at this moment know enough to solve the problems that have plagued humanity,* or at least *we can find out how to solve them.* The problem of poverty, for example, has been greatly reduced in those countries that have incorporated scientific means of production and intelligent principles of distribution; sometimes in these countries, so much is produced that the supply, for a brief while, exceeds the demand. The same kinds of principles that enabled Europe and North America to produce abundantly can be applied elsewhere, although variations in techniques of production will be necessary, and we must beware of our tendency to export our own techniques without careful study of the other country and corresponding modification of the techniques. You must not forget that you live in the first generation to have a justified hope of solving the great classical problems of war, poverty, caste, tyranny, and disease. Let us exploit our hopes; perhaps we may have some successes where others have failed.

[1] Albert Schweitzer, *The Philosophy of Civilization,* New York, The Macmillan Company, 1949, p. 2.

Symptomatic Solutions
and Causal Solutions

Solutions to problems are of two important kinds: solutions may reduce the causes of a problem. If a physician, for example, discovers a patient with fever of 107° he might try to attack the cause of the problem by first discovering the germ causing the difficulty, and then prescribing an antibiotic to destroy that particular germ. On the other hand, at 107°, the patient is literally burning up and can live for only a few hours. The physician might feel that the fever is too high to permit time for full diagnosis; proper laboratory tests to discover the bacterium responsible might take several days. The patient's condition nearly forces the physician to give immediate symptomatic treatment; therefore the physician may administer a drug known to reduce fever, or in special cases, may place the patient in an ice bath. Although such treatment would be given in ignorance of the causes of the patient's condition, it might save his life. We may direct solutions either at the causes of a problem or at its symptoms and the speaker must know which direction he is taking.

To understand these two kinds of solutions, let us illustrate them further. We might treat the problem of crime by increasing the sentences given those who commit crimes. Such a solution is symptomatic because it does not inquire into the cause of crime, and it can be applied only after the criminal act is committed. Punishment is always a symptomatic solution. To treat crime causally, we would have to find some way of reducing or preventing its causes.

To take another example, is a high protective tariff a symptomatic solution or a causal solution? In order to be sure of the answer we must identify the problem that the tariff is designed to solve. That problem is that foreign countries can produce some goods less expensively than American producers and hence sell them at lower prices. A causal solution would require either the raising of the wages of laborers abroad or reducing the costs of production at home, or both. These causal solutions would tend to bring the prices of domestic goods in line with prices of foreign goods. The tariff reduces the symptoms of the problem by adding a certain amount to the price of these goods, but leaves unchanged the factors that cause the price differences.

Both symptomatic solutions and causal solutions may be effective if they are properly chosen. Each of these solutions, however, has its own limitations and dangers, and when either is inappropriately used, the result may be failure to solve the problem, or even a worsening of the problem. Let us, therefore, see the special characteristics of each of these major types of solutions.

The Advantages of Symptomatic Solutions

Symptomatic solutions have at least two advantages: First, such solutions often may be applied with great ease and rapidity. When, as small children, we overstepped the bounds of propriety, traditional symptomatic treatment may have been administered—the spanking. Often such symptomatic treatment prevented further recurrence of the problem. To uncover the causes of even minor behavior problems could take months; and to treat these causes could consume far more months. Just as it is easier to take aspirin for a headache than to find the cause of a headache, so symptomatic treatment usually may be applied faster and more easily than causal solutions.

Secondly, symptomatic treatment may be applied where the causes are either unknown or not agreed upon. Many of the problems about which we speak are so complex that the causes are uncertain. At the time we were not completely certain about the causes of the Great Depression of the 1930's; at least economists did not, then, agree on the matter. Yet even though we did not agree on the causes of the depression, we had to treat it. The New Deal attempted many symptomatic solutions. Today most people would agree that the New Deal was relatively successful; at least, few of the reforms of the New Deal have been repealed. But the reforms were almost entirely symptomatic reforms. Thus symptomatic treatment may be valuable because often it can be applied easily and quickly and because it can be applied when we do not know the causes of a problem.

The Disadvantages of Symptomatic Solutions

One danger in attacking the symptoms of a problem is that the symptoms themselves may be of value. For example, a fever may be useful (although physicians still debate the matter) because it may kill harmful bacteria that have invaded the system; to reduce the fever sometimes permits the bacteria to prosper. A cough may be an unpleasant symptom, but helps clear the bronchial tubes of irritants; to quiet the cough leaves the irritants intact where they might cause damage. Symptoms may also have value in social problems. The reading of comic books is a symptom that may have unrecognized value; the popularity of these books may be a reaction to the drabness of the city. They may offer a vicarious way of finding adventure and thrills, and may help prevent antisocial and illegal behavior. Similarly, foreign competition that frequently threatens American industries can produce beneficial results. Such competition may spur domestic industries to improve both their products and the means of producing them. Since World War II, Russia has posed a threat to the free world, and that threat, dangerous as it has been, has been one of the most stimulating irritations the free world has had. Particularly in our own country has the symptom of tension between ourselves and the communist world been beneficial. Because of the threat, we have spent increasing amounts of money on education and science; we have been forced to re-examine our educational policies and our rationale for scientific research; we have found it necessary to help less affluent societies with the result that at least some of them are close to economic "take off" and others are rapidly becoming affluent; we have searched our nature and our history for a sense of national purpose, and in some respects the cold war has given at least some of us a greater sense of the uniqueness of a democratic society. Probably much of our energy has been misdirected, but no one can doubt that the cold war has been energizing. Such symptoms, because they can energize, may have more value than we commonly realize.

Another danger in treating symptoms is perhaps more common. Symptomatic treatment may not be effective because the original causes may continue operating. Unless the cause of a fever is finally removed, the disease will persist. If an overweight person is treated only symptomatically by being put on a diet, his weight will likely not come down, especially if the cause is psychological or physiological. The cause of his overeating may be, for example, that he realizes that if he is overweight, he has a socially acceptable reason for not competing in certain kinds of social situations; in truth, he may feel he is a dull person and unable to compete in such situations, but his weight protects him from recognizing his "dullness," and thus, being overweight is a temporary palliative. Since the cause of his overeating persists, so does his weight. Thus when only the symptoms are treated, solutions may be ineffective. Just so, however, have we treated many of our problems. We have treated the symptoms of juvenile crime, and juvenile crime continues to increase alarmingly. We have treated the symptoms of poverty, and even in our rich country, one fifth of our people is impoverished. We have treated some of the symptoms of war, and war threatens the extinction of us all. These problems may persist until we can treat them in a more fundamental way by locating their causes and trying to reduce the potency of these causes.

Drug addiction provides an interesting example of the relative effectiveness of symptomatic and causal treatment. In the United States, we have treated the problem symptomatically by trying to enforce the law better and by giving those who deal in narcotics sterner penalties. Yet the problem of drug addiction remains with us. England and Sweden have had greater success in combatting the drug problem. Their reasoning is more clearly causal: A man usually sells dope to procure money to buy dope for himself. The "pusher" is himself an addict who must spend up to seventy-five dollars a day to prevent the withdrawal effects that occur when he has been without narcotics. These effects are so discomforting and painful that one who has not suffered them cannot imagine their severity. A man might, to avoid them, even kill to purchase "a fix." But the habit can hardly be cured. Barely 2 per cent of the addicts who have been taken away from dope stay away from it. Nevertheless, if we could prevent withdrawal symptoms, we could reduce the "pusher's" motivation to sell dope so significantly that he would not want to risk the danger and would stop "pushing." One way to keep this kind of person from feeling withdrawal effects is to give him, under close medical supervision, just enough narcotics each day to keep him from having withdrawal symptoms. The cost of such treatment is hardly fifty cents a day. The man himself remains a useful citizen who, although he should not be permitted to run complicated and dangerous machinery, can perform many tasks that will be of use to others and that will permit him to retain his own self respect. Such a system has been practiced in certain European countries for thirty years, and by reducing the motivation of the "pusher" to sell dope, has greatly reduced the amount of dope addiction. In all of England there are fewer addicts than in any one of America's five largest cities. (A new drug, Methadone, may prove effective in "curing" addicts; its present value is, however, uncertain.) Perhaps we should use the European causal solution.

A final limitation to symptomatic solutions is that much symptomatic treatment often results from anger and masks a desire for vengeance. We are sometimes most apt to administer symptomatic treatment to our children when we have become angry with them. We increase the penalties against criminal acts despite evidence that these penalties do not reduce crime. But we fail, in these cases, to attack the causes of the problems, and the problems remain undiminished. Moreover, anger blocks our thinking and reduces the chances of solving our problems. Symptomatic treatment given in anger and for vengeance may, finally, bring forth a powerful reaction and thereby, increase the problem. We should be suspicious of symptomatic solutions.

Summary

To speak intelligently about solutions, we must decide whether or not we will treat the causes or the symptoms of a problem. We know of no general rule that can help us decide which choice to make for knowledge in these matters is slight and much depends on the specific problem. We might remember, however, that symptomatic treatment often is more quickly and more easily applied, and that it can be applied in complex situations where the causes cannot be determined with certainty. But we must also remember that sometimes these symptoms are of benefit, and that when we fail to remove the causes of a problem, the problem may remain. Finally, we should remind ourselves that much symptomatic treatment is given in anger and is not a problem-solving response. Within this framework, the speaker must select the best solution.

PRESENTING SOLUTIONS TO AUDIENCES

Once the speaker selects or devises a solution that he believes will help solve the problem, he has already gone through a long preparation. If he has been thorough, he has tried to understand the problem and its effects on others and on his audience; he has tried to understand the causes of the problem; he has studied various solutions; and he has selected the one he thinks most appropriate. Now his task is to find ways of convincing the audience that his solution merits adoption. There are no invariable rules to follow, but we can offer some general suggestions.

Analogy

One of the best ways to convince an audience that a solution is a good one is to show how a similar solution has worked under similiar conditions. This technique requires the use of the analogy. The analogy has two purposes: (1) *The analogy may be used to show that something that was true elsewhere may be true in a similar situation.* When Galileo discovered that Jupiter had moons that revolved around it, he furnished a strong psychological support for the heliocentric theory of the Solar System because people felt that if Jupiter had moons revolving around it, then, perhaps the Sun might also have satellites. (2) *The analogy may be used to show a solution that worked elsewhere might work in a similar situation.* Let us illustrate this use of the analogy. Some have argued, for example, that forced racial integration reduces prejudice because when the merchant marine integrated several years ago, prejudice against Negroes seemed to drop proportionally to the number of times men had worked together on ships after segregation ended. Although 54 per cent of the men were opposed to desegregation at first, by the time crews had taken two voyages on an unsegregated basis, only 25 per cent of the men reported dissatisfaction with desegregation and by the fifth voyage, only 9 per cent remained dissatisfied.[2] What worked in the merchant marine to reduce prejudice, one might argue, might work in the schools. To use another analogy, one might argue that a city ought to have a city manager

[2] Ira N. Brophy, "The Luxury of Anti-Negro Prejudice," *Public Opinion Quarterly,* IX (1946), pp. 456–66.

form of government instead of a government headed by a mayor, and support this idea by describing how successful the city manager system has been in other cities.

Such use of the analogy requires that the speaker take great care to convince the audience *that the solution worked well elsewhere.* If one is trying to convince the audience of the value of the city manager form of government, he must show that in other cities it reduced the possibility of graft and corruption, that these cities have maintained or increased the services performed by the city and did so at less expense to the taxpayer than would have been the case under a mayor. If one wishes to convince the audience that the honor system is the solution to student cheating, he must demonstrate that it has worked in other universities. Perhaps the speaker would, for example, tell about the honor system at the University of Virginia, where, for over a hundred years, that system has had the hearty endorsement of students and faculty. He would want to include testimony from faculty and students about how well the system works, studies of the system, and, perhaps, surveys of opinion about the system. To take another example, if one wishes to demonstrate that automobile accidents might be reduced by raising the speed limit, he would select statistics from states that had raised their speed limits, and compare these statistics on accidents before and after the limit was raised. (Surprisingly, the number of accidents usually goes down.) But whatever solution the speaker recommends, he must use facts, figures, examples, and testimony to demonstrate that his proposed solution worked well elsewhere.

The speaker must also convince the audience *that the two situations are similar.* If one were arguing for forced integration in the schools and used as support the way integration reduced prejudice in the merchant marine, he would then have to argue that the situation in unsegregated schools is similar in all significant respects to the situation in the merchant marine. An opponent could argue that a man working on a ship away from home is different from a high school student living with his parents and surrounded by his friends. The student would find it much more difficult to give up his prejudice because such prejudice is sometimes a condition for acceptance with his friends and is often approved and reinforced by them and his parents. Thus the central task of using the analogy is often to convince the audience that the situation where the solution worked well was similar in all significant respects to the situation where the solution is recommended. But what are the *significant* respects? As we have emphasized throughout this book, there are no certain and fixed rules that will lead one to correct conclusions, and especially is this lack of certainty true in the use of the analogy. What is significant must be discovered by thorough acquaintance with the two situations and by careful thought. To judge whether or not the merchant marine was comparable to the situation in a Southern high school would require careful thought and analyses of the two situations, if not a sociological study. The more the speaker knows about the two situations, the more he will be able to decide what is significant, the more evidence he will be able to furnish the audience, and the fewer mistakes he will make in analyses.

In some cases the speaker need not find closely similar situations in which a solution has worked. For example, if one is attempting to show that better street lighting reduces crime, one might show that in some areas of New York City, crime was reduced by installing more and better street lights. If one can get examples, statistics, and testimony to show that better street lighting also reduces crime in a suburban area, in a country town, in small cities, in cities from various geographical areas, and in poor districts as well as in wealthier areas, he need not show that the situations are similar to the one for which he proposes the solution. Here the speaker has shown that the solution works in a *diversity* of situations, and consequently, might be expected to work *anywhere*. In such cases, one need only have a variety of situations, and show with reasonable care that the solution was successful.

Some texts state that the analogy is the weakest form of support. In our opinion, it is no weaker than the example, than statistics, or than any other form of support. As with all forms of support, it is possible to make mistakes and no known system of reasoning or logic guarantees freedom from mistaken conclusions. The analogy is no more subject to error than any other form of support. On the contrary, the analogy has a unique usefulness, for through analogical thinking we can use the experience of people in similar situations. If we find that one system for speeding up the process of education works at one university, we may argue that it might also work at ours. Or if we find that one method of reducing juvenile delinquency worked well in Chicago, we might, by analogy, wish to try it in Los Angeles. If we find one way of discovering how to help an under-developed country increase its national wealth, perhaps that way of discovering a solution might be applied to similar countries. If one school system is successful in turning out good students, good citizens, productive scientists, or effective statesmen, perhaps other school systems will find the same methods useful. Far from being useless, the analogy is indispensable to human thought because it permits us to use the experiences of others. Without analogical thinking, no man could profit from the success or failure of another. Far from being either weak or useless, the analogy is both necessary and useful. If your friend finds a good dentist, by analogy, the same dentist may be good for you. If you find that a certain professor has profound anesthetic effects on your friends, use analogical reasoning and avoid his class. Thus the analogy is not only useful, but indispensable. Of course, like other forms of support, it is open to error, but inasmuch as it enables us to use the experience of others, we not only can but must use it.

Other Methods

Solutions can be supported by means other than the analogy, and frequently, these other methods may be appropriate. The speaker should try to use a variety of these methods. Inasmuch as the student already has been introduced to these methods in previous chapters, only a brief treatment of them is necessary here.

1. *Explain that the solution will remove the cause.* If a speaker has chosen a solution that is causal, he may wish to use one of the forms of causal argument discussed in Chapter 10. To summarize the kinds of causal argument that may be useful in presenting solutions, the student should remind himself of the following kinds of causal arguments:
   a. Demonstrating that a solution will remove the cause by describing how the cause will be removed.
   (1) Chain of causes
   (2) Multiple causes
   (3) Method of consequences
   b. Demonstrating that a solution will remove the cause by showing that it has done so in other cases.
   (1) Method of agreement
   (2) Method of difference
   (3) Method of correlation

Thus causal reasoning may be used to support the idea that your solution could remove the cause of the problem. To illustrate, you might use a chain of causes to explain how lower prices to the farmer may not solve the problem of agricultural surpluses. Thus, a speaker concerned with the problem of surpluses such as characterized our country from World War II to about 1965 might urge that the problem be solved by *raising* prices offered to the farmer. The following example uses multiple causes in the first paragraph, a chain of causes in the second, and the method of correlation in the third:

Consider the farmer who knows that because of lower prices he will get 20 per cent less than last year for each bushel of corn he raises. If he gets less, you'd think he would raise something else. But he can't. His equipment is specialized. A corn cultivator, for example, can't be used for anything except cultivating corn. A corn picker will not harvest potatoes or soy beans, but only corn. Moreover, his knowledge is specialized so that he cannot easily switch to raising, say, vegetables for the big city produce markets. He doesn't know the efficient ways to raise them, what the best seeds are, how to harvest them quickly, or even where to sell them. So he has to stay a corn farmer.

Because he will make 20 per cent less on the same amount of corn, he decides he will raise more corn. He plows up another hundred acres, buys better seed than the previous year, adds more fertilizer to the planting, and makes use of new chemicals to control weeds and pests. As a result, he maintains his income, but he raises more corn. And in years of surplus, we will pay the bill. If we want to solve the problem of surpluses, we must be sure that the farmer is paid a decent return on his labor.

Because prices to the farmer went down during the Eisenhower years, the surpluses went up. At the beginning of the Eisenhower-Benson farm program, we had 2.4 billion dollars of surpluses. By the end of the administration, prices the farmer received had gone down, and we had more than eleven billion dollars worth of agricultural surpluses. The less money the farmer received, the more crops he raised.

2. *Explain that the solution will prevent the symptoms of a problem from occurring.* One could, for example, recommend reducing juvenile delinquency by imposing a curfew. The explanation of how such a curfew might prevent the symptoms from operating is simple: most delinquency occurs after ten o'clock at night; if no juveniles were allowed on the streets after this hour, then no juvenile delinquency could occur—on the streets, at any rate. Again, the speaker will be using causal argument, but using it to show that the solution will cause a reduction of symptoms.

3. *Show that the testimony of well-qualified experts supports the idea.* For instance, the testimony of agricultural experts to the effect that certain kinds of farming would increase the productivity of underdeveloped countries will help convince the audience of the value of your solution to the world food shortage. See pp. 45–48.

4. *Whenever possible, use a combination of ways of supporting solutions.* If the speaker can show that a similar solution has worked elsewhere, that the solution will remove one of the principal causes of the problem, and that experts believe the solution to be a good one, this kind of variety adds logical and psychological strength to the speaker's solution. Because our survival depends on the quality of our solutions, we do well to expend energy, intelligence, and care in selecting and presenting them to others.

SELECTING CAUSES FOR SOLUTION

One should be careful about the causes he chooses to remove by his solution. As Protagoras, an ancient Greek philosopher and teacher of speech, pointed out, every event has many causes: If a javelin thrower at an Olympic game accidentally kills a spectator, one may say that the cause of death was that the javelin pierced the heart of the spectator. But someone else could argue that it was the bad aim of the javelin thrower. Perhaps the city council would insist that it was the fault of the manager of the event who permitted spectators to stand too close, whereas a more philosophical mind might allege that without the desire for thrills and spectacles, no crowd would have assembled in the first place. A more hot-headed person would have recommended firing the teacher of javelin-throwing because he failed to produce a student who was both careful and accurate. The causes one selects must depend upon many factors. If one is a doctor, he will choose to treat the wound; if one is a trainer, he will try to prevent future injuries by giving safety precautions to our athletes; if one is the manager of the event he may try to erect barricades between the performers and the spectators. The kind of cause treated depends on one's interests, skills, and analysis of what he believes to be easiest and most desirable. Therefore, when a cause is selected for removal, the speaker should often explain why he selected a particular cause.

SOLUTION SPEECH

Once one understands the importance of a problem and tries to analyze its causes, he is in a position to find a solution for it. Finding solutions is of utmost urgency for us. In the past, many societies understood that they had problems, but were unable to meet the problems with the rigorous research and creativity necessary. These societies perished. If our society is to grow, or even to continue to exist, we must solve the problems that beset us. Each problem represents a sign of weakness in our culture; some problems such as war, poverty, disease, immorality, and caste destroyed previous civilizations. In this society, our existence is not assured unless our speakers can diagnose our problems, grasp the causes of these problems, select solutions and make them palatable. In this assignment, you are asked to present a solution to a significant problem.

Assignment

Give a five- to seven-minute speech in which you present a problem of significance and offer a carefully-supported solution.

Technique of Presenting Solutions

Needless to say, you must spend a few minutes making the audience realize the significance and nature of the problem before offering a solution. Your introduction should be short and as directly relevant to the problem as possible. Follow your introduction with a short but excellent example of a "problem speech." It may be possible to present a solution to the problem you dealt with in your earlier speech. If so, refer to that speech quickly, remind the audience swiftly but concretely of the significance and nature of the problem, and present a solution. Select from the following methods to show that your solution is a sensible one.

I. Analogy
   A. First show that a similar solution worked elsewhere. Show that the solution removed the problem, or a significant part of it, that its cost in time and effort was not prohibitive and that it brought with it no new problems that were insurmountable.
   B. Then show the audience briefly that the two situations are comparable in significant respects. Significant parallels can often be found in places far removed in time and distance. At all costs, one must avoid an analogy in which the two situations are not similar. If, of course, you choose solutions from a variety of conditions, as described on page 193, you need not demonstrate that the situations in which your solution works are similar to the one in which you recommend it because you have shown that it is likely to work whenever tried.
II. Testimony
   Show that qualified experts believe the solution to have merit.
III. Explanation
   A. Explain how the solution will prevent the cause from operating, or reduce the effectiveness of the cause.
   B. Explain how the solution will prevent the symptoms from occurring.

Subjects

No list of solutions is given because the appropriate ones should be arrived at after careful study, discussion, and debate. Through the competition of ideas one can best discover both the problems to be solved and the best solutions to them. Furnishing this competition is one of the most valuable contributions of speakers in a free society.

12 ▯ Thinking and Speaking About Meanings: Definitions

Not long ago, a painting by Leonardo da Vinci entitled "Ginevra de Benci" sold for $5,800,000—the highest price ever paid for a single painting. The price of a painting, however, is not always an index of its greatness. Many a great artist, unable to sell his work, lived and died in poverty. On the other hand, lavish sums were often paid for landscapes and paintings of animals during the nineteenth century; today these paintings are stored in museum attics and basements. If the cost of a painting is not necessarily an index of its greatness, the problem emerges: Is Leonardo's painting a great one? To solve this problem, we must first define *great painting*.

The same kind of problem emerges if we ask, "Is it just to execute a man for murder?" for here, again, if we are to solve the problem, we must begin with a definition—this time, of *justice* and, perhaps of *murder*. One day, if not several times already, you will wonder whether or not you are in love. But you cannot solve that perennial and important problem unless you first can carefully define *love*. Definitions, which are mistakenly considered to be dull, are a prerequisite to solving some of the most crucial and most lively problems we face.

The Importance of Definitions

Definitions and Problem Solving

Good definitions are essential to problem solving. We cannot solve the problems about great art, justice, or love without a definition of each of these terms. If we wish to know whether or not President Kennedy's "Inaugural Address" was a great speech, we must first define greatness in speaking. We cannot know how to search for happiness until we have a sound definition of happiness—and such a definition is not easy to compose. Nor can we know how to increase our intelligence—or even if it can be increased—until we obtain an adequate definition of intelligence. For some kinds of problem solving, therefore, definitions are not merely useful; definitions are a prerequisite to any solution at all.

Not only is a definition a prerequisite to solving some kinds of problems, but the solution to such problems will be commensurate with the quality of the definition. In the following case the solution can be no better than the definition used to arrive at a solution: If we defined a great painting as "any painting bringing a high price," then, "Ginevra de Benci" would be a great painting, indeed. But, so, too, would be the trite landscapes and romanticized animal scenes from the nineteenth century, because these also once brought a high price. And with such a definition, we would be forced to the untenable conclusion that paintings of Van Gogh were not great while he lived but were great after 1930, and that Landseer's country scenes were great in 1900 but not after 1930. Inasmuch as greatness implies *permanence of value,* a definition implying that greatness can fluctuate wildly is unsatisfactory and leads to a poor solution of the problem. We would have done better to recognize that we arrived at a poor solution because we started with a poor definition. We should have worked to improve the definition rather than to "solve" the problem in a way that is unsatisfactory. Indeed, even if it seems that the problem of defining greatness in art is unsolvable, we would be on safer ground to admit this fact than to use a poor definition. Such a decision is still an intelligent one, and more to be prized than an untenable "solution."

Definitions and Knowledge

Definitions are necessary, also, for certain kinds of knowledge. If one asks: "Does history happen according to certain laws?" the answer cannot be given until one defines laws. If, by laws, one means inevitable cycles that repeat themselves, then almost surely there are no "laws" in history. If, on the other hand, one means "general principles of cause and effect based on the examination of historical cases" then, most likely, there are known (and unknown) laws in history, such as "Civilizations sometimes may fall because creative people are persecuted." Much information requires definitions if the information is to be understood. Certainly, if we are to know whether or not "neurobiotaxis is the cause of learning" we must first know what neurobiotaxis is. When the definition tells us it is "neural growth producing interconnections among nerves," we can understand the statement and begin to search for evidence of it. Perhaps the best example of the ways in which definitions lead to knowledge is contained in Euclid's *Geometry*, where, with some axioms, postulates, and definitions, Euclid proves all manner of complicated theorems, putting these theorems in the realm of certain knowledge. Definitions are necessary for knowledge, at a simple level and at more complex ones.

Definitions and Clarity

Definitions are necessary to assure understanding and to guard against being misunderstood. When one uses a term with which the audience is unfamiliar, or when one wishes to give a precise meaning to a vague word, he must define that word. If one uses the term *socialized medicine*, for example, one must define it; it has meant everything from health insurance to total government employment and management of the medical profession. *Underdeveloped nation* has sometimes meant only those nations with a per capita income of below $50 a year (which would exclude India), all the way to nations such as Mexico whose productivity has increased as much as 14 per cent in a single year and whose wealth ranks her in the upper fifth of nations. "If first you would debate with me, define your terms," said Voltaire, in a much quoted statement. He knew that speakers should guarantee clarity to listeners by supplying careful definitions, and he was, as we should be, suspicious of those who fail to give careful definitions of their terms.

KINDS OF DEFINITIONS

We will examine three important kinds of definitions, each of which has different uses and limitations. Each of these concepts of definition springs from completely different ideas about the world or about the nature and function of words. Let us begin with that concept of definition that is the oldest and, perhaps, the least understood.

Platonistic Definition

Plato believed that certain concepts could transform men and society. These concepts—which today we call *values*—exist as Ideas only. According to Plato, in the World of Ideas are concepts which, if we truly understood them, would change our behavior, our laws, our nations, and our entire culture. Ideas have great power because, according to Plato, every Idea has the following characteristics:

1. *Ideas are the models or achetypes of our popular concepts.* We can clarify the way in which the Ideas serve as archetypes if we apply Plato's Theory of Ideas, for a moment, to chairs (but we must keep in mind that Plato himself was not the least bit interested in objects, but only in values): We can observe many kinds of chairs, some with arms, some made of wood, some beautifully upholstered, some hand-carved and gilded, and others constructed from the cheapest sorts of material. But all these chairs might be conceived of as imitations of the Idea of a chair. All chairs, whatever their dimensions, materials, or qualities, are thus imitations of the Idea of a chair, and if we had no such Idea, we could not make any chairs at all. Just so, the values in Plato's World of Ideas are the archetypes or models for our concepts. Thus, Plato believed that there is an Idea of Justice, of Courage, of Love, of Patriotism, of Happiness, of Art, and even of the subject you are studying—Rhetoric.[1]

2. *Ideas are perfect in the sense that when they are understood and applied they can transform men and society.* True love can transform us remarkably and magnificently into something better; the lack of it, at best, leaves us incomplete, and neurotic love can destroy us. Just so do other Ideas change us. A few examples may illustrate the surprising fact that Ideas transform; geometry, for example, is a system of Ideas. Geometry sets out the properties of circles, triangles, and cones, even though nowhere are there any circles, triangles, or cones, or even anywhere straight lines (because under a microscope all these are most imperfect); and yet, geometry sets out the properties of these Ideas, and does so for *any* triangle, circle, or cone in *any* universe. From the time the Egyptians used geometry to measure the fields and, thereby determine who owned which fields, after the Nile flood (thus creating a more just society) to the present when we use geometry to navigate around the earth and to build fantastic cities, this system of Ideas has transformed us. Presumably Plato got his notions of the World of Ideas from geometry, for he had inscribed above the entrance to The Academy the words, "Let none enter here without a knowledge of geometry."

Perhaps a better example of the ways Ideas transform is Western culture itself. Its differences from other cultures are all traceable to two Ideas: There are no good names for these Ideas, but first Western culture has the Idea of what we might call love of the individual and respect for him,

---

[1] Platonistic Ideas are capitalized (Justice, the Good, and so on) to indicate that the writer is referring not to what people generally mean when they use the words *justice* or *good* but to the archetypes of our ideas, and not to imperfect imitations.

or what we call a dedication to freedom, or what is sometimes called Democracy. Secondly, our culture possesses another Idea that we might label respect for knowledge, or curiosity, or love of learning, of which philosophy and science are the two highest developments. These two Ideas: which, somewhat superficially we can call Democracy and Science, have transformed Western culture in ways that have made it more vigorous, more powerful, and in some ways, kinder, than the ancient Empires of Egypt, China, India, or Mexico. We differ from other cultures in that we are dedicated more or less to the Idea of freedom and the Idea of the search for knowledge. These Ideas have given us our strength and have shaped us. As they are more fully realized, they will shape us further. One can see that Ideas transform: If we knew what Justice is, we could judge others justly; all of us at times must judge, but being ignorant of Justice, we judge poorly. Moreover, we could judge whether a law is just or unjust and either follow that law courageously if it is just or break it if it is unjust. Even more important, if we understood justice more perfectly, we could create just laws and create a just society, and even a just world. Plato was corret; Ideas do transform, and great Ideas can transform greatly.

3. *Most manifestations of Ideas on earth are imperfect imitations of the Idea.* In contrast to the Ideas, our earthly imitations of Justice are hopelessly imperfect, so imperfect that our misconceptions of Justice can work great evil, just as an electric chair or the dunking chairs of Salem's witch-hunting days may be said to be evil imitations of the Idea of a chair, so have men's concept of Justice and other values been evil. Once we thought it just to cut off a man's hand for stealing a loaf of bread, and to sell people into slavery. These practices were evil misconceptions of the Idea of Justice. Had we understood that Idea, we could have acted Justly as individuals, created laws that were truly Just, and built a Just society.

4. *Knowledge of the Ideas is everlasting.* Much of our learning today, rather than being everlasting, is ephemeral. By the time an engineer has been out of school ten years, perhaps 50 per cent of the knowledge he learned in engineering school will be outmoded. But once one truly understands one of the Ideas—such as Justice—the knowledge is timeless. Thus, if one comes to understand what Justice is, that understanding would have been true in the fifth century, B.C., and would have been true yesterday, just as it would be true for all cultures on earth and on any other planet. A contemporary anthropologist might be tempted to quarrel because societies sometimes seem to have very different ideas of what is just. The Eskimos believe it proper to abandon their aged in the cold and snow when they reach a certain age, whereas we think it best to care for them. Yet even the Eskimos abandon the older person so that he may not endure the pangs of old age; Eskimos feel that they act out of consideration

for the older person himself, just as our actions are done for the sake of the aged. There may be, therefore, one common idea underlying both kinds of behavior. Plato might reply that if we truly understood Justice, we would all agree on its nature; too frequently we have grasped only another imitation of the real thing, and not Justice itself; hence as time goes on, we change our concepts of Justice, but as we come closer to an understanding of Justice, our ideas will change less and less.

5. *Knowledge of the Ideas is extremely difficult to discern.* One cannot develop perfect and timeless knowledge of the Ideas easily. Plato believed that no one in fifth-century Athens had a knowledge of even a single Idea. This lack of knowledge, Plato believed, accounted for the evil that was rampant in the world. Plato himself never offered, in any of his writings, a single definition of an Idea, although he lived until he was past eighty and his *Dialogues* are nearly as long as the *Old Testament.* Perhaps he offered definitions in his lectures, but we have no record of them, and one who reads the *Dialogues* will note that Plato, in those dialogues in which definition is important, overthrows and refutes other men's definitions but offers none himself. Nevertheless, if Plato is correct and there are Ideas that are perfect and everlasting by which we may transform ourselves and our society, it may be possible, twenty-five hundred years later, to discern these Ideas with greater proficiency. The promise that Ideas might fulfill is worth a good try.

JUSTIFICATION FOR PLATO'S THEORY OF IDEAS

But is such a notion of definitions as Plato's justifiable? Is there, in any sense, a World of Ideas? We can see some utility in the concept of Ideas if we try to operate without it. Suppose, for example, we wanted to make an elaborate study to answer the question, "What are the effects of democracy on people?" To make such a study—which would require large sums of money and several hundred investigators—we would have to study what happens in democracies. In other words, we would have to observe cases of democracy. So we might, for example, decide to study democracy in our own country, in England, Holland, Switzerland, France . . . Ah! But surely someone would say, "France is not a democracy; it is ruled by a near-despot." Then we would have to examine the Idea of democracy. We would have to state a definition of democracy and that definition would serve as a criterion by which we select the cases that determine the results of our study. We might find, indeed, that there were no "real" democracies on earth, and that all seemed to be hopelessly imperfect imitations of the Idea of democracy. We could not proceed without such a definition, and the definition itself would certainly be an Idea. There is merit in Plato, for indeed, we have Ideas, and the use of these Ideas is not only desirable but sometimes inescapable.

Not only are there Ideas, but these Ideas seem to be models, if not archetypes. In some senses, there are countries that have been more closely modeled after the Idea of democracy than others and still other countries seem to be the palest imitation of the Idea of democracy. The Idea, moreover, seemed to come prior to the imitation of it, thus supporting another aspect of Platonism.

Moreover, an Idea represents a kind of perfection that is not achieved on earth. We would be more apt, for example, to discern a perfect definition of democracy than we would be to find perfect examples of it. We can, perhaps, after great difficulty, find a good definition of Love, one that rises above the imperfect imitations that are manifest in infatuation, or in neurotic love, and that Idea helps suggest the transforming power of Love that men have felt and have written about through the centuries. Such a definition of Love indeed could help to transform us. Not only do these Ideas exist in some sense of the word, but they also have some power to change men and society, as we see on pp. 201–202.

Plato may have been wrong about whether or not a definition can state the timeless, everlasting nature of some things. Contemporary existentialists, among others, insist that some things are always changing their natures, always growing, always decaying, always altering so that their natures cannot, therefore, be defined as Plato wished. Undoubtedly these existentialists are correct about _things_. But by no means is it certain that they are correct about values and Ideas, even though our notions of certain values and Ideas may change.

At least this much is certain: Working hard to find the perfect, unchanging and transforming meaning of values is stimulating to one who tries it. The process may lead him to new discoveries about the value he is defining, and enable him to speak with greater insight, greater clarity, and greater precision. The promise of Plato's concept exceeds the promise of any other concept of definition, and is worth taking seriously.

DEVISING A PLATONISTIC DEFINITION

Perhaps Plato's theory of definition is of greatest use in defining values. Let us see how one might arrive at a Platonistic definition of a value. The first step in searching for such a definition is to understand thoroughly the characteristics of a Platonistic definition, so that one does not immediately select an inferior one. Thus to define a value, one must search for a definition that expresses the Idea of the Value—the Idea of which all earthly manifestations are but imperfect imitations; the definition, moreover, must be one that is perfect in the sense that if it were completely understood and followed it would create a better life. One must attempt, moreover, to define a concept so that the definition will apply always and everywhere. Finally, the Platonistic definition will be difficult to attain. But because the definition does arrive at knowledge that is archetypal, transforming, unchanging, and everlasting, Plato's concept of definition is as worthwhile as it is difficult.

The second step is to learn all one can about the concept to be defined by reading the best works by the best minds on the subject. Thirdly, one should examine cases of the Idea to be defined, for although these cases are imperfect, they may jog the mind and stimulate it in such a way as to lead to the best definition. To devise a good Platonistic definition, fourthly, requires especially careful contemplation of the Idea. One must use one's mind, struggling to devise a definition that meets the characteristics of Platonistic definition. Fifthly, one must try out, and probably, discard, several definitions until one finds one that seems to be best.

Aristotelian Definition

Aristotle had a different conception of the function of definitions. To him, a definition classified a thing into its categories. Plato's concept of definition is more intriguing and romantic than Aristotle's, but the latter's can be applied more surely and more frequently. *To Aristotle, the act of definition is merely an act of classifying a term; to classify anything one must always use at least two classifications of it: First, one must place the term in a large general class or genus.* If we were defining a circle, we might first put it into the class of "a closed plane curve." But having put the circle into this class does not define it because other figures such as ellipses are also closed plane curves. *Therefore, we must show how the term differs from all other members of that general classification. We can do this by adding a second class, called the species; the species makes clear how the term differs from other members of the same genus.* To define the circle, we might add to the phrase "a closed plane curve" the additional classification, "all points of which are equally distant from a given point." No closed plane curve except the circle fits this definition. Hence, by classifying a circle into a genus and species, we have successfully defined it. Thus, if we were defining a chair, and put it in the genus, "a piece of furniture" and the species "made for sitting on," we would have to add a subspecies to separate chairs from benches inasmuch as both fall into the same genus and species. A definition may have as many subspecies as are necessary, although the speaker should have as few as possible so that the definition is easy to comprehend.

One may be somewhat hesitant to furnish definitions that are Platonistic because of the difficulty of devising them, but it is less difficult to find good examples of Aristotelian definitions. We might try to define *Intelligence.* We would fail if we resorted to the rubric of some psychologists and said that "intelligence is what the intelligence tests measure." This definition not only has no clearly marked genus and species, but it says nearly nothing, for we still must ask, "What do intelligence tests measure?" The obvious answer, "intelligence," does not clarify the matter. We might define it as "Skill in problem solving." Here we would have a clear genus: Intelligence is a *skill*; we would also have a clear species: it is not any skill, but skill in *problem solving*. The definition, so far, seems to meet Aristotle's requirements. But is intelligence only skill in solving problems? Aristotle would be not a guide, for nothing in his theory of definition reminds us that skill in solving problems is not necessarily a sign of intelligence. Skill in solving problems in wood-carving may, for example, be the result of *practice*, not of intelligence. Or they may be the result of excellent instruction. Nevertheless, we may be able to salvage the definition if we add one more species and say that intelligence is skill in solving problems *with which one has not previously been confronted*. Here we have, perhaps, an adequate definition of intelligence; Aristotle and perhaps even Plato might have accepted it.

COMBINING PLATONISTIC THEORY AND ARISTOTLE'S RULES OF DEFINITION

Plato's mode of definition and that of Aristotle's can often be used in the same definition. We might try to define *Justice*, using both the Aristotelian and Platonistic methods. Plato, even if he did not define Justice, wrote so much about it that, by putting together his writings on the subject from the *Republic* and some other dialogues, such as the *Gorgias*, we can arrive at something like a definition. To Plato, Justice seemed to be "that condition of society in which each person received the most satisfaction possible and in which he gave the most satisfaction possible to others." Here we have a broad genus: Justice, to Plato, was not merely an action of the courts, as we are apt to think of it, but a condition of a *whole society*. There are two species: This condition of society is one in which the person *receives* the most that he needs and in which he *gives* the most that he can. Thus we have tried (perhaps vainly) to apply Aristotle's theory of definition to a Platonistic Idea. At any rate, the two concepts of definition can be used together. Even though Aristotle did not conceive of definitions in Ideal terms as did Plato, and although the former looked on definitions only as means of classifying, the two theories are not necessarily incompatible. One can attempt to define the Idea of something and in so doing, state its genus and species. The two methods work well together, for in searching for the genus and species, one may often hit upon the Idea of the term being defined. The definition of the circle offered earlier, although Aristotelian, still states the Idea of a circle; and it does so although nowhere is there a perfect circle, nor is there likely to be. Yet the Aristotelian definition arrives at the Platonistic statement of the Idea of a circle, of which all our earthly circles are only imperfect imitations! Thus the two methods of definition may work well together. Plato may direct one toward the perfect, the everlasting, and the transforming, but Aristotle furnishes useful *rules for the composition* of precise definitions. The student using Plato's theory should try to apply Aristotle's rules for defining.

Operational Definition

Sometimes it is impossible to state the Idea to be defined as Plato would have us do, or to classify the word in such a way that no one will disagree with our classification. In such situations, operational definition may be of help. For example, take the word, *psychology*, whose meaning has changed through the years. To some, at the beginning of this century, it was the attempt to analyze the content of one's consciousness. Freud, Adler, Jung, and their followers, however, emphasized that psychology should also analyze those things of which we are *unconscious* but which still influence our reactions. Under Watson, psychology was the study of human behavior, and to behaviorists, the study of the content of consciousness was considered not to be the domain of psychology. Today, educational, clinical, industrial, animal, social, physiological, and phenomenological psychologists have added their own meanings so that the boundaries of psychology have expanded. Presumably it will change further in the future.

Moreover, we cannot state the Platonistic Idea of psychology, (because psychology is not a value and Plato was interested only in values), and hence we should avoid a Platonistic definition. For these reasons, it is difficult to assign the term to precise categories, as Aristotelian definition would require. If we do, we may leave out some aspect of psychology that is under study, or may omit some aspect that someone one day will be studying.

These difficulties have led to the operational definition in which no attempt is made to state the timeless nature of a thing or to place it in rigid categories, but in which an attempt is made to describe a thing *by what it does—the way it behaves, the properties it has, or the things people do when they practice it.* Thus, in defining *psychology*, operationally, we would attempt to describe what people who call themselves psychologists have done when they study what they call psychology. Or, if we were defining electricity operationally, we would be able to define it only by what it *does*, because we do not yet understand exactly what it is. The operational definition contrasts with the Platonistic and Aristotelian concepts, but follows a notion advanced by the pragmatists: *that a thing is what it does and nothing else.* The operational definition is particularly useful to debaters who are arguing a resolution. With most terms that

need defining in such debates, neither Platonistic nor Aristotelian definitions are of much use.[2] In the resolution, *Resolved*, that the basic industries should be nationalized, the term *nationalization* must be defined.
One doubts that there is a Platonistic Idea of that term, and perhaps
Aristotle's system of genus and species is insufficient. Here, we need to
know the precise plan of nationalization; would it constitute confiscation
of the industries by the government? A forced sale of these industries?
What agency of the government would "possess" these industries, and
to what end would they be operated? More precisely, in debates on a
resolution, the definition of some of the principal terms must be an
operational definition of the *plan* implied by the proposition.

Thus, the student who chooses to define things operationally must
define the reactions of the thing being defined, or what men do when they
use it. Operational definitions, therefore, are often longer, more tentative,
less pontifical and, under some conditions, more useful than the other
two kinds of definition.

Some Difficulties with the Three Kinds of Definition

The Platonistic and Aristotelian definitions (and sometimes the operational as well) have a special difficulty. When one states what he thinks
the Idea of a thing is or classifies it into categories, he is apt to attach too
much importance to his own definition and so fail to keep an open mind
toward it. For example, those who defined psychology as "the study of the
contents of consciousness" probably circumscribed, limited, and even
stultified the thinking of at least some persons so that psychology was not
as easily conceived in more useful terms. Such a definition denied that the
study of learning, adjustment, morale, groups, physiological psychology,
and psychotherapy was the province of psychology! Psychology has become
enriched by more liberal definitions of it. We must, therefore, whenever
we use the Platonistic or Aristotelian definitions, be willing to be skeptical
about our own definitions and be willing to permit changes in them. At
all odds, we must not look upon them as a kind of dogma to be enforced.

At the same time, much sloppy thinking results from operational definitions. One is restricted by the discipline of stating the nature of a concept or by that of classifying it. Those not so restricted and who define
operationally—especially if they are amateurs at such kinds of definitions
—may construct overly long, verbose, and fuzzy definitions. Nevertheless,
the clarity and discipline required by the more ancient approaches to
definition would eradicate much of the verbiage of these definitions. Pla-

---

[2] See the article on the subject, "On Definition in Argument" by Robert P. Newman
in *Pennsylvania Speech Annual*, XXIII (Sept. 1966), pp. 30–39. One must agree with
the article, provided one is discussing only school debates. In other speeches, however,
in which the meaning of a value is crucial, the Platonistic or Aristotelian mode of
analysis may be more helpful than an operational definition.

tonistic and Aristotelian definitions, although they may lead to some rigidity in thinking, have clarity, precision, and terseness. These merits are difficult to find in many operational definitions.

For these reasons, often a good way to begin working on a term is to try to state the Idea of the term, as Plato would require, and in so doing to classify it into its genus and species as Aristotle preferred. If, after careful attempts, it seems impossible to use such a combination of methods of definition, the student may wisely make use of an operational definition.

CHARACTERISTICS OF GOOD DEFINITIONS

1. It may seem commonplace to say that a *definition should include all necessary characteristics of a term*, but too often this requirement is overlooked. Particularly is it overlooked with certain kinds of words that "everybody" understands. When "everyone" knows the meaning of a term, it is not uncommon to find that no one understands it. Take the term *history*, for example. Most people would define history as "that which happened in the past." Yet this definition does not contain the slightest suggestion of what some historians are trying to do. To confine the work of a historian merely to noting that certain things happened in the past is not the most useful meaning of what the historian does. Such a "history" would result in a compilation of events and dates. Yet this kind of history, as every school child knows intuitively, is relatively useless, meaningless, and dry. Some historians insist that the purpose of history is to state the *significance* of events in the past. Thus a historian would try to explain the import of the French Revolution to the French peasant, to the English noblemen of the time, and to us today. But the significance of history changes. Pearl Harbor meant something different to the American people on December 7, 1941, from what it does today. Inasmuch as meanings shift, history changes with the times so that each age must write its own history. Thus to include all the necessary characteristics of the term *history* requires a search that takes us beyond the obvious.

To find all the salient characteristics of any term requires more than a peek into Webster. It requires thorough knowledge, study of technical works on the subject, painstaking examination of cases of the term, and careful thought. Thus to define a term with something like universal validity, we should, in the case of history, study what historians have said that history is, and what historians seem to have done when they wrote history. None of these kinds of study is easy, but all of them together will result, if not in a perfect definition, at least in one that will stimulate some thinking in both the speaker and the audience.

2. Besides containing all the necessary characteristics of a term, a definition *should not contain what Aristotle called "accidental" properties.* If

for example, I defined a chair as a "piece of furniture usually made of wood . . . ," I would have included an unnecessary quality because chairs are made not only of wood, but of metal, plastic, and other materials. There is nothing about "chair" that requires the concept of wood, and hence this part of the definition should be omitted. The inclusion of such unnecessary properties results in cluttered definitions that are unnecessarily verbose and misleading.

3. Finally, *good definitions should not contain words whose meanings are not clear to the audience.* Samuel Johnson wrote the first dictionary of the English language. It was a stupendous feat for one man. He did not, however, always take his task seriously. He humorously defined *net* as "a reticulated fabrication decussated at regular intervals with interstices at the intersections." The definition is brilliant and precise, and displays Johnson's mental and verbal abilities, but it is a poor definition because the term *net* is itself clearer than the definition. Definitions should not include words the audience cannot reasonably be expected to understand nor words whose meanings may be different to different members of the audience. Neither should definitions include the word being defined. If, for example, someone were to define *Buddhism* as "a religion based on the teachings of the Buddha," he would not be answering the most basic problem posed by the term, namely: "What are the teachings of Buddha?" A definition that contains no unclear words may sometimes be difficult to construct (and, occasionally, we must admit, impossible). Yet a definition filled with words of uncertain or fuzzy meanings is often useless. The speaker can, of course, define terms in the definition, although he may sacrifice some interest in doing so. Still better, the careful student will use the greatest care in defining so that the definition will be self-evident.

Whether one is using the Platonistic, Aristotelian, or operational definitions, he must be sure that his definition contains all essential aspects of the term being defined, that it contains no accidental properties, and that the words of the definition are clear to the audience.

DICTIONARIES AND DEFINITIONS

Nowhere in this chapter have we advocated that speakers open that useful tool of scholars and students, the popular dictionary. We have not, because the aim of these dictionaries is not to state the nature of an Idea, as Plato would have us do, nor to classify it as Aristotle suggested, nor to describe its behavior as the operationalists wish. The aim of nontechnical dictionaries, such as *Webster's*, is not necessarily to do any of these things. The popular dictionary tries to state only the ways in which people *have used terms.* (Contrary to popular belief, a dictionary is not a kind of a law-book of language but only a record of what people have meant by a term.) These ways may not be the most useful ways of using words. Hence, we do not believe the student will gain much from exploring his collegiate dictionary. On the other hand, *specialized* dictionaries do try to find the most useful meaning of terms, and students who are defining an economic, psychological, philosophical, religious, or other such term should consult several dictionaries in these special subjects. At the same time, we do recommend the use of *Webster* for the student who wishes to know the common meaning, pronunciation, or spelling of a term; the student should recognize, however, that the purpose for which the popular dictionary is compiled makes it serve some purposes but not those we have in mind in this chapter.

Supporting Definitions

Definitions, although they are valuable tools, are always general statements and tend to be, therefore, somewhat dull and unclear. For this reason, definitions should be supported, and by an abundance of examples, comparisons, contrasts, and the like. In this respect, the student should review Chapter 3, "Supporting Ideas." We will here examine the kinds of support that are particularly well suited to making definitions clear and interesting.

First of all, *explanation* may often help clarify a definition. Note how explanation may be used to clarify Spinoza's definition of *God*:

Spinoza defined *God* as "That which is the cause of itself." This definition means that God is not created by an outside force; He is not influenced by anything outside Him; only His own nature can change Him; Not even the most cataclysmic crashing together of galaxies can attract His attention, unless His own nature chooses to note the matter. God is that which, alone, of all the items of the universe determines Himself. He can choose, if He wishes, to note the slightest whisper of the wind but what He does, He does only because it is consistent with or determined by His own nature.

One should be cautious about explanations, however, for explanations can be quite general.

Perhaps a better way of clarifying a definition is by the use of *illustrations* and *contrasts*. For example, if we define *intelligence* as "skill in solving problems not previously encountered," then note how illustrations and contrasts can be used to bring out the definitions:

The engineer is intelligent when he designs a new bridge, or lays out a new highway that will be as nearly accident-proof as highway engineering permits. The surgeon who develops a new mode of operating is being intelligent. The engineer may not be very intelligent when he votes, for he does not have highly developed skills that inform him about who is and who is not a good candidate; the surgeon may behave quite stupidly when he gives his opinion about foreign policy, or even about the way socialized medicine works in England, for his skills have taught him how to make incisions, how to excise tissue, and how to sew up abdomens, not how to view political and social systems.

Contrasts are a favorite way of clarifying definitions. Robert M. Hutchins, when President of the University of Chicago, borrowed the definition of a university from Cardinal Newman and clarified it by contrasting instances:

A university is a community of scholars. It is not a kindergarten; it is not a club; not a reform school; it is not a political party; it is not an agency of propaganda. A university is a community of scholars.

Comparisons likewise may help clarify a definition. We might make clear what the *intellectual* is by comparing him with the intelligent man, and then by contrasting the two:

If we agree that the intelligent man is he who can solve problems, what, then, is the intellectual? The intellectual is very much like the intelligent man. Sometimes the intellectual is indistinguishable from the intelligent man, but there is one important difference. The skills of the intelligent man are for sale; these skills are commonly put to work for those who pay for the skills. The engineer is paid for the company that hires him. You and I may buy the skills of a surgeon. But the intellectual is not for sale. His most salient characteristic, apart from his possession of intelligence, is that he chooses the ends for which he shall work. More particularly, *the intellectual chooses the problems he will solve.* He is not like the bright chemist who goes to work for the large corporation to solve the chemical problems of that corporation. The intellectual works for ends he himself determines. And this difference is why the intellectual often doesn't fit well in a firm and why he sometimes causes so much friction in society. But this difference is also why a democratic society cannot ever do without intellectuals, and why it can never have quite enough of them.

Illustrations, comparisons, and contrasts are the best ways to make definitions meaningful and interesting.

Just as necessary, however, are *repetitions* of the definition. When the speaker gives his definition, he should watch the audience closely to see that they understand it; if the definition is a complex one, he may need to repeat it immediately. Throughout the speech, the speaker would be wise to repeat the definition frequently, not only for clarity, but for emphasis.

Other methods of support are not, as a rule, so interesting as illustrations, comparisons, and contrasts. Nevertheless, with certain definitions they may be appropriate and helpful. The student should however, avoid these methods unless they clearly make a strong contribution to understanding, to clarity, and to the vividness of the definitions:

1. Support the definition by *division*. If one, for example, defines *psychology*, he might add some clarity to his definition if he divided psychology into its many aspects: educational psychology, abnormal psychology, clinical psychology, general psychology, social psychology, physiological psychology, and others.

2. Support the definition by *synonyms*: To define *ethics*, for example, one might say, "Ethics is best conceived of as being closer to 'fun,' to 'happiness,' to 'enjoyment' than it is to their opposites. When we understand ethics, we find that the ethical man is the man who has the most fun, who is the happiest, and enjoys life the most. Our Victorian ancestors have done us a disservice by equating ethics with 'Don'ts' and 'Thou shalt not's.' "

3. Support the definition with a brief *etymology* (linguistic history) of the term being defined. To define *liberal arts*, it is instructive to discover that the word *liberal* is from the Latin word *liberare*, meaning *free*. Where etymology illumines a term, use it. But somehow or other, the idea has seeped into the colleges and high schools that etymological considerations are absolutely essential. To the contrary, they are not, for what was originally meant by a root term may have little or no significance for what the descendant of that term means several thousands years later. Therefore, use etymology where it adds interest or where it contributes to understanding but do not use it where it adds nothing.

When a good definition has been made interesting by the use of supporting material, it is more apt to become a compelling value for the audience, and to shape the choices that they make. In so operating, definitions may help enrich our civilization.

The following assignment will help the student realize the significance of definitions and techniques by which they may influence the value systems of an audience.

DEFINITION SPEECH

Introduction

If someone wants to know if he is in love, or if a certain painting is beautiful, he cannot find out unless he knows, in the first case, what love is, or in the second, what beauty is. Careful definition is often, therefore, a prerequisite to knowledge. Moreover, one of the ways of clarifying the values that are the basis of our choices is to try to define them. When we can define what we consider to be true and false, good or bad, ugly or beautiful, useful or useless, we are in a better position to understand why we make the choices that we do. We must define these values, because they determine the course of our civilization. A highly developed civilization gathers much of its fire from taking the nature of certain values as problems. The values of art, science, truth, the good life, and the like must be clarified and defined if we are to understand them and to reap whatever rewards they offer. Thus, the act of defining certain kinds of values helps us understand one of the forces that can contribute to our civilization. For these reasons, we should inquire into the nature of some of the ideas that have made our culture the rich, outstanding, and complex culture it is.

Assignment

Give a six- to eight-minute speech in which you present a definition. The objectives of the speech should be to (1) arouse an interest in any of the following concepts; (2) present a carefully phrased and intelligent definition; and (3) make the definition clear and interesting. You may be cross-examined by the class on your definition to test its merit.

Techniques of Using Definitions

DEFINING A TERM
Use any of the three kinds of definitions described in the text.

1. Platonistic definition: Attempt to state the Idea of any of the terms listed in the assignment.
2. Aristotelian definition: Attempt to classify the term by putting it in a large family or genus, and to show how it differs from other members of the same family by putting it in one or more species.
3. Operational definition: Define any term by what it does, or what people do when they follow or practice the idea.

The definition should contain the following characteristics:

1. It should avoid superficiality by probing deeply into the most important characteristics of what is being defined.
2. It should not contain characteristics that are accidental or irrelevant.
3. It should contain no terms whose meanings are not clear.

SUPPORTING THE DEFINITION
One should use the most vivid supporting material possible to clarify the concept and to give the audience a lasting interest in it. The following

forms of support are useful: "a", "b", "c", and "d" are especially recommended. The remaining kinds of support should be used with caution and only when they clearly add to our interest in the concept and understanding of it.

a. *Illustration:* Give real or hypothetical, detailed or undetailed illustrations that are vivid and varied.
b. *Comparisons:* Both literal and figurative comparisons may be used to help the audience understand the concept.
c. *Contrasts:* Tell what the concept is not; give negative examples of it.
d. *Repetition and restatement* of the definition should be used frequently.
e. *Division:* Often, breaking a concept into its parts helps us understand the concept; division should not be used, however, unless it does clarify the definition or add interest.
f. *Synonym:* Sometimes a synonym will help clarify the concept. Avoid synonyms, however, unless one would work particularly well.
g. *Etymology:* Sometimes a concept may be clarified by giving the original meaning of the word, or by explaining what it means in another language. Often, however, etymology is a poor guide to meaning.

SUGGESTED SUBJECTS

Many of the following subjects are values and need the clarity of a good definition to make them understood. Others are not values, but have one or more values as their essential characteristic. In both cases, the clarity furnished by a definition and the support of the definition will help stimulate thought about the value systems of our world and the basis of our choices.

Art, beauty, Buddhism, Christianity, civilization, communism, Confucianism, deduction, dialectic (Hegelian or classical), economics, eloquence, energy, Epicureanism, ethics, evil, freedom, God, goodness, health, history, Hinduism, idea, Islam, induction, idealism, intelligence, Judaism, justice, law, literature, materialism, mathematics, metaphysics, music, normal, mysticism, perfection, personality, phenomenology, philosophy, physics, poetry, psychology, pragmatism, reason, rhetoric, science, socialism, sociology, Stoicism, Taoism, thought, theology, time, transcendentalism, truth, wealth, Zen.

In order to find or devise an acceptable definition, use the following procedure:

1. Consult some general works first such as the *Oxford English Dictionary* (which is the most comprehensive dictionary in the English language and many times the size of *Webster's Unabridged*), *The Syntopicon* by Mortimer Adler, and *Encyclopedia Britannica*. An exception to this

suggestion should be made in the case of psychological, sociological or economic terms; for these words the student should read about the concept in texts and consult several professional dictionaries.

2. Consult works in the specific field of your definition, looking up the concept in the index of a number of recent books.

13 ∬ Thinking and Speaking About Values: Consequences

THE NATURE OF VALUES

Light can play strange tricks. In ordinary light, certain kinds of rocks appear grey; but when fluorescent or ultraviolet light is turned on them, the dull greys are replaced by irridescent blues, yellows, greens, and reds. In sunlight, a green sweater appears green, but in pure red light it looks black. Like the light, values and value systems color our world and give it brightness or dullness. By the light of various values civilizations find the unique paths they follow and from that light cultures are given their distinctive hues. The light cast by these values, moreover, either reveals our problems to us or blinds us to them. But like the light, which is itself invisible until it strikes an object, our values and value systems also remain invisible, until they are reflected in a decision. Even then, values are not always perceived. Because of the pervasive influence of values, we cannot speak intelligently without understanding something of their nature.

A value is a standard on which, consciously or unconsciously, we base our choices. We may, for example, favor aid to a certain foreign country because we have already promised to help it; in this case, the desire to uphold our public integrity is the value on which we have based our choice. We may be opposed to foreign aid because it will cost a large sum of money, in which case a wish for economy may be the value underlying our choice. *Values may be defined as concepts that express what men believe is right or wrong, important or unimportant, wise or foolish, good or bad, just or unjust, great or mean, beautiful or ugly, and true or false, and that, therefore, underlie all choices.* Intelligent speaking demands that we locate, understand, and analyze the bases for our choices.

THE IMPORTANCE OF VALUES IN CIVILIZATION

High civilizations do not owe their superior development over lower ones entirely to their wealth and power. Their superiority comes in a substantial degree from their commitment to certain kinds of values. Carthage, for example, was wealthier and more powerful than Athens, but never developed a civilization comparable to that of Greece. No other civilization borrowed or imitated Carthaginian ideas, techniques, or culture. Their civilization appears to have been merely rich and powerful and to have lacked the values that have earned for Athens the admiration of all who have known her. The story of Athens, however, is much more than a story of accumulations of wealth and of imperial growth. Greek values shaped Greek greatness.

These values not only were reflected in the origin of Greek philosophy, but were a cause of its development. The first philosopher, Thales, asked, "What is the most fundamental constituent of matter?" Questions about the nature of the world and matter had been asked before by the Egyptians and Persians. The questions, however, produced poor answers because the value system of these peoples permitted explanations involving the gods, demons, and spirits they believed to exist. Thales' contribution was that he posed a question to be answered in the light of a special value: reliance only on that which could be *observed*. This value, which was Thales' conception of the way to arrive at truth, was his most important contribution. Thus the nature of matter was taken *as a problem to be solved*, and the solution required a "natural" and "rational" rather than a superstitious answer; with the choice of such a problem and with the use of such a value system, Greek philosophy could begin, and for better or for worse, the world would never be the same again.[1]

It is not surprising that Thales found the wrong answer to the question, for we cannot, even 2,500 years later, produce a perfect answer. But the

[1] Thales' answer was that the most fundamental component of the Universe was water. He probably arrived at this conclusion by observing that water fell from the sky, and was presumably, therefore, part of air; that water seeped into holes in the ground making it appear that it was part of earth; that water accumulated on a cold dish held over the fire, making it appear that it was part of flame; and that watery fluids were present in plants and animals.

example of Thales inspired other philosophers to do as he had done, namely to take the nature of matter as a problem and to search for natural explanations. Heraclitus, Parmenides, and others did so and found, not too surprisingly, contrasting answers. When many people accept the same problem, the same values, and the same method of attack and still find divergent answers, the effect is often stimulating and causes further questioning.

The stimulating effect of such questions and values caused the Greeks to wonder about things other than the nature of matter. The same kinds of questions and the same kinds of values were used to explore the nature of mathematics, political activity, the good life, truth, and especially, the nature of man. One reason Greek culture achieved superiority is that the Greeks valued understanding, valued human reason based on observation, and valued questions about the natures of art, science, life, governments, animals, drama, goodness, and the like. In fact, the desire to understand the nature of things became a characteristic value for the Greeks and directed their thinking more than it had any previous civilization, and more than most subsequent civilizations. Such values produced the memorable things about Greek civilization. The value attached to the problems of the nature of Justice and Goodness inspired Plato's *Dialogues*. Moral and religious problems inspired Aeschylus, Sophocles, and Euripides to write plays that can be compared favorably to Shakespeare's. Athenian sculpture, in the fifth century, mirrored the Athenians' concept of the ideal man and thus reflected another of the Greek value systems. Greek poetry sharpened the Greeks' perception both of man's promise and of his dilemmas. Thus Greek civilization arose partly out of a desire to understand the nature of things, and grew because the Greeks' sense of values dictated a unique choice of problems.

Moreover, the values that demanded a rational answer based on observation forced the development of *tools* to solve the problems the Greeks were posing. The Greeks developed dialectic, democracy, induction, deduction, debate, and literary, rhetorical, and artistic criticism. Thus the value systems of the Greeks not only dictated the choice of problems, but also brought forth new tools. The new values and the new tools initiated new studies that were to change the world: medicine, biology, political science, psychology, logic, ethics, metaphysics, history, physics, music, mathematics, and rhetoric. *The Golden Age arrived, not only because Athens was rich and powerful, but because she had a value system that was unique among the civilizations of the world.*

That civilizations follow the lead of their value systems is illustrated by the differences between Greece and Rome. The Roman never quite caught up with Greek civilization, although the Romans admired it enough to try to adopt it. The Roman was not so concerned with the nature of things as was the Greek; and the practical Roman preferred to accept, rather than refine, the formulations of the Greeks. Consequently, Rome never developed a science, a philosophy, mathematics, or arts that were above the level of imitation. Moreover, Roman imitations of Greek culture were generally inferior, just as Cicero was inferior as an orator to Demosthenes, and Plautus was inferior to Aristophanes in the art of writing comedies. No Roman philosopher could match Socrates, Plato, or Aristotle; Roman sculptors imitated the Greeks, as did Roman architects. As one might expect, no new ideas about the nature of man and no new formulations about the universe were produced in Rome, for the Roman system of values did not press the Empire's citizens to exceed their Greek teachers.

The Roman, however, had his own values and they, too, had merit. Roman values emphasized order and the techniques for securing it. This order gave the world more prosperity, peace, and even more freedom than recent motion pictures would lead us to believe. Rome forged her own tools for securing these values: codes of law, civil service systems, and limited self-government for her provinces. These tools enabled the Empire to operate in spite of insane emperors, incompetent Senates, and vast differences among her peoples. The peace brought about by Rome may have preserved the culture of Greece on which our own culture is based, and without which Western culture would lack much of its richness and variety. Roman values differed from Greek values, but nevertheless preserved Greek culture, and made a contribution of their own.

Thus the kinds of problems a civilization chooses to solve and the means used to solve them determine the richness or poverty of a civilization. In this way also, the value system of a culture determines the nature and the worth of the culture. A few brief illustrations may serve to reinforce the point. The Persians placed little value on the individual and never developed a democracy. The Greeks placed little value on civil order and never developed a nation. The Orientals placed small value on material things; partly for this reason, only recently have most Oriental nations begun an industrial revolution. The Americans prized acts and deeds, and passed by the value of contemplation that is so important to Eastern philosophy and religion. We have each gone down the paths our values lighted for us. Because values underlie choices of such magnitude that they determine the nature of our civilization, intelligent speaking demands that we understand and analyze these values.

THE IMPORTANCE OF VALUES IN CHOOSING PROBLEMS

Our value systems determine, in part, which problems we recognize as requiring solution. If we are not interested in the nature of art, we shall not try to think about problems of art, and if we are not moved by human beings who suffer, we may not try to understand the causes of poverty. We recognize a problem because our values give us a generalized picture of an ideal and because the problem at hand represents a marked deviation from that ideal. Values, therefore, are basic to problem solving.

Because values furnish the light by which problems can be seen, it is often necessary for a speaker to heighten or even inculcate certain values before an audience can perceive a problem. (It would be useless to point out to a savage that his explanations of thunder are not rational explanations until he first valued such explanations.) Inasmuch as values are the bases of our choices and because they are our idea of what is right, good, true, or beautiful, there is always at least one value that underlies the recognition and acceptance of a problem demanding a solution. Successful speakers will be aware of such values and will attempt to judge the extent to which an audience will require that the value-background of a problem be established or heightened.

THE NEED FOR ANALYZING VALUES

Most of us would agree that justice is better than injustice, that health is better than sickness, that freedom is better than slavery, and that beauty is better than ugliness. But what precisely, supports our certainty that justice is better than injustice? What makes one value superior to another? How, when we are faced with a conflict of values (such as choosing between peace with slavery or war with the possibility of eventual freedom), do we choose among values? Although defining what we mean by justice, peace, or freedom will help clarify these values, we must do more than merely define them. We must find some further ways of making clear which values are most worth securing.

The Chinese philosopher Mencius once said that if one put in a heap all of the customs that are somewhere considered good, and then takes from the heap each that is somewhere considered foolish or evil, nothing would remain. He was saying, in effect, that there is no way of deciding which things have value and which do not on any intrinsic basis, except insofar as the person himself assigns a value. Thus, a painting has "value" if someone wants it, and only if someone does. Values, in other words, are sometimes thought to be relative to the person. The twentieth century abounds in this kind of relativism and such relativism is an intelligent corrective to earlier dogmatism and to discussions of value without regard to the circumstances of the person choosing values. At the same time, however, values do not depend entirely on one's perception or on one's idea of them. Milk absolutely has a value for drinking that gasoline does not and could never have, regardless of the subjective feelings of the drinker. It is possible to clarify these values further and to make clearer the extent to which they should influence our choices. Values are the light by which we see our world; they are the bases of our choices; they determine which problems we believe are important; they give our civilizations their distinctive hues. Therefore, we must understand how to analyze values and how to persuade others to accept them if we are to make intelligent speeches.

ANALYZING VALUES: STATING CONSEQUENCES

What makes one value important and another less important? Let us consider an example. A college education may be said to have a certain value, and an expensive automobile to have another. In these days, both may cost about the same. Assuming that we could choose one or the other for ourselves, which would be the first choice? The question can be answered intelligently only when we study the effects that each will produce. The consequences of an act or a value make it worthless or worthwhile. The consequences of drinking gasoline make it a poor source of health, and the consequences of putting milk in the gasoline tank are also not beneficial. Just so, whether to choose an expensive car or a college education may depend upon the consequences of each act.

These consequences, however, cannot be easily discovered. One consequence, for example, of choosing a college education may be that you may (quite without knowing it) influence others to take the same step, just as choosing an expensive car may influence others to keep up with you. Another consequence of a college education is that you may meet friends and professors who will influence you the rest of your life, just as the trip you take in your new car might make lasting impressions on you. In fact, you cannot foretell the effects of a choice or of a value completely. Yet the further you explore the consequences of selecting a certain value, the more rational your choices can become. Even if we cannot know all about the effects of any particular value or decision, it does not mean that we shall not have intelligence in the matter, for even if we are not free of all error, we shall have been freed of some errors.

Persuading Audiences to Accept a Value

In a speech or any part of a speech in which it is important that an audience accept a value, the student can select one of several lines of approach. Following are a number of lines of argument that are particularly useful in persuading an audience.

We have not listed, however, all the possible ways of persuading an audience to see the consequences of a value, and the student may find that for his particular audience and value there are more appropriate ways than those described. At the same time, the following list of methods, when strongly substantiated by examples, testimony, statistics, and similar support, will help an audience accept the value the speaker has in mind.

1. *This value has produced desirable effects in the past.* One might illustrate the use of this idea by explaining that one reason ancient Greek civilization reached such high peaks in so short a time was that the Greeks had a passionate belief, for a brief time, in freedom.

In our country, during World War I, we renamed sauerkraut "Liberty Cabbage," and in World War II we could not see such operas as *Madame Butterfly* or *The Mikado*. The ancient Greeks were in some respects freer than we. *Lysistrata*, for example, was an antiwar play produced in Athens during time of war—and produced at state expense. No one asked if it supported the Greek national aims, or the war effort, but only whether or not it was a good play. As things turned out, it won the prize as the best comedy of the year. It is hard to conceive of such a thing in the United States during any of the wars of the twentieth century. In Greece, freedom stimulated a multitude of ideas about philosophy, politics, man, religion, and nature that could hardly have been uttered, much less debated, had the Greeks not lived in a free atmosphere where ideas could compete. Destroy Greek freedom and Greek thought would die with it—as it did when Athens no longer governed her own destiny, and when Athenians persecuted the creative minds.

Several variations of the idea that the value has produced good effects in the past may be applied:

a. Failure to use the value produced harmful consequences.
b. The opposite of the value produced harmful consequences.
c. Where the value was tried and seemed to fail, the conditions were unfavorable for the application of the value; today the conditions are more favorable.

2. *The best men accept this value, whereas less admirable ones do not.* One consequence of the soundness of a value is that people who possess good sense (experts, authorities, admirable people, and the like) choose it. This consequence can be used, likewise, to persuade an audience to accept the value. If the value is honored by one whom the audience reveres, they are more apt to accept the value. Thus if the audience is known to think highly of a certain statesman, a philosopher, an industrialist, or a labor leader, and that person also is devoted to the value in question, the audience is more likely to accept the value. Many of us accepted the values of our teachers—when we liked the teacher—just as we might have rejected some value when we disliked the person advocating it. Thus a value may be reinforced by the example of one who accepts it or by the testimony of such a person.

Moreover, if it can be shown that groups of people worthy of emulation have accepted the value, whereas less admirable ones have not, the speaker can sometimes influence the audience: For example in a section of a speech designed to inculcate a desire for freedom, one could tell of the Greeks, of the struggles of the early settlers in the United States, and of the Hungarian Freedom Fighters, thus making the point that admirable men struggle for freedom. The theme would be particularly strong if the speech shows that other groups have made greater sacrifices to secure or keep freedom than the audience will need to.

There are some worthwhile variations on this theme that may be applicable to the situation facing the speaker:

    a. Admirable societies and groups accept the value.

    b. Unadmirable societies and groups do not accept the value but despise or fear it.

    3. *The value fits the needs of the audience.* We discussed motivation in Chapters 5 and 9. Values must appeal to people, or they cannot be values. If the value does not fit the person and his circumstances, it will not exert a strong influence on his behavior. The situation can be compared to the soil conditions for a plant. If the soil is too acidic, as clay soils tend to be, the plant cannot make use of the nitrogen, phosphorus, and potash in the soil and will not grow well. In the same way, a value may be desirable because it can produce better conditions for growth of the individual by supplying crucial human needs. These growth needs are difficult to characterize but would include genuine satisfactions instead of momentary pleasures; the possibility of happiness instead of merely gratification; the possibility of transformation of one's self rather than the maintaining of an uneasy neuroticism; and the possibility for inventiveness and creativity rather than of a stolid conformity. In a sense, understanding the nature of these growth needs is the task of the whole of education, and even of the whole of one's life, and can hardly be settled with finality here. Nevertheless some readers will immediately understand these needs and recognize that they are basic, and others, one hopes, will begin the search for goals that bring the deepest and most permanent satisfactions.

    4. *The value can be justified by reasoning.* One consequence of a sound value is that it can be subjected to tests of logic and reasoning without being found invalid. Philosophers have invented many kinds of logic and many kinds of reasoning; he who has studied the history of philosophy and, particularly of epistemology, will best understand the following categories listed here and their significance:

    a. *The value can be stated as a principle that all men should follow.* Immanuel Kant asserted that one test of the goodness of a thing is whether or not it can be *universalized*: that is, if we believe a value is good, we ought to be able to recommend it to everyone. Thus, for example, we may not like to stop at traffic lights, but we can hardly justify such a dislike because if everyone failed to stop, the resulting chaos would make driving far more dangerous. Therefore, stopping at traffic lights is likely a good thing. Kant's test has some ambiguities, but with it, we can rule out many practices as unethical and can develop some certainty about others. Sometimes the variations of this theme may be quite persuasive: This value can be universalized; its opposite cannot be universalized; the lack of the value cannot be universalized.

b. *The merit of the value is self-evident.* In the sixteenth century, philosophers developed a "new logic," which was the basic logic used by Thomas Jefferson in writing the *Declaration of Independence.*[1] Certain ideas can be seen to be true if one merely gives one's attention to them; argument is not necessary to establish their merit, but only the complete understanding of these ideas. Once we completely understand that value, we will accept it. But the value *itself* must be grasped, not merely words about it or arguments for it.

We are no longer so certain that there are self-evident truths as were the philosophers of the sixteenth and seventeenth centuries; at least, we know that what seemed self-evident to them does not seem self-evident to us. Despite the ringing words of the *Declaration*, we know that all men are *not* created equal, and if they are endowed by their creator with certain inalienable rights, enough of them are in chains and serfdom to make one question the efficacy of the "right." Nevertheless, one way to lead men to accept a value is to present it and to present it so completely and so fully in its beauty, its power, and its significance that by the perception of the value itself, men are led to accept it. The last two hundred years have not uncovered self-evident truths, but then there may be self-evident *values.* Indeed, one suspects that a value is either that which, when understood, compels one's belief in it, or it is no value. Far from being a method to be despised, the full and poetic expression of a value may, indeed, be the best "argument" in its favor.

c. *The denial of the value is contradictory and serves to assert the value.* Sometimes to deny a thing logically implies the thing itself. For example, if one asserted that "there are no such things as thoughts," he would already have implied that there are thoughts, because the denial of a thought is, *itself*, a thought. Or if, again, I assert, "Communication cannot occur among people," I have just refuted myself, for I have communicated some ideas, and, therefore, my denial of communication implies communication. This system of logic, known as *noncontradiction*, began with René Descartes. Later philosophers developed the method of noncontradiction more fully than did Descartes, who did not clearly understand it. Perhaps speakers in the twentieth century are more sophisticated in using varieties other than noncontradiction. And, perhaps, values cannot be established by this method. Nevertheless,

[1] See Wilbur Samuel Howell, "The Declaration of Independence and Eighteenth-Century Logic," *William and Mary Quarterly*, XVIII (October, 1961), p. 478.

since the advent of experimental science, this method has not been used with the frequency and intelligence it might have been. It may be time to try it again, and this time, to try to see if it can establish a logical defense for a value.

Other Themes

One could add indefinitely to the list of means for arousing audience acceptance of a value. One could include such approaches as: "These values are within the grasp of the audience," or "Where the value produced good effects, the conditions were much the same as in our case," or "This value is easy to attain." Any stereotyped formula, however, will not be so effective as the speaker's selecting and phrasing of ideas so that they fit the unique audience and particular subject with which he is dealing. The speaker must seek ways of convincing an audience that the consequences of adopting a value, whether in the past, in the present, or in the future, are desirable.

Finally, we believe that some values are of supreme importance because unless these values are realized to some degree, no human life, as opposed to animal life, is possible; these values are of such nature, furthermore, that not only are they responsible for our humanness but they can also transform our lives, provided we commit ourselves to them. The identification of these values leads to a standard of values for the speaker.

A STANDARD OF VALUES FOR RHETORIC

The speaker needs a set of values applicable to speaking that will help him choose ideas, select supporting material, and decide which basic themes are of greatest worth to him and his audience, aside from their utility as persuasive devices. Such a consideration of values requires an introduction to the ethics of speaking. In addition to the preliminary discussion of ethics in Chapter 1, much of this book has been concerned indirectly with ethics. We have advocated the use of valid and honest supporting material, the choice of subjects involving problems of weight, and choice of solutions most beneficial to humanity. It is now time to grapple more directly with ethics.[2]

The standard of value is to be found in the nature of man and in those aspects of his nature that separate him from other animals. The unique nature of the human being seems to originate with two complicated and

[2] The ideas presented here were first published by Henry Nelson Wieman and Otis M. Walter in "Toward an Analysis of Ethics for Rhetoric," *Quarterly Journal of Speech*, XLIII (October, 1957), pp. 266–270, and are reprinted here by permission.

interlocking processes that generate all capacities that we call *human*, and which turn the biological man into a human being. They are, further, of such nature that they can enable man to transform himself so that he can achieve the highest success of which mankind is capable. In these two capacities, therefore, should lie the ultimate standard of value. These capacities are man's use of symbols and his capacity to be influenced by other men in a way that no animals are influenced by their fellows. Let us see how symbols can make one human and can enable man to transform himself.

Symbols

Certain peculiarly human performances such as the creation of litera-ture, art, mathematics, and science have their roots in symbols. The func-tion of the human brain itself, according to Suzanne Langer, is to convert the raw data of sense experience into symbols. The brain, therefore, is not to be conceived of as merely a kind of telephone switchboard, but as a powerful transformer:

The current of experience that passes through it undergoes a change of chac-acter, not through the agency of sense by which the perception entered, but by virtue of a primary use which is made of it [the sense experience] immediately: it is sucked into the stream of symbols which constitute the human mind.

Because our brain is only a fairly good transmitter, but a tremendously pow-erful transformer, we do things that . . . [the cat] would reject as too imprac-tical, if he were able to conceive of them.[3]

Langer traces the origin of dreams, ritual, magic, and speech to the process of transforming the raw data of sense experience into symbols. But the symbol itself changes the world of man into which it is introduced. Ernst Cassirer also emphasizes the power of symbols "not in the sense of mere figures which refer to some reality . . . but in the sense of forces each of which produces and posits a world of its own."[4] Because the brain trans-forms the raw data of sense experience into symbols, the human being lives in the world of these symbols, which further change his world in a way unknown to animals. Thus the human being will live, fight, and even die for symbols which he believes represent supremely important realities. Professor Karl R. Wallace writes:

This capacity to symbolize abstractly, to combine abstract symbols into patterns, and to employ symbols in referring to past events and to the possible and probable future—symbolism in this way is, so far as we know, uniquely human. . . . The symbol is man's peculiar mode of ordering his experience,

---

[3] Suzanne Langer, *Philosophy in a New Key*, New York, The New American Li-brary, 1948, p. 34.

[4] Ernest Cassirer, *Language and Myth*, New York, Dover Press, 1946, p. 8.

extending his experience, and refining his behavior. The growth and development of symbolization is almost synonymous with human growth and development; and learning, problem solving, organizing and evaluating involve high-level symbol behavior.[5]

Clearly, then, the capacity for symbolism is an essential element for the existence of human personality. Without symbols, of course, there can be no language. Without language much that is peculiarly human is impossible, for there can be no extensive thinking or problem solving. Without symbols, we cannot develop into human beings; we can only become animals that are biologically human but psychologically no different from other animals.

Symbolism is also indispensable for the continued growth of human personality. Forming concepts, discovering new concepts, and refining older ones are all impossible without symbols. When the process of growth is interrupted by interference with the process of symbolism, as in aphasia or senescence, the possibilities for refining, ordering, and expressing experience are severely limited.

Finally, symbolism can transform man creatively and progressively. Without symbols, as we have said, there could be no mathematics, no history, no science, no philosophy, or art. Nor could there be any love—that is, the recognizing and appreciating of the needs and interests of other persons and adopting them as our own. Likewise there could be no faith, in the sense of giving one's self in supreme devotion to what one believes to be the guide and goal of life. These human monuments have transformed human life. Symbols, moreover, can extend this kind of transformation beyond any known limit. In this extension lie our greatest possibilities.

Our Need for Others

But symbols can be used either destructively or creatively. We seek a guiding principle enabling us to use them creatively. The search will lead us to the second peculiarly human quality, which shares with symbolism the responsibility for the origin of human personality, the nurture of personality during its growth, and the capacity to transform it. This quality is *the unique need of human beings for other human beings*. To be sure, animals need other animals for food, for reproduction, and apparently even for companionship—some die when placed in isolation. But this need of animals for each other is not the same as the need of the human being for other human beings, and it must not be confused with mere gregariousness. George H. Mead asserts that man needs other people

[5] Karl Wallace, "Education and Speech Education Tomorrow," *Quarterly Journal of Speech*, XXXVI (1950), p. 179.

in order to generate and develop these uniquely human aspects known as "mind":

Mind arises in the social process only when that process as a whole enters into, or is present in the experience of any one of the individuals involved in that process. When this occurs, the individual becomes self-conscious and has a mind.[6]

Not only is "mind" developed by association with others, but only by *taking the attitude of another person toward himself* does man form a concept of "self":

The human individual experiences himself as such not directly, but only indirectly, from the particular standpoints of other individual members of the same social group, or from the generalized standpoint of the social group as a whole. . . . For he enters his own experience as a self or individual not directly or immediately, not by becoming a subject to himself but only insofar as he first becomes an object to himself just as other individuals are objects to him . . . and he becomes an object to himself only by taking the attitudes of other individuals toward himself.[7]

Thus taking the role of others generates our mind and self. We may call this need of man for others, for understanding them, and for being understood by them, the need for *mutual understanding*.

Like symbolism, mutual understanding is essential, not only to the generation of human qualities but to the continued growth of the human being. *Others* frequently provide the motivation for the individual's activity, and make possible shared knowledge and the healthful give-and-take that can stimulate further growth and development. Even the development of language requires the presence of other people, because we create symbols to communicate with others. We can use language to communicate only when we can mutually understand symbols. To understand symbols, we must know something of what is in the mind of the other person; otherwise we could not grasp the meaning of words or use language. Thus symbolism and mutual understanding are inseparable, even if distinguishable, processes, and all growth as a result of language requires at least some degree of mutual understanding. Without this interchange, one cannot continue to learn from others or increase what one can know, appreciate, and control.

This need for other people also has possibilities of transforming man beyond his present state. On this matter Mead says:

In the conception of universal neighborliness there is a certain group of attitudes of kindliness in which the response of one calls out in the other . . .

[6] George H. Mead, *Mind, Self and Society*, ed. Charles W. Morris, Chicago, University of Chicago Press, 1934, p. 134.
[7] *Ibid.*, p. 138.

the same attitude. Hence the fusion [of interests] . . . which leads to intense emotional experiences. The wider the social process in which this is involved, the greater is the exaltation, the emotional response, which results. . . . This, we feel, is the meaning of life—and one experiences an exalted religious attitude. We get into an attitude in which everyone is at one with each other insofar as all belong to the same community. As long as we can retain that attitude we have for the time being freed ourselves of that sense of control which hangs over us all because of the responsibilities we have to meet . . . but in . . . the religious situation, all seem to be lifted into the attitude of accepting everyone as belonging to the same group. One's interest is the interest of all. There is complete identification of individuals.[8]

The Transformation of Man

The creative transformation of society comes about through the joint operation of symbolism and mutual understanding. When one, by virtue of his unique individuality, creates some further symbolism, this creation is added to the culture only if that unique individuality is understood by others.

Mutual understanding of the unique individuality of the other does not mean approval of all his thoughts, feelings, and actions. One cannot, however, justly disapprove of anything until after one has first achieved an understanding of it. Therefore, mutual understanding is the necessary prior condition that must be met before disapproval is justified. To be sure, we are caught every day in circumstances which require us to condemn before we achieve any high degree of understanding; but to realize this circumstance is only to realize that human life falls short of perfection. Mutual understanding is, then, the basis on which any judgment must rest, which morally approves or disapproves the conduct of a human being.

Mutual understanding ends in mutual influence. Through this mutuality of concern the purposes of each may be brought to fulfillment even when they are very different. To bring these purposes to fulfillment often requires modification of our purposes and desires, but it does not require that our purposes or desires be the same. On the contrary, in mutual influence, this modification is apt to be most profitable when one finds the purposes, needs, and desires of the other interesting and valuable to one's growth and development.

There are, then, two inseparable processes that are distinctively human: the process of symbolism and that of mutual understanding. These two processes are *constitutive needs* of the human being. That is, these processes build the *human* mind and *human* personality, save it from dis-

[8] *Ibid.,* p. 274.

integration, sustain it in its growth, and, finally, transform the human being progressively beyond any known limits. These processes, therefore, are the most fundamental of all human values.

If this analysis of the unique qualities of the human being and their significance is correct, it follows that an ethical act is one that enables the organism to meet its constitutive needs for symbolism and mutual understanding; an unethical act is one that destroys, prevents, delays, or otherwise limits the possibilities of meeting these needs. The moral law derived from this ethic might be stated thus: *Always act to provide conditions most favorable for mutual understanding between yourself and all concerned.*

Speaking, if it is to be ethical, must create conditions favorable to the expansion of symbolism and mutual understanding and influence. We define ethical rhetoric *as the discovery of the means of symbolism which lead to the greatest mutual understanding and mutual influence.*

The highest values have the highest consequences. When we use these values in speaking, we may enable man to transform himself and his society. To this end, speaking must commit itself if it is to serve us best.

Value Speech

Introduction

When we have studied the problems of our culture, we have gazed upon the cesspools and sore spots of our civilization. Such a view is incomplete without a glimpse of the greater moments of an advanced culture. In addition, more is required of us than that we solve our material problems, for it is not enough to sleep in safety with stomachs filled with food. We need to capture the aspirations and the visions given us by those who made great cultures possible. The solution of our problems may permit us to live, but a keen perception of values will make life worth living and can transform us, beyond any known limit, into the best we can become. Let us, then, search out these values and learn what they may hold.

Assignment

Give a six- to eight-minute speech in which you select a single value and build the most powerful case you can for that value. You may, if you wish, choose to attack a popularly held value that you believe to be false. The speech should aim at changing our ways of thinking and feeling; it should, ideally, change our lives.

Technique of Presenting a Value

A value must be made clear, perhaps by defining it as suggested in the previous assignment. The value may then be made both interesting and persuasive to the audience. This task may be performed by explaining the consequences of the value, particularly by showing that (1) the value has produced good consequences at other times for other people; (2) the value has been adapted by those the audience admires or rejected by those the audience disparages; (3) the value can fulfill the highest needs of the audience, or (4) the value can be justified by reasoning. Each of these ideas, however, must be phrased or modified to fit the value selected and the audience. Moreover, it must be undergirded by the best supporting material the speaker can find, for the richness of the supporting material will in part determine whether or not the value gains a wide acceptance among members of the audience.

Subjects

Subjects such as the following should be chosen:
The value of reason, love, music, art, literature, learning, or religion.
A value taken from other cultures, e.g., stoicism, epicureanism, or Taoism.
A value taken from another civilization, e.g., Inca, Aztec, or Chinese.
The value of a specific piece of literature—a poem, play, novel.
The value of a particular period—the romantic, classical, or contemporary.
The value of a particular man—a composer, scientist, teacher, writer, or
   politician.
The value of an attitude toward life.
The negative values—those that harm, destroy, stultify, or limit human
   achievement.

14 ▯ Discussing Problems and Values

Man lives with other men who face situations similar to his or who are involved in the fabric of his own search for a satisfying life. In this environment, which does not yield its secrets and resources easily, man is forced to communicate. Thus far in this book we have concentrated on one form of oral communication, public speaking. The liberally educated citizen in a free society must possess the knowledge, skills, and attitudes that will enable him to conceive ideas and to communicate them purposively to groups of his fellows; but further, the knowledge, skills, and attitudes that are necessary for speaking to audiences will form a useful foundation for other forms of oral communication.

In a free society, men and women share interests, share responsibilities, and share rights. The same sort of problems that prompt individuals to address audiences under various situations may in other circumstances stimulate individuals to speak informally together seeking answers. It is common to call this informal, purposive speaking *discussion*. It is because interests, responsibilities, and rights are shared that we find so much discussion about us. Few of us will go through a week without being involved in talking with others in an attempt to reach some mutual understanding of problems that we face. Each individual, whether he knows it or not, interprets events that surround him and conducts himself according to

233

some set of values. Members of groups share values, and, if these groups are to persist and function, the members must recognize these values. This recognition must be constantly renewed. Often the recognition, the renewal, or modification of shared values depends upon discussion.

Undoubtedly the impulses and conditions that lead to discussion are as old as human society. In one of Plato's dialogues, Socrates says, "I think that all of us should vie with each other in the struggle to learn what is true in the matters under discussion, and what is false; for it is to the common good of everyone of us that this should be made clear."[1] Discussion was developed to such a degree of excellence by Socrates and Plato that the results of their thought have persisted throughout the history of Western culture to influence nearly every age. Although we shall be infinitely more elementary than these Greek philosophers in considering the theory of discussion and the practical use of our techniques, we should recognize that we undertake an activity that has proved deeply meaningful in human expression and communication.

A DEFINITION OF DISCUSSION

"I do not deal in definitions . . ."[2] George Bernard Shaw once wrote. When one thinks about defining *discussion*, he is tempted to adopt Shaw's attitude. The word is used in contexts that differ vastly. The public speaker, for example, often says, "I want to discuss several issues with you," when obviously he intends to talk while we sit and listen. Although we can define the term in such a way as to exclude this speaker and others, *discussion* must remain a vague word, that is, there will be many instances in which we cannot confidently assign the term nor clearly justify not assigning it.

First of all, a discussion involves a group (we sometimes speak of *group discussion*). How many? The lower limit is easily stated—two, but the upper limit is more difficult to set. In general, the more persons involved, the more difficult it will be to discuss problems informally. Two to six can discuss; six to ten may be able to; if more than ten are involved, discussion is possible, but becomes increasingly unlikely to occur. A group is not simply any aggregate of people; ten people waiting for a bus are probably not a group as we use the term here. A group has some more or less clearly defined purpose for existing—the members share interests, problems, values. They recognize some need for working together.

Sharing some need to work together, the members of the group co-

---

[1] *Gorgias*, trans. W. C. Helmbold, New York, Library of Liberal Arts Press, 1952, 505.
[2] *Quintessence of Ibsenism*, New York, Brentano's, 1910, p. 28.

operate; in discussion, they talk together making a situation in which each may address himself to whatever points arise as they arise.

Discussion, then refers to the effort of a group of individuals who talk informally together in order to solve commonly recognized problems or to arrive at an understanding of values. This definition implies that the desired end product is agreement, that the group intends to arrive at a plan acceptable to all for attacking a problem, or that the members are able to inquire into the meaning of value statements in such a way as to arrive at meanings with which everyone is satisfied. Whereas complete agreement ought to be the goal of those involved, complete disagreement may be the result. There are situations that demand some sort of final group decision. Recognizing this, the group may produce a compromise which the members decide represents the most nearly complete agreement they can reach.

Although disagreements in discussion ought not be considered failure, discussions are not as productive of understanding as they ought to be and can be, for a very simple reason. Too many people say to themselves, "I can discuss. I discuss constantly. What is there to learn?" As a matter of fact, a life-time of learning is necessary, not only for the scholar who may make a career out of studying group processes and interpersonal relations, but also for the man or woman who seeks effectiveness in working with others and who desires to understand himself more deeply.

This chapter is a brief introduction to discussion. The student should gain a sharpened awareness of discussion and begin to form some attitudes and learn some techniques that should prove useful in developing effectiveness in discussion.

ATTITUDE IN DISCUSSION

If anything is the essence of discussion, it is the attitude of those involved. If they have the proper attitudes toward their task and toward one another, they probably cannot fail to have a profitable discussion; if they do not, they probably will be unable to discuss at all.

The key descriptive phrase is easy enough to state and remember, but extremely difficult to learn and practice at a meaningful level; it is *friendly cooperation*. Before that healthy cynic in every sophisticated student breaks forth and cries, "How juvenile. What next? Three choruses of 'The More We Get Together'?" let us caution that it's not as simple as it may sound. But perhaps we are a different sort of people from those Plato found in ancient Athens, judging by one remark he puts into the mouth of Socrates:

I imagine, Gorgias, that you, too, have taken part in many discussions and have discovered in the course of them this peculiar situation arising: people do not find it easy by an exchange of views to arrive at a mutually satisfactory definition for the subjects under discussion, and in this way bring the argument to an agreeable end. Rather, when they disagree on any point, and one declares the other to be guilty of incorrect or vague statements, they grow angry and imagine that everything that is said proceeds from ill will, not from any concern about the matters under discussion. Some of these arguments end most disgracefully, breaking up in mutual vituperation to such an extent that the bystanders are annoyed at themselves for having become auditors of such people.[3]

If we believe that Plato observed the ancestor that still lives in us, we should turn our efforts toward developing an attitude of friendly cooperation. These suggestions may be useful in the development of a productive discussion attitude.

Repress the Disposition to Take Offense

If others do not immediately agree with our sage observations, we should resolve to put firmly aside our disposition to take offense. All too often we quickly assume that others disagree out of bad motives. *Even if, and especially if, we find another's manner distasteful to us or believe that he is trying to be irritating, we should make every effort not to be antagonized.* We know that this is difficult advice to follow; each of us has observed and perhaps participated in discussions of religion in which the participants, professing faith in a belief that teaches humility and non-violence, descend into the bitterest personal denunciations. We should take as our guide Montaigne's statement, "When any one contradicts me, he raises my attention, not my anger: I advance towards him who controverts, who instructs me; the cause of truth ought to be the common cause of both the one and the other."[4] Too often, however, to use Montaigne's words, "Instead of extending our arms, we thrust out our claws."

What does one gain by taking offense? To answer the question, ask another: why does one take offense? Probably not simply because one finds another's remarks in and of themselves offensive, but because he supposes that the other *intends* to slight, disparage, or to insult him in some way. In short the motivation one *suspects* to lie behind the remarks triggers the offense.

At this point we should repeat one of the most common pieces of good

---

[3] *Gorgias,* 457.

[4] "Of the Art of Conference," *The Essays,* ed. W. Carey Hazlitt, trans., Charles Cotton, London, Reeves and Turner, 1892, III, p. 158. This delightful essay, one of the finest ever written on the subject, is, fortunately, available to the student in an inexpensive edition under the title of "The Art of Conversation," *Great Essays,* ed. Houston Peterson, New York, Pocket Books, 1954.